D0063222

This book is for my mother
MA-BLOKE
and to the memory of my father
JOSEPH
who was killed by the Sophiatown
which they bulldozed
into the dust

Bloke Modisane

Blame me on History

AD. DONKER / PUBLISHER

AD. DONKER (PTY) LTD
A subsidiary of Book Marketing & Distribution (Pty) Ltd.
P O Box 2105
Parklands
2121

First published 1963
First paperbook edition 1986
Reprinted 1990

ISBN 0 86852 098 5

Printed and bound by Creda Press (Pty) Ltd, Cape Town

Chapter One

SOMETHING in me died, a piece of me died, with the dying of Sophiatown; it was in the winter of 1958, the sky was a cold blue veil which had been immersed in a bleaching solution and then spread out against a concave, the blue filtering through, and tinted by, a powder screen of grey; the sun, like the moon of the day, gave off more light than heat, mocking me with its promise of warmth—a fixture against the grey-blue sky—a mirror deflecting the heat and concentrating upon me in my Sophiatown only a reflection.

It was Monday morning, the first working day away from work; exactly seven days ago I had resigned my job as a working journalist on *Golden City Post*, the Johannesburg weekly tabloid for the locations. I was a free man, but the salt of the bitterness was still in my mouth; the quarrel with Hank Margolies, the assistant editor, the whiteman-boss confrontation, the letter of resignation, these things became interposed with the horror of the destruction of Sophiatown. I was a stranger walking the streets of blitzed Sophiatown, and although the Western Areas removal scheme had been a reality dating back some two years I had not become fully conscious of it.

In the name of slum clearance they had brought the bulldozers and gored into her body, and for a brief moment, looking down Good Street, Sophiatown was like one of its own many victims; a man gored by the knives of Sophiatown, lying in the open gutters, a raisin in the smelling drains, dying of multiple stab wounds, gaping wells gushing forth blood; the look of shock and bewilderment, of horror and incredulity, on the face of the dying man.

My Sophiatown was a blitzed area which had suffered the vengeance of political conquest, a living memorial to the vandalism of Dr Hendrik Frensch Verwoerd; my world was falling away, Martha Maduma's shebeen was gone, she had moved her business to Meyer Street, but the new shebeen lacked the colour and the smell of the long passage, the stench from the puddles of urine. I walked through the passage, the puddles were dried up and the smells were gone; and at the end of it was the door into Martha's shebeen, but she was not there.

Across the door over the corrugated iron fence was destruction, the tenement houses were razed to the ground; and somewhere among the ruins was the room of Nene, a boyhood friend, who had grown up to be a murderer doing a seven-year term of imprisonment; he would never see his room again or the woman he lived with. I hurried away from the scene, through the long passage and back to Good Street, past Aly's fish and chip shop which always smelt of old dripping. I stopped at the Odin Cinema to look at stills; the films were always the same blood and thunder tuppenny horrors with memorable titles like: *Two Guns West*, *The Fastest Gun Alive*, *Guns Over the Prairie*.

Over the street facing the cinema was one of those enormous communal yards accommodating thirty-two families in thirty-two rooms; the people had been removed and the four blocks of eight rooms each had not been demolished yet, but the roofs, doors and window-frames had been removed. Only the walls remained, the walls with the gaping wounds. On the walls of two of the rooms were slogans painted, perhaps hurriedly, and the paint bled down from the letters: 'WE WON'T MOVE', 'ONS POLA HIER', 'HANDS OFF SOPHIATOWN'. Against the background of the demolition the slogans were only a dusty mockery of the boast.

The building structures, the naked walls, seemed unprotected and helpless against the bulldozers, like trees, their leaves blown off by autumn winds, standing bare and numb to the winter cold; as I had stood on Christmas day three years ago in front of the cinema with the muzzle of a ·38 revolver pointing at my stomach.

'Just open your mouth, Bloke,' Lelinka had said, 'open your mouth and I'll shoot you.'

I stood there numb with fear, I was helpless, unarmed, I did not want to die.

'You bloody shit house,' he said.

Gilbert 'Kwembu' Moloi, former non-European heavy-weight boxing champion, employed as the bouncer doorman, pleaded for my life persuading Lelinka to put away the gun; and ten minutes later, during which my life had hung in the balance, ten minutes of obscenities thrown at me, Lelinka put his gun away. I had won yet another reprieve.

I was working as an emergency usher in the Odin Cinema, and it was during the Christmas day matinée; suddenly a woman screamed in the one-and-tenpenny stalls.

'You better see what that's all about,' said Mr Berman, the manager.

'That's where the Americans are sitting,' I replied. 'You're a white man, they won't start anything with you.'

'You're not afraid, are you?' he joked. 'Don't worry, they'll touch you over your dead body.'

I walked up the aisle to Row R and there was this girl crying, I flicked on the torch.

'Fock off,' a voice said.

I flashed the torch in the face of the speaker; it was Lelinka, the knife-happy rough-house brother of Selenki and Boykie, the foundation members of the Americans, Sophiatown's best-dressed boys, whose fashions came straight out of the pages of *Esquire*.

'Lelinka, that girl's making noise,' I said.

'What do you want to see, Bloke?' Lelinka said, rising from his seat and removing his hand from under the girl's dress. 'I said, fock off, shit house.'

We exchanged words, insults and vulgarities, down the aisle out into the foyer, and it was only out in the light that I became aware of the revolver; I became silent immediately when I looked into his eyes.

The gaping scars of the bare walls began to frighten me, I hurried down the street, past Dr Bayever's surgery and Dr Wolfson's, stopping opposite the petrol filling-station; the 'Thirty-Nine Steps', Fatty's famous shebeen, was demolished. I reconstructed in my mind the rickety steps—thirteen in all —which led up into the shebeen with neon lighting and contemporary furniture, and the seductive Fatty. It was perhaps the only shebeen which served ice cold beers; and definitely a famous Sophiatown landmark. It was gone.

Gone too were the stories which grew out of the 'Thirty-Nine Steps', stories of excitement and of terror; like the night The Spoilers, the gang from Alexandra Township, came to Fatty's and taunted the Durango Kid; word had gone out that the Durango Kid was going straight, that he was no longer carrying guns. The Spoilers had come to Sophiatown in their De Soto and inside the 'Thirty-Nine Steps' they taunted the Durango Kid, baiting him into a fight; but the Durango Kid was patient, refusing to be provoked, and in the end when the threats were becoming more explicit, he got up.

'Wait for me,' he said, 'I'll be right back.'

A quarter of an hour later he was walking down Good Street with two guns, like his namesake, and at that particular moment The Spoilers were leaving the shebeen in the De Soto; the Durango Kid started shooting, from both hands, and the De Soto jerked away like a jet, with the Durango Kid shooting until it went out of range.

All that was gone.

Walking down Good Street and up Gerty Street was like walking through a ghost town of deserted houses and demolished homes, of faded dreams and broken lives, surrounded by rousing memories, some exciting others terrifying; for Sophiatown was like our nice-time parties or the sound of the penny whistle, a mounting compulsion to joyousness, but always with the hint of pain. Sophiatown was also like our week-ends, it was the reason, or rather the excuse we used to stop the progress of time, to celebrate a kind of wish fulfilment; we cherished Sophiatown because it brought together such a great concentration of people, we did not live in it, we were Sophiatown. It was a complex paradox which attracted opposites; the ring of joy, the sound of laughter, was interposed with the growl and the smell of insult; we sang our sad happy songs, were carried away by our erotic dances, we whistled and shouted, got drunk and killed each other.

I stopped opposite 21 Gerty Street, there was only the debris of the house in which Emily lived; the memory of happy nights spent there rushed back to tease and irritate me, and it was then that the loneliness penetrated. The people I had known, and loved, were gone; the relative, the friend, the childhood sweetheart, last year's beauty queen, the nice-time girls, the shebeen queens, the beggars, the thieves, the frauds, the gangsters, the killers; they were all gone, and with them had gone the only world I knew. The music had gone, the colour, the violence, only the desolation remained.

I drifted aimlessly into yards reconstructing the hovels, the shacks, the slum dwellings, from out of the debris and the dust; avoiding the open gutters, walking round the garbage cans, the lavatories, knowing that these were the things I hated most in Sophiatown and because they were no longer mine to complain about I loved them. And there in the rubble was a piece of me.

The pride of having grown up with Sophiatown shrivelled inside me; I had failed my children as my father and my forefathers and the ancestral gods of my fathers had failed me; they had lost a country, a continent, but I had failed to secure a patch of weeds for my children, a Sophiatown which essentially was a slum. I stood over the ruins of the house where I was born in Bertha Street, and knew that I would never say to my children: this is the house where I was born, that when I was a boy Sophiatown was a bare veld; that there once was a tree here, perhaps the only one in the location, round and about and into which we played, dreamt a little and built a fairy location with parks and gardens beautiful with flowers; a location with playgrounds like the ones white children played in; that the dreams we weaved were bold. But not for them even the pleasant reminiscences, only the interminable tragedy of dispossession; all that I can bequeath to them is the debris and the humiliation of defeat, the pain of watching Sophiatown dying all around me, dying by the hand of man.

The house in which I had been born was now grounded into the dust and it seemed especially appropriate that I should be standing there, as if to witness the closing of the cycle of my life in its destruction; my friends were leaving the country, Ezekiel Mphahlele had taken a job in Nigeria, the Millners were gone to Ireland, Arthur Maimane was in Ghana, and soon Elly and Lionel Rogosin and the crew of 'Come Back Africa' would be leaving. Then Mr De Wet Nel, Minister of Bantu Administration and Development, under Section 9 (7) (f) of the Natives (Urban Areas) Act No. 25 of 1945, threatened that 'the Minister of Bantu Administration and Development may, unless the local authority objects, by notice in the *Gazette*, prohibit a social gathering in a private home in a town, at which an African is present, if, in his opinion, such gathering is undesirable having regard to the locality in which the house is situated. Any African attending such a gathering is guilty of an offence and liable to a fine not exceeding ten pounds or to imprisonment not exceeding two months or to both such fine and such imprisonment.'

The Minister then proceeded to publish the names of thirteen white South Africans, prohibiting them from having parties or, in the words of the Minister, he barred the thirteen citizens of Johannesburg from 'attending, holding or organising, directly or indirectly, any gathering at which an African is present'. These mixed gatherings are being held by 'irresponsible persons, and which are un-South African and subversive in nature, in direct contravention to well-known South African custom', and the Minister concluded, inferring dark and strange events, that 'lately, liquor has flowed freely at such parties, and the results can be left to the imagination'.

It was a tactical move on the part of the Minister, the announcement was sufficient in itself, it was not necessary to solicit the consent of the local authority; the liberals buckled, they had been intimidated, and became careful not to be listed with 'the thirteen', most of whom had been banned under the Suppression of Communism Act and were treason trialists.

White friends who had usually invited me to their homes for that 'illegal drink' became appropriately careful, and when they did invite me the rendezvous was my room in Sophiatown. I was incensed by this; it was objectionable enough for the Government to regulate our public lives, but this intrusion upon private freedom made me recalcitrant. I invited more white friends to my home as a registration of protest, hoping to inspire in them a physical objection to this intrusion; but the Minister had put the fear of the tyrant in them, and when I fully realised this, that they were afraid and were accommodating this intolerable situation, the country began to die for me.

I began to suffocate, and with Sophiatown dying my whole world was falling apart; my marriage had been festering away and my wife, Fiki, had taken my daughter and 'gone to mother'. The quarrel with Hank Margolies closed the ring; I did not have to resign my job, I could have swallowed my pride and allowed the assistant editor the privilege of being white. There was an unwritten law that on 'Drum' publications we were equal, black and white, if in nothing else but in that as human beings we were equal, but apparently this had not been brought to the attention of the assistant editor.

'Mr Margolies,' I said, 'If it's possible I wish to be excused from working this afternoon.'

'Why should you be excused?' Hank Margolies said, all forthright and American.

'Monday afternoon is our day off, and I made alternative arrangements,' I said. 'If we had been told on Saturday I wouldn't have committed myself.'

'What's so important that can't wait?'

'I'm helping Lionel Rogosin with the shooting of his film.'

Hank Margolies smiled benignly and adjusted the cigar in his mouth; he clanged his teeth into it.

'I don't understand you,' he said, 'what's more important to you? Your job or Rogosin's film?'

'Hank, the notice came out this morning,' I emphasised. 'I've made promises.'

'Modisane, your first loyalty is to your paper,' he said, smiling in that superior way he had. 'It's your life. What kind of a journalist are you?'

'Opening envelopes couldn't be that important,' I said, 'one more or less won't make any difference.'

'Look, Modisane,' he said, jabbing a finger at me, 'I don't want to argue with you. You either do the job or take your hat and go—I don't want to argue.'

'But, Mr Margolies. . . .'

'I'm not arguing with you, Modisane,' his voice boomed, turning his back and walking to his desk.

It was a terrible confrontation; my colleagues were embarrassed and sympathetic, half hoping I would precipitate a showdown which would finally resolve the dichotomous relationship between the black journalists and the white staff; the cub reporters were surprised that a senior member had been confronted like a cub. They were all staring at me, anticipating, silently urging on a dramatic situation. I sank into my chair, formulating my decision, and some minutes later I lifted the receiver and dialled Lionel Rogosin's number.

'Lionel? Bloke,' I said. 'Look, Lionel, something important has come up in the office, I can't meet you this afternoon. Meet you tonight? Your flat, about eight, okay. Sorry, Lionel.'

Conversation through the lunch hour was halting, Simon Mogapi, the sport's editor, was mumbling something like, 'he'll never talk to me like that', mostly we ate in silence; too many things wanted to be said, and I did not intend to discuss my decision which had been an arbitrary one since I did not have a wife at home to discuss it with. We returned to the office by way of the shebeen which was on the roof of the office building, and right through the afternoon we opened envelopes, checking entries sent in by readers. It was the weekend following the July Handicap, South Africa's Derby, and *Golden City Post* awarded annual prizes for the correct forecast of the first four horses; there were thousands of entries and the opening of envelopes, sorting and checking took us through to seven o'clock that evening.

Lloyd, the copy boy, came round collecting signatures of the journalists who had sacrificed their afternoon off; a compensation of fifteen shillings would be paid against the signatures. I refused to sign.

'Look, Bra-Bloke, this is money,' Lloyd said.

'Yes, I know,' I said, 'but I didn't do the work for money, it was out of loyalty. I donate mine to 'Drum' publications.'

The work was done, the winning entries locked in the safe,

the rubbish cleared, I sat behind my desk and typed out my letter of resignation; I was obliged to give a month's notice, but the company owed me three weeks' holiday which I submitted as part of my obligation, to be deducted from the four weeks. I worked one week and walked out of the office a free man. The editor, Cecil Eprile, who was a personal friend, was disturbed by the remarks I made in my letter concerning the white attitudes on the paper. I was disappointed that Mr Margolies seemingly failed to realise the significance of what I had done.

Perhaps the concentrated impact had not crystallized in my mind; at the time it had seemed the heroic thing to do, but standing there on the ruins of the house in which I was born I seemed to be looking at my whole life, the body which contained that life reduced to dust; I kept remembering a line of Omar Khayyám: 'I came like water, and like wind I go.' Sophiatown and I were reduced to the basic elements, both of us for the same reason: we were black spots.

Sophiatown died, not because it was a social embarrassment, but because it was a political corn inside the apartheid boot. The then Minister of Bantu Administration and Development, Dr Verwoerd, condemned Sophiatown because it was a slum; true there were no parks, playgrounds, civic halls, libraries; true that a large number of people lived in what was described as 'appalling conditions', in corrugated iron shanties, subdivided by cardboard walls; true that on 50 by 100 feet areas, up to eighty people were huddled in back-yard shacks; but it is also true that Moroka was an approved shanty started in 1946 as an emergency camp where every family was housed in hessian shacks.

If the Government was concerned with alleviating the living conditions of the Africans, the shanties of Moroka, Edenvale, Eastern Township, deserved this consideration far more than did Sophiatown, where the real problem was overcrowding;

14

the shanties of Sophiatown were erected behind solid houses; but the politicians saw political gains and the sociologists and the race relationists saw only textbook solutions—new townships, with recreation centres, parks, schools, libraries, playgrounds; poverty it seems is less disturbing to the public conscience if it is suffocated in model housing estates.

Sophiatown belonged to me; when we were not shaking hands or chasing the same girl or sharing a bottle of brandy, we were sticking knives into each other's backs. The land was bought with the sweat, the scrounging, the doing without, and it not only was mine, but a piece of me; the house was mine even if the rain leaked through the roof and the cold seemed to creep through the cracks in the ceiling, and crawled through the rattling window-frames and under the door.

It was widely conceded that Sophiatown was a slum, and slum clearance was a programme the principles of which were generally accepted; but it was Sophiatown the 'black spot' which had to be ravaged, and as Can Temba said: 'I have long stopped arguing the injustice, the vindictiveness, the strong-arm authority of which prostrate Sophiatown is a loud symbol.'

Chapter Two

WHATEVER else Sophiatown was, it was home; we made the desert bloom; made alterations, converted half-verandas into kitchens, decorated the houses and filled them with music. We were house-proud. We took the ugliness of life in a slum and wove a kind of beauty; we established bonds of human relationships which set a pattern of communal living, far richer and more satisfying—materially and spiritually—than any model housing could substitute. The dying of a slum is a community tragedy, anywhere.

It was especially true of Sophiatown, the most cosmopolitan of South Africa's black social igloos and perhaps the most perfect experiment in non-racial community living; there were, of course, the inevitable racial tensions, which did not necessarily flare up into colour-caste explosions. Africans, Coloureds (mixed-bloods), Indians and Chinese, lived a race-less existence. It is true that as racial groups, we were placed, socially and economically, on different levels of privilege; white was the ultimate standard and the races were situated in approximation to this standard: the Chinese were nearest to white, they were allowed into white cinemas and theatres and some restaurants; the Coloureds, nearer white, and the Indians, near white. Social mixing was difficult, but community spirit was high.

As children, mixing was easier, and together we had our normal—by South African standards—racial skirmishes with the white boys from the adjoining working-class white area. There was a mud pool in the buffer strip which divided Sophiatown from Newlands, and as a lad I joined in the fights for the right to swim in the mud pool. Whichever group got there

16

first imposed its right to use, and continue using the pool; we threw stones at each other. The white boys usually dominated the contest in the end, invariably resorting to pellet guns. At the beginning it was for the right to use the pool that we fought, but this rationalisation soon lost its validity—it was for the sake of fighting that we went to the pool.

I was in the water when one of these fights started, and they threw stones at me and trying to ward off the stones I was drawn deeper into the water, until suddenly the earth under my feet gave way. I struggled against drowning until I preferred death to the agony. My hands searched for a weight to keep me down. During the struggle to stay down I was grasped by a hand and guided out; and once out of the water I threw stones with one hand, at the same time as trying to pull my trousers on with the other. I have never learned to swim.

The African children, as a race group, did not fight Indian, Coloured or Chinese children, as race groups; but we fought each other in gang wars in which opposing factions would be made up from individual members of the group units. Yet we would unite as a Sophiatown gang—a non-white group—to fight the white boys from Newlands or Westdene; children divided by the race attitudes and group conflicts of our society.

Like America, South Africa has a frontier or voortrekker mentality, a primitive throw-back to the pioneering era, the trail-blazing days, when the law dangled in the holster and justice was swift, informal and prejudiced. Instant justice, lynching and horse-whippings are deep in the traditions of these countries; both are compulsive addicts of horse operas, we are always playing cowboys and Indians. The mud pool was the Wild West of America or the dark interior of Africa; and to us, out there in the pool, the white boys were the Red Indians, and we were the cowboys. The symbols were undoubtedly reversed in the white camp; and in the rivalry for the mud pool we ravaged each other, desecrating the sanctity of the body of our society; we, the colour pieces of a colour society, inflicted festering sores on each other, and on the society; rehearsing our roles, arranging and dividing ourselves into the colour groups determined by our society. We were the warriors of Dingane, commemorating, celebrating the victory over the wiles of Piet Retief; we were the heroes of Africa: Tshaka, Hintsa, Moshoeshoe and Sekhukhune.

As a boy growing up in the Sophiatown without play-grounds we improvised our own games, the games of the children of the streets; our repertoire included games like dodging traffic, stealing rides on horse-drawn trolleys, getting on and off whilst in motion, and the more proficient we became the more ambitious we got, graduating to the green Putco buses. During riots we would be in Main Road stoning cars driven by whites, and the red tramcars which carried white commuters between Johannesburg city and Westdene and Newlands. We were part of the riot programme, stoning the police and being shot at, and hit, like everyone else. I learned early in life to play games with death, to realise its physical presence in my life, to establish rapport with it. The children of Sophiatown died in the streets, being run over by the Putco buses and the speeding taxis and were shot during riots.

Standing over the death of Sophiatown, another death came into my consciousness; I remembered the room in Gold Street, the all-in-one room which was kitchen, bathroom, bedroom, maternity room and a room for dying; thoughts of my sister, Nancy, who died of starvation, delicately referred to as malnutrition. For twenty-four hours a day, every day for the days of one week, relatives, friends and neighbours mourned over the body, the hymnals were sung as a kind of religious ode to death. I was impressed by the ceremonial of the wake, by its symphonic solemnity; the women were wailing a chant of mourning, seemingly talking to each other, throwing phrases at each other; one group stating the melodic line of sorrow, the other singing the harmonic complement, a consolement almost causing a sort of unintentional counterpoint.

There was solemnity about the lighted candles over the body; they moved my sister, Suzan, to tears and she was permitted to cry because she was a girl.

'A man does not cry,' an uncle stressed.

Seeing Ma-Willie, as my mother was called, crying was unbearable, and trying to be a man was difficult; the sight welled up that tear which I brushed off so discreetly; but death failed to horrify me, except that I hated it for what it did to my mother and perhaps blamed Nancy for dying. On the day of the funeral Ma-Willie was overcome with grief; the aunts, the other women and the girls broke down into weeping fits, a cousin became hysterical, seized by epileptic spasms, shrieking aloud and writhing on the ground and fainting. She was carried to another part of the yard and laid on a rug and fanned by a neighbour. The plain white coffin with silver handles left our house, irrevocably, and I was never to see Nancy again; it was this fact, alone, which emphasised the permanency of death.

If my father had not walked up to me at that precise moment I would have most probably disgraced my masculinity; he took me into the house of a neighbour; and thus death had made his first personal intrusion into my life.

I switched off the memory machine, but there was another kind of death gaping at me; I turned away from the ruins of the house where I was born in a determination not to look upon this death of Sophiatown. I removed my hat and stood still while a modest funeral train drove past; it was an open lorry carrying a small white coffin and not more than a dozen people.

Another child victim, another Nancy. Those of us who

survived the clutches of malnutrition, the violence of the streets, lived with another kind of ugliness; the dry-breast barrenness of being black in white South Africa. There are times when I wish I had been born in a bush surrounded by trees, wild flowers, vales, dongas and wild life; to have grown gracefully like the seasons, to have been spring's simplicity, the consciousness of summer, but I became, as they say, a man before I was a Boy.

My father, Joseph, was always the signal of authority, unapproachable, the judge symbol; the only time he came close to me was to administer the cane or lay down the law of Moses, and this six-foot-two giant towered above my world, the only real force I ever feared, the authority I respected; perhaps I should have loved him too. One afternoon he came carting a rough bird-cage with seven pigeons and leading a dog which he presented to me, then wrung from me a pledge impressing upon me the seriousness of my responsibility for the protection, the maintenance, the sustenance of the pets.

I was excited and together we constructed a kennel for Rover, the dog, and a compound cage, the top half for the pigeons and the bottom for the fowls Ma-Willie wanted to keep; the working together brought us close and all through that time he became a friend I could touch, even if I pretended, with calculated casualness, that it was accidental. After the construction he retreated into his tree-top tower, to become again the symbol of authority. I prepared the feeds for the dog and the pigeons, and was punished if I fell behind with the schedule.

I resented having lost him, felt enslaved to the pets because the schedule made encroachments into my playtime; friends would whistle signals for me to join them in play, but the house duties: fetching water from a communal tap fifty yards away and having to fill two ten-gallon drums; washing dishes, cooking the feed for the dog, nursing the baby, kept me away from the streets, away from my friends until just on sunset, and after sunset I was not allowed out of the yard.

I risked the cane, disobeyed my mother, disappeared from home, neglected my duties and was away until an hour before sunset; then I hurriedly started the fire in the mbaula, brazier, fetched the water, cooked the dog's food and washed the dishes, and by seven o'clock my dog would be fed; the tight schedule worked except that the time for my school work was wasted, all my energy would be sapped. This arrangement was disorganised the afternoon my father returned from work earlier than expected, and I was playing in Good Street when I saw the dread figure, a whip in his right hand; I disappeared into the nearest yard, jumping fences and cutting across to Gold Street, round into Victoria Road and into the yard. I preferred to be whipped at home.

I loaded three four-gallon tins on to my push-cart and hurried to the tap, rehearsing excuses, selecting the approach most likely to soften my father, the appropriate manner of apologising, begging for forgiveness; when I returned with the first load he was in the room with Ma-Willie who was ill in bed, and Suzan, realising the trouble I was in, was trying to start the brazier fire.

'Thanks, Suzie, I'll do it,' I said. 'Is he very angry?'

Little Suzan was too terrified to speak, she was biting her bottom lip, signalling with her head. I started the fire and rushed out to the tap again, when I returned I lighted the Primus stove and boiled water for tea which I served to my parents. My father remained silent. I heated more water and washed the dishes, and Suzan drank her tea between wiping dishes. Whilst the supper was cooking, the fowls locked in and Rover whining for his feed, I knocked on the door.

'I've done most of the work, father,' I said, with all humility. 'I'll wait in the kitchen.'

He joined me ten minutes later, locked the door and

administered to me a whipping to remember, a whipping I took without a squeak, but with plenty of tears; and when it was over I dried my eyes and went into the bedroom to collect the cups.

'Would mama like another cup of tea?'

She shook her head, I looked at my father and he said 'No', then I started for the door.

'He's not a bad boy,' Ma-Willie said, as I closed the door behind me.

It was the statement which was to blackmail me all my life; I wanted to live up to it, to embrace the responsibility implied in that statement. It became important for me to have it changed to: he's a good boy. When my friends were pilfering I would conveniently be on an errand for my father, I chickened out of street fights, concentrating my efforts into being a 'good boy'. But one afternoon during winter vacations I fought Uncle Louie, the Gold Street strong man.

We had been playing marbles and I had won all his beautiful coloured marbles which we called 'glass eyes'. Then suddenly he demanded them back and they had been the most beautiful I had ever owned; he was the street bully, so I gathered them into my marbles bag and handed them to him. He had hardly closed his fingers round the bag when I snatched it and dashed for home with him on my heels. About five yards from the gate where I lived he tripped me and I fell flat on my face, when I looked up Ma-Willie was looking down at me; the humiliation was unbearable, I lashed out at Uncle Louie flaying him with fists from all directions. He was so surprised that he put up a clumsy fight and when we were separated I kept my winnings.

There was a glint of pride in my father's eyes when the story was related to him; we began to grow closer, he spoke to me directly more often, and his image took on another stature. One afternoon he defended me when I had been punished unjustly by a stranger at the tap; I went home to report to him and without another word we returned to the tap together, with me carrying a fighting stick.

'I agree that a naughty child should be punished,' my father said, 'but my son says he was not impolite.'

'He tells lies,' the man said.

'My son does not lie,' my father emphasised. 'And if he has deserved a beating it is I who will give it.'

This demonstration of faith in my integrity filled me with pride and admiration, and almost as an objection to being called a liar I struck out against the man with the stick I had, and drew blood with the second blow.

'Don't do that,' my father said, taking the stick away from me.

My father apologised for me and the man apologised for having punished me; the image of my father ennobled itself in my mind. Our relationship grew stronger, he seemed to grow fonder of me, we talked about my school work, what I wanted to be, and when I informed him that I wanted to be a doctor his mind fastened on something else.

'A doctor is a man,' he said, with an abnormal emphasis on the word 'man'.

He had in the past punished me, not so much for what I had done, but for the lies I had told in the desperate attempt to escape the cane, and it took me a long time to understand this. I was seldom punished if I told the truth; we discussed what I had done, and I would usually be filled with a sense of shame, not a guilt complex. He insinuated into my consciousness the separation between the emotion of shame and the sense of guilt which he said was a sterile and introversive form of torture which dissipated itself rather than focused on the enormity of the wrong; guilt swamps the individual while ignoring the deed itself. My father fastened on the deed, exploiting the emotion of shame, and in this way I turned away in disgust because of the shame, and it was this sense of shame which has motivated me from hurting people by word or deed.

Then the walls of my world came tumbling down, everything collapsed around me, wrecking the relationship. My father shrunk into a midget. There was a Pass raid and two white police constables with their African 'police boys' were demanding to see the Passes of all adult African males.

'Pass jong, kaffir,' demanded the police constable from Uncle George, a distant relation of my father. 'Come on, we haven't all day.'

He would not dare to address my father in that tone, I bragged, my father is older than he.

'And you, why you sitting on your black arse?' the constable bawled at my father. 'Scratch out your Pass, and tax.'

I was diminished. My father was calm, the gentleness in his face was unruffled, only a hardness came in his eyes; he pulled out his wallet and showed his documents, an Exemption Pass certificate and a tax receipt for the current year. My hero image disintegrated, crumbling into an inch high heap of ashes; I could not face it, could not understand it, I hated the young constable for destroying my father; questions flashed through my mind, I wanted to know why, and I think I resented my father, questioned his integrity as a man. I turned my face away and disappeared into the bedroom, searching for a parting in the earth that I could crawl into and huddle up into a ball of shame.

In my little prejudiced world of absolutes my judgement was cruel, imposing upon him the standards of my own world of fancy; we lost each other from that moment, and in his own way he tried to recover his son, but I was hard and monstrously unjust, and so he again became the harsh hand of authority, the authority I could no longer respect. I began to fear him, keeping out of his way and in the end I saw only the cruelty, never the man. I grew closer to Ma-Willie and the four of us, Suzan, Marguerite and I arranged ourselves against him, united by our fear of him; he must have been the loneliest man in our little black world; I knew very little about him, never got to know whether he had parents, brothers and sisters; I knew vaguely that he came from the Pietersburg area, that there were some kind of relations in Medigan.

Once when Ma-Willie pushed me he became very angry and threw a chair at her, and watching my mother shrink away from him filled me with a loathing for him and a sympathy and closer attachment for Ma-Willie who was the only parent that was real to us; she took us on shopping expeditions to town, supervised and bought all our clothing, the school uniforms, the school books, took us on our first day to school and helped with the homework.

Walking up Toby Street I passed the beautiful house of the Mogemi family, they had not yet sold their property to the Resettlement Board, but everything else around it was levelled with the dust; the Lutheran Mission Church, Berlin Mission, stood erect among the ruins, and a hundred yards up the road was the palatial home of Dr A. B. Xuma with two garages. I turned south at Edward Road and stopped at Bertha Street and the sight to the east was deadening, my eyes spread over a desert of debris and desolation. Suddenly I needed my father, to appeal for his protection, to say to him: Do you see, my father, do you see what they have done to our Sophiatown? But he was only a patch of earth with a number at the Croesus cemetery, he was a number I had burned into my mind that day we buried him.

It was on the afternoon of February 16, 1938, that he died, and I was at school unable to help him that moment when he needed it desperately; he had lived alone in himself and died so, alone and lonely, the children were at school and Ma-Willie had gone to visit her relations in Alexandra township. It was shortly after the lunch break when I was summoned to the principal's office. Mr G. Nakeni, headmaster of the Dutch Reformed Mission School, Meyer Street, Sophiatown, was waiting for me as I walked out of the classroom. I followed him to the fence next to the street.

'Was your father sick?' Mr Nakeni said.

'No, sir,' I said, thinking it was a rather pointless question, not worth interrupting the history lesson.

'You better go home.'

'Now, sir?'

'Yes.'

I returned to the classroom, reported to the teacher and gathered my books; I walked home leisurely, playing with a tennis ball along the way. There was a crowd gathered outside the corrugated iron which fenced in our yard, I slithered through the crowd and standing next to the gate were two African police constables and between them was a manacled man. I walked through the gate and as soon as Dorothea, a neighbour, saw me she started crying; she told it to me as simply and as gently as she could, leading me to the spot.

She informed me, between sobs and sniffles, that the battered and grotesquely ballooned nightmare, hardly recognisable as a human being, was my father; the swollen mass of broken flesh and blood, which was his face, had no definition; there were no eyes nor mouth, nose, only a motionless ball, and the only sign of life was the heaving chest. Recognition was impossible, I felt only revulsion and pity for the faceless man; he could have been anybody and the horror would have been the same, I shuddered at the brutality of the assault. I looked at the man back at the gate, who could have had the heart to do such a thing; he looked like other people, there was nothing visible which could set him apart from others, and I did not feel anything towards him.

The story was that there had been a quarrel with this man,

that both parties had stormed away from each other in anger and later my father went into the extension of our yard in the hope that both of them had cooled down, but the man surprised him with a blow on the face which knocked him down; the man then proceeded to pound him with a brick until my father lost consciousness, from which he never recovered.

I returned to the blood-splashed spot where lay my father, and gazed at the distention, hoping to find something familiar in that mass, anything to bring the man closer to me, some mark of recognition, some sign of identification; and I could not cry, I wanted to break out and collapse at his side, but suddenly I could not remember his face and there was nothing to remind me; all through the interminable wait for the ambulance I did not, or could not bring myself to cry, I have never cried since that day when I was fourteen.

Death is never familiar and each death has its own special pain, each pain kills a little something in us, and I have looked upon death masks so often there is nothing left in me to be hurt by it. The pain of death has slithered into my mind, I use it as a weapon of vicarious vengeance, as a gesture of mercy, and at times, to punish myself, I arrange gory accidents for those I love; when I am annihilated by a sense of shame, arising directly out of my action or from the force and impact of events by which a friend suffered a moment's pain, I run away because of shame and rather than face them I kill them off in ugly accidents; then the horror and the pain of death would focus on the nightmarish sight of my father, and I fall into a state of anxiety and develop an itch all over my body, scratching until my skin bleeds; the pain becomes a reprimand, the physical moment of punishment.

Ma-Willie had been informed of the accident and returned home by way of the hospital, a widow.

'We are cast-offs in the wilderness,' Ma-Willie said, in Sesutho. 'We are orphans, our shield is gone.'

'I hear you, mama.'

'O serithi sa rona from today,' she said, 'we are your children, to live from today in your shade.'

'Ee, 'me.'

'You must tell all our relatives, all our friends, send telegrams,' she said. 'Arrange for the children to be sent to Alex, it is you who must make the funeral arrangements, report to the Burial Insurance Society and they will do the rest.'

'You're the man now,' Uncle Lekoba said.

From that day I became a fourteen-year-old man responsible for a family of four; with some help I moved out the furniture from the bedroom and set it up for the ceremony of the wake; I changed into my only pair of trousers, bought the candles and the provisions for the all-night mourners, prepared and served supper to the children and Ma-Willie, who had officially assumed the traditional mourning dress.

She was joined later by all her sisters and brothers, their grown-up children, friends, neighbours and acquaintances, and the commemorational rites to death began over the body of the man who had passed on into—to nourish—cosmic life; they sat round the room in a circle, night and day, and sang through the requiem hymnals, the sad songs of the tebello, the wake, which most of the mourners knew off by heart. None of the people seemed to be horrified by the death, it only made them sad and full of pity. I received the sympathisers, acknowledging their condolences.

'It's a sad thing,' a sympathiser said, 'he was a good man; he was not rough, he didn't deserve the death he died.'

'To die like that,' another said, 'it's a shame; to die like an animal, like a tsotsi. God will see that man.'

'We all die our own death,' a man said, 'but this is not the death for this man, this is not the death he has made for himself; life has cheated him.'

More people arrived and each had kind words for me, all

lamented the fact that life had mocked at my father, and since life was not transferable they were mystified that he should have died a dog's death. It was this riddle of life which seemed to disturb them more than the fact that a man had died.

'It's a bad sign,' a man said, shaking his head, 'it's not a good thing; it portends a very bad thing.'

'I swear by the truth,' a woman said.

'The poor man has gone to the ancestors.'

They spoke in Sotho, Zulu and Xhosa, and most of the imagery, and the relationships of the symbols intended, escaped me; I made polite gestures that the catering help was asking for me. My cousins had set a catering section in the yard; a brazier fire with enormous water kettles was next to a table on which was an enormous teapot, cups and saucers, five loaves of bread, butter, family-size tins of jam. Around ten o'clock they served the first round of tea.

More people arrived, women came singly or accompanied by their husbands or sons, young girls in pairs or escorted by brothers or boy friends, wearing black shawls or wrapped in blankets, wearing black doekies, head scarves or black berets, to commune with the bereaved during the ritual of the wake. Men moved out of the room to make space for the women, and the wake grew so great that it overflowed into the yard where we had to set up benches; the cousins distributed blankets to the few women who had not brought their own, and the men sitting round the brazier in the yard gave up their fire to the women who sang the hymns from the benches out in the cold. I asked Betty, my favourite cousin, to start another brazier fire.

I was to discover, that night, and during the week of the wake, the many friends my parents had; neighbours brought things they thought we might need: cups and saucers, benches, braziers, outsize teapots, spoons, masses of things; it was a pleasant lesson, I was touched by the spirit of community, although my conservative Aunt Letty was upset and uncomfortable.

'Tomorrow people will say we are askers,' she said. 'You don't know how some people can talk.'

'But we didn't ask for anything, Auntie,' I said.

'Tomorrow we'll fetch our own things from Alex,' she said, with finality.

I was surprised to notice that the girls on the benches were not looking into their hymn books, they knew by heart the entire range of hymnals, and it was much later that I discovered the reason or could articulate the fact that so large a number of people attended the wake; I could not then understand the implications of a conversation I overheard.

'There are many people,' a young man said.

'Hm, many people.'

''Me Ma-Willie goes to other people's tebellos.'

I learned that attending tebellos and going to funerals was a necessary social function; the more funerals a person attends, the more people he can expect when death comes into his house. It is considered either a disgrace or a social slight or a sign of unpopularity, to have a small insignificant funeral. Since life and death exist together in our lives, and death is so close, we live in a state of preparedness for death; women usually have a funeral ensemble in their wardrobe, and most men own a black or dark suit; we belong to burial societies and attend tebellos so frequently that we know all the hymns.

'Can you take my collection now,' a man said to me, 'I have to go to Pretoria tomorrow. I want to sign the collection book so you'll know I gave something.'

'We thank you,' I said, 'I'll fetch the book.'

This was one of those rites which attended death, people gave as much as they could to help with the funeral expenses; I had not been warned to keep a register of signatures against the monies contributed, so I took one of my exercise books to use as the collection book.

'Here's the book, uncle, ' I said.

By midnight the cousins, under the supervision of Aunt Letty, served a dish of samp mealies—a sort of hominy dish—with meat followed by more tea; the catering help worked through the night serving the needs of friends during the wake. Around three I was tired but I could not steal a nap, I was a man, carrying a load of responsibility, and it would probably have been interpreted as impolite; if strangers could sit through the night commemorating the death of my father, as his son I had a stronger obligation to stay up.

And although death had intruded into my life before, when Nancy died my life was not really changed and death had still seemed something which happened to other people; but now I came to know the vacancy it left in our lives, and the poor lonely man came to be missed and loved.

It was a big funeral, the first I ever attended; the instruction from the mortuary for the coffin not to be opened cheated the family from the customary last look at the corpse. The bearers carried the coffin out of the house, the yard, and into the hearse, and as they passed by me I noticed that 'William Modisane' had been inscribed on it in error. The shock of seeing my name and not my father's on the coffin confused and frightened me, but it seemed symbolic somehow; I was officially dead, something I was later to exploit emotionally.

The funeral service was an emotional drain, I pretended an appearance of maturity, but the strain was too much for a practising adult, and although I did not shame myself or desecrate my masculinity by breaking out and crying unashamedly, I missed the fantasy of childhood, to wish myself to another place, in another time, where I could be myself, a boy choking with tears. During the consecration service a shovel of sand was held out at me and I understood that I was expected to sprinkle a handful of sand over the coffin, but I could not persuade my hand to throw sand over my father; it seemed to be a symbol of contempt, a profane ceremony, like throwing mud at an ancestral god. I was suffocating with emotion, I could not explain this to the man who held the shovel, then an uncle manipulated my hand, like a mechanical device, guiding it over the shovel, scooping up sand and opening it over the coffin; I shut my eyes as my hand was manœuvred.

When the mourners returned from the cemetery two tin bathtubs with water had been placed outside the yard next to the gate, and in turns we washed our hands before entering the yard, in a kind of ceremony of purification or cleansing, to wash away death from our hands. The day of the funeral was also the day of prime slaughter and feasting, a celebration to death itself.

Chapter Three

MY MIND recoiled with anger and a little with fear, I had not realised the scope of the destruction; it was a wasteland, like a canvas by Salvador Dali, with all the despairing posture of mass desolation, then it began to look picturesque as a slum would to the tourist; there seemed to be a pattern, a design, in the arrangement of the destruction: the bulldozed walls, the bricks, the sand, the door and window-frames, the deserted dustbins, the skeletons of motor-cars, of propped-up trolley carts, a promiscuous assortment of discarded possessions; and rising like tombstones or desert cactus among the desolation were the structures of outdoor lavatories and the rebellious isolated houses which stood defiant against the authority of the bulldozers; these structures were the proud indestructible soul of Sophiatown, defiant erections among the ruins, an undying symbol for those who loved Sophiatown, and those who feared it.

The house of Dr Xuma had always been the model for my landed security. There was a tiny plot in Gold Street next to the Diggers Hall, opposite the house of Mr Dondolo and the shebeen, 'The Battleship', which I had hoped to purchase after becoming a doctor and on which I would construct my palace; but that dream has been annihilated, it is languishing among the ruins like black South African dreams, yet behind me stood the house of Dr Xuma, bold and majestic, like the man inside it, the man Ma-Willie wanted me to emulate.

After the funeral service, when even the relations had returned to their homes, Ma-Willie and I had a long talk; she spoke with gentleness and care, almost feeling her way around the very words.

'The wayside corn does not grow,' Ma-Willie said, in Pedi, a northern Sotho dialect. 'Things will be heavy now; to be a doctor, I would have liked to have been able to bear the burden.'

'Yes, 'me, I hear you,' I said. 'I want to look for work, I want to be the one to look after you.'

'When my strength is tired it'll be time for you to work,' she said, 'but first, you must go to school.'

'School is for children,' I said, 'I am a man, I must work and look after you and the children.'

'I will work,' she said, firmly, 'you will go to school.'

'Where is the money to come from?'

'We'll see,' she said, 'God is living.'

To be a doctor like Dr Xuma would be to be respected, to live in a big house with separate bedrooms, a room for sitting, another for eating, and a room to be alone, for reading or thinking, to shut out South Africa and not be black; a house in which children would not be sent out if someone wanted to take a bath, we would not have to undress in the dark or under the blankets. Dr William Modisane, I love the sound of the title, the respectability and the security it would have given our family and eased the handicap of being black in South Africa. Money and social position would have compensated for this, maybe even bought us acceptance; I was not particularly concerned with the groans of suffering humanity, was not dedicated to wiping out malnutrition, malaria, or dysentery, I had no pretensions to such a morality, I wanted solely, desperately, none of these things—only to pull my family up from the mud level of black poverty.

Ma-Willie and I had always pointed with pride to Dr Xuma, the African doctor who had studied in America, Glasgow and London; he had success, wealth, position and respect, and my mother was suddenly seized by the vision of a Dr Xuma in the family.

'You will be a doctor,' she said, determined.

She turned our home into a shebeen, worked fourteen hours a day brewing and pressing home brews called skokiaan and barberton, and from the proceeds she educated me to high school level and the two girls to primary school level. They dropped out because they could not visualise the immediate benefit of education; but the value of it had been indelibly impressed into my mind.

Moralists and reformists, like Dr Xuma, whose existence did not depend on shebeens spoke out publicly against the medical dangers of these concoctions, but prohibition anywhere places a premium upon the restricted commodity, and thus the churches, the welfare department, the cause-followers fastened on the campaign to stamp out the traffic, focusing on altruistic motives like: the health of the Native, the destitute family of the addict bread-winner; but the police departments, which put up half-hearted banner campaigns, were more realistic than the correctionists who overlooked the human factor; the Africans, like everybody else, wanted to, and would drink, whether it was or was not prohibited.

To the police departments shebeens were a source of unlimited funds, the tariffs for liquor offences were worked out with careful attention, reasonably steep but not calculated to discourage or inconvenience the budget of shebeen queens. The liquor squad was made up of 'reasonable men' always willing and prepared to listen to the pleas of the shebeen queens, to make accommodating adjustments. My mother always paid, and I often wondered why she had not taken out an insurance policy against this hazard.

Life in a shebeen exposed me to a rude introduction to the South African police, they made me realise the brutal, dominant presence of the white man in South Africa. I saw my mother insulted, sworn at and bundled into the kwela-kwela, the police wagon, so often it began to seem—and I perhaps accepted it—as a way of life, the life of being black. Listening to the young constables screaming obscenities at Ma-Willie emphasised the fact that we were black, and because my mother was black she was despised and humiliated, called 'kafir meid' and 'swart hell'. I was helpless in the coffin of my skin and began to resent the black of my skin, it offered no protection to my mother from the delinquency of the police constables who saw only the mask representative of a despised race; but Ma-Willie was not black, she was my mother, and if I had been white the whiteness of my skin would have protected her honour. I wished I was white.

Every night was Saturday night, house full, in the charge office of Newlands Police Station, new arrivals waiting to be charged were sardined in the yard immediately behind the office; a continual buzz flowing from the shebeen queens, the drunks, Pass offenders, thieves and all sorts, in a conspiracy of voices, making arrangements, sending out messages, to relations, to friends, about funds, fines.

Tell my wife.

Mother.

Friends.

Ten shillings.

It was always the same, the same voices, the same desperation, the same pleas, and throughout all this I waited outside the police station, waiting for my mother to be charged, fined and released, waiting to escort her home. The police clerks behind the desk were pedantically methodic in their job, and sitting out there with nothing to do I would find leisure in timing the changes of working relays. The offenders were shouted into the charge office.

'Stand against the wall,' the police clerk said. 'Shake up, this isn't a bed.'

'Silence, you devil,' the other shouted. 'You, you with the black face, shut your stink mouth.'

The offenders pushed against each other into a straight line against the wall. The clerk placed the pad in front of him, arranging two carbons between the pages, selected an indelible pencil, sharpened the lead and generally prepared himself for the session.

'Right,' he said. 'Name? God, these bloody names. Guilty or not guilty?'

'Guilty, my crown.'

'Two pounds.'

'My wife is bring it, my baas.'

'Lock him up.'

'Is coming, my baas,' he said, 'the money.'

'Silence. Next. Name? God. Guilty or not guilty? Eight pounds. Good, stand one side.'

And so it went on for two hours the clerk working like a robot, questions and instructions rattling away almost as if by reflex action, and at the end of that time the offenders would be ordered off into the yard.

'Hey, Ephraim, open a window,' the clerk shouted at the attendant African police boy. 'This place stinks.'

For the next half-hour the clerks would stretch, smoke and drink coffee and chat together; Ephraim would be fingering the roller and inking the pad.

'Ephraim, tell me,' the clerk said, 'what is it about you people that smells so bad?'

'Don't know, baas.'

'Like shit.'

'Yes, baas.'

'Bring those stink pots out.'

When all the offenders had been charged, there would be another break, then those with funds paid the admission-of-guilt fines and took their turn at being finger-printed by Ephraim; this done they wait against the wall whilst the receipts are being written out, then the names are called out against the receipts and the offenders start hurrying out through the door where the women find their escorts waiting. This would be around one-thirty and I would consider myself lucky if Ma-Willie was in this early batch.

My mother accepted her life, and, I suppose, so did the other shebeen queens; they chose this life and accommodated the hazards, my mother wanted a better life for her children, a kind of insurance against poverty by trying to give me a prestige profession, and if necessary would go to jail whilst doing it. And in our curious society going to jail carried very little social stigma, it was rather a social institution, something to be expected; it was Harry Bloom who wrote: more Africans go to prison than to school.

On the way from the police station Ma-Willie and I would make interminable stops delivering messages from people inside.

The responsibility mounted upon me by the death of my father transformed my entire life, exposed a print of living which appalled me; I became a part of shebeen life and the spectacle of so many drunken people behaving like children horrified me: women breaking into crying fits, men quarrelling and fighting over a trifle, people staggering into drunken sprawls, getting sick and lying in their own vomit was too much for my young and puritanical mind. I loathed the sight, the smell and the taste of liquor, until I imagined myself behaving shamelessly, being unable to realise the weight of the shame.

I observed them before that first drink; when they arrived they were normal, almost as noble as my father, I could not help thinking that any one of them could have been my father, then gradually the similarity would wash away and the man would corrode into a something I could only despise; and yet at that moment of drunkenness they were boldly happy in their stupid argumentative state, singing and dancing, whistling and shouting, unbottled by the drink, existing on another level.

Even against my impulses an admiration for them sneaked through my prejudices, they became less formidable as they became less like a family figure, were human in a free sense, almost approachable; but it had always to be after that drink, before which I could see only the sadness in their eyes, the nervousness in the fingers clutching the scale of skokiaan which was rushed down into their system; to drink was to get drunk, there seemed to be a compulsion to get drunk, it was in the manner they drank the skokiaan, in the way they paused almost to feel the drink taking effect. It seemed there was something in their lives which they detested, wanted to destroy almost; I felt that for them getting drunk was a purposeful destruction of the pain of their lives, a drowning of themselves in this orgiastic expenditure. They were breaking out, escaping from themselves in the very noise which was part of it and of themselves.

Noise was among the pet hates of shebeen queens, for it, too, was an intoxicant; people got drunk with it, and when they were dizzy with it they fought and injured each other; it was also the pied piper which attracted the police and gave the shebeen a bad name, but the noise was that part of drinking that laughter is to joy, and if they had to make a noise then there must be a provision made against police intrusion. So I was trained to be the watch dog capable of spotting a policeman fifty yards away; but the element of risk was a strong potential, the liquor squad was changed much too frequently, and the blank periods before I could recognize the new squad were dangerous to my mother.

By seven o'clock every night I would go on duty and over the week-ends remained on my post until after midnight when the last of the boisterously happy men staggered into the night which would give life to another day, to another night from which they would return to obliterate it from their consciousness. I would go to bed for three hours and be on the post again at three whilst Ma-Willie pressed the brew, and ninety minutes later I would cuddle into my bedding which I made on two long benches placed together; I hated sleeping on the floor and it was uncomfortable sleeping in a foetal position on the bench.

The schedule was unchanging and on top of this were the school hours, the masses of homework done by candlelight with my eyes blearing out; but school was exciting, and history was stimulating. I learned of the rise and fall of man, the dark ages of his soul which he survived, and then his proudest hour, the renaissance of culture, man's most productive age. I could not resist the glorious history of ancient Greece, the civilisation which was to influence one section of the world and to subjugate and dominate the other; I was excited by the architecture, the philosophy, the drama, and the concept of democracy and government, which provoked a comparison with South Africa, a constitutional democracy; I was aroused by the gallant history of Rome, the Gallic wars of Caesar, the conquests of the world's first fighting machine, the culture which produced Leonardo da Vinci, Michelangelo and others; we were taught that the cultures of Greece and Rome have left their standard on the whole world, that even in South Africa the architecture of the Colosseum, the Johannesburg white cinema, was by influence an example of Roman architecture; but we were not allowed into the galleries to see even copies of the art masters, and all I knew about the 'Mona Lisa' was that it was a painting of a smiling woman.

What the history books and the teacher did not point out was that this civilisation initiated and institutionalised the degradation of the human spirit, that it was maintained and sustained by slave labour; tyranny has still to be officially included among the legacies of the civilisation that was Rome.

40

South African history was amusing, we sat motionless, angelically attentive, whilst the history teacher recounted—as documented—the wars of the Boers against the 'savage and barbaric black hordes' for the dark interior of Africa; the ancestral heroes of our fathers, the great chiefs which our parents told stories about, were in a class described as bloodthirsty animal brutes; Tshaka, the brilliant general who welded the Mnguni tribelets into a unified and powerful Zulu nation, the greatest war machine in South African history, was described as a psychopath. A group of us confronted our teacher.

'My lessons come from the history books,' he said, 'and if you want to pass exams you must reproduce the history lesson, straight from the book if you like.'

'What's the truth?' I said.

'That you must learn for yourself,' he said. 'This is only a historical phase, the situation may be reversed tomorrow and the history may have to be rewritten.'

'How did it happen?' I said. 'Why?'

'Your history lessons may answer that.'

The question has not been fully answered, but the history revealed that truth may have a double morality standard; the white man petitioned history to argue his cause and state his case, to represent the truth as he saw it; he invoked the aid and the blessing of God in subjugating the black man and dispossessing him of the land. It was impossible to understand history, it showed a truth I could not accept, so I learned my history of South Africa like a parrot, I reproduced the adjectives describing African chiefs, and for external examinations I added a few of my own adjectives to flatter the white examiners.

'Which adjectives did you use?' I asked classmates, after writing the examinations. 'I described Dingane as malicious, venomous, ferociously inhuman, beastly, godless; I should get a good mark.'

And there in Sophiatown I seemed to be walking on the pages of history, a broken, defeated soldier, crushed and humiliated, walking among the human wrecks along the banks of the river which ran red with blood after the battle of Blood River; my eyes surveying the wasteland of mutilated bodies of the once proud army of Dingane, and as then, I knew that defeat was to lose the land by annexation. By interpolation the bodies became the homes, the blood the sand; I walked along Edward Road, turning south at Good Street, then the awareness of the silence surrounding me keyed up my senses, I listened to this silence which was so unusual for Sophiatown; children did not seem to be playing or just being about, I missed the boys practising on the penny whistle, the rickety, squeaking horse-drawn trolley carts, the rattling crocks, the coal, the empty bottles, the dry bone vendors, shouting like village criers; somebody had switched off the noise, the bang-up noises of Sophiatown; the silence was screaming in my head, the echo deafeningly loud. I hurried along the street looking for children at play at dice, banging against the electric standards, hide and seeking among the ruins, in the school yards, but all that I could find in the streets was the silence echoed back at me.

Only the silence came across the broken-glass-decked high walls girdling in the Coloured children's orphanage in Milner Road, the same silence from the white cemetery across the hill; about and above the screaming silence filtered the depression of loneliness. I dreaded returning to the empty home without Fiki and my daughter Chris, who had gradually begun to fill the emptiness of my life, for more and more I had found myself turning to a fifteen-month-old child for perhaps the only meaningful affection I ever felt; she had become an amalgam of all the people I had ever wanted to love me, and in many respects, even at that age, she was very much like me, and I think Fiki resented this.

For the two weeks during which a kind of cold war raged between Fiki and me we battled for the affection of Chris, she seemed to be observing us as children must do, playing between us, and at us, reminding us perhaps of the link which brought us together; she drifted between us apportioning her attention and love, showing neither preference nor favour, I think she treated us as the children we deserved to be treated as, dividing herself equally between us.

'We want to go to Natalspruit,' Fiki said, after the first week of the silent seige.

'What for, sweetie?' I said. 'You've only just returned from being with mammy; you stayed away for three months.'

'We'll only be away for two weeks,' Fiki said.

'Sorry, sweetie,' I said, 'perhaps if you told me why. I'm tired of being a sometime husband; I'm tired of being on hire purchase, you spend five months a year at your mother's. What am I supposed to do when you're gone? Last time I heard you had been at a dance function in Payneville, I don't want my wife going to shows eighteen miles away.'

'I didn't go with a man.'

'That's hardly the point, sweetie,' I said.

'You stay next to your mother,' Fiki said, 'I also want to be next to mammy.'

'I see,' I said. 'All right, sweetie, take your things and go to mammy; but I need a clarification here, you're either married to me or to mammy, if it's mammy, then go.'

A terrible scene developed, Fiki was hurt and began crying, I was raging with crystal-cold anger, speaking slowly, my voice controlled and incisive; we lived two strangers in the same house, in the same bed, in a state of constructive desertion, and when our bodies touched, accidentally, we itched away mumbling apologies. Fiki suffered more from the silence, several times she made overtures to a settlement, but I was vengeful and spiteful, intending her to beg on her knees for forgiveness, all that mattered was to teach her a lesson.

A week later her mother, Mrs Plaatje, came to visit us, I immediately suspected a conspiracy and determined this was going to be the first time I would refuse her something, and the prospect was unsettling; she was too wonderful a human being to refuse anything, and like most women I loved she could play on me like an mbira, manœuvre me into any situation. I evaded talking to her, knowing I would finally agree for Fiki and Chris to go to Natalspruit, that I would hate myself for it; I saw the lonely nights ahead, the physical absence of Fiki, I would miss the antics of Chris jumping into my bed and reading with me the newspaper flat on our backs, tucking close and resting her head on my shoulder. I would miss the morning tea Fiki served us in bed, the fuss she made about getting late for work, the minutes Chris and I spent playing on the bed; the songs I sang to her, the way she sat up against the wall listening excitedly and applauding the spectacle of me standing in the middle of the room in pyjamas, doing comedy routines, the song and dance man; I seemed to live for the glowing smile on her face, its thousand shades and variations; I was dedicated to doing this and the rewards were bounteous; Chris was almost too perfect a child.

That was what I would miss most, but an even greater and more enveloping fear was the loneliness of being alone, the nights behind the typewriter, working into the small hours, afraid to get into bed, afraid of the being alone; I would be afraid of the compulsion that would come over me, to throw myself at people, to surround myself with them, and whenever Fiki left me, this affliction would come over me, sitting in the room my ears tuned to the slightest noise, in anxious anticipation of that knock at the door. Then Princess would come in and we would play records, have a drink and make love; Princess was haunted by the lyrics of the song, 'May the Good Lord Bless And Keep You', it made her introversive and tearfully affectionate, conveying a sense of premonition that the song might some day have real meaning; perhaps she understood and suffered in anticipation the pain of a permanent parting.

Her name was Margaret, and I called her Princess. Her love remained constant, survived the marriage to Fiki, and it was she I ran to when confused and uncertain about my marriage. She did not burden me with questions or demands, she was there when I wanted her, understood that it was Fiki I wanted to be married to. Princess talked to me about the men she was going out with, brought them round, I suspect for approval, but something usually happened and she would employ my shoulder to cry them out of her system. My mother was very fond of her, they spoke together for hours, exchanging recipe dishes, and when a relative died in Alexandra Township Princess accompanied her to the tebello, working in the catering; she was the ideal makothi, the African daughter-in-law, but it was Fiki I had married, and for some reason Fiki and Ma-Willie were never really close.

Fiki came from a middle-class background of Coloured influence; her mother was Coloured, her father was a court interpreter, the son of the famous author, Sol T. Plaatje. There was a snobbishness about Fiki which perhaps was responsible for the relationship with Ma-Willie, who was a shebeen queen. There were times when I would be embarrassed with and for her, and twice she raised the question of moving away from my mother, something totally inconceivable; I was tied to Ma-Willie by responsibility, family unity, custom, I was the eldest son, she and the children were under my protective support, the shield, as she called it; Fiki had probably forgotten the responsibility of this.

Mrs Plaatje was waiting for me to settle down, I had exhausted all the excuses for avoiding the issue.

'Mammy, how's daddy?' I said, formally pacing the

conversation with the customary formalities of laying the ground with the introductory trivialities.

'Daddy's all right,' she said, with a perceptible nodding of the head. 'His legs have been giving him trouble, but not too much.'

'I'm sorry to hear that, mammy,' I said. 'How was daddy this morning?'

'Not very bad,' she said, 'it's at night when they trouble him; the doctors can't do a thing for him.'

'Doctors of today are not as good.'

'They are too young,' Mammy said. 'But daddy's problem is loneliness, he longs for Chris, and I long for Fiki.'

'I see, mammy.'

'The house is so quiet without Chris,' Mrs Plaatje said, 'only yesterday daddy said it would be nice if the children came for a week or two.'

'But, mammy, they've just been to see you.'

'I know, my son, but it's a holiday for Fiki,' she said. 'Why don't you all come down?'

'Thank you, mammy,' I said, 'but I'm busy writing a book and I need Fiki in the house.'

'You see, both of you need a holiday,' Mrs Plaatje said pushing the point. 'Fiki looks tired, she needs a holiday.'

'Holiday from what, mammy?' I said, amazed at the sudden boldness. 'Fiki doesn't work too hard, Chris is sweet, doesn't give trouble. It's dreary here, mammy, without them.'

Mrs Plaatje smiled with her teeth, her eyes were bewildered, refusing to understand, and believe, that I had actually refused her request; it probably came as a surprise to all three of us, Fiki was furious.

'We'll all come down for Christmas, mammy,' I said, in a desperate assurance that no malice was intended.

'You don't love mammy any more.'

'No, mammy, that's not true,' I said. 'I love mammy very much and mammy knows it.'

'All right, my children,' she said. 'Where's Chris?'

'I'll get her mammy,' I said, rising. 'Would mammy like some tea? No, Fiki, sit down and talk to mammy, I'll make it. Okay?'

Fiki's interpretation was that my attitude was disrespectful, accused me of having presumed to disregard her mother's intervention; and instead of a thaw our relationship was deteriorating like a festering sore, she retreated into a silence, began to lose weight, a condition which was noticed by our friends, Myrtle and Monty Berman. It did not occur to me how deeply I had hurt her until that evening when she broke down.

'If you don't love me, why don't you divorce me?' she said. 'I can't live with a man who won't talk to me; Bloke, I'm going mad. Asseblief, Blokie, please.'

'Sweetie,' I said, contrite with shame on seeing her explode in anger and tears. 'I'm sorry, sweetie, I'm very sorry; I didn't realise, I'm sorry, I thought you didn't want to talk to me.'

'You're doing it purposely, you want to drive me out of the house,' she said. 'All right, Blokie, you win; I'm going home.'

'But, sweetie, you are home.'

'I want to go home.'

'Okay, sweetie,' I said, realising the determination in her voice. 'You and Chris can go for two weeks.'

Ma-Willie came into our room as the gentle arbiter, appealing to our responsibility as adults and parents.

'The children can hear you,' Ma-Willie said. 'Chris is sad.'

'Sorry, ma.'

It seemed we had gone over and past the crisis, we spoke together, went out to cinemas and parties, spent the Sunday with Margaret and Morris; laughter returned to our little room, we played our records, loud, danced and dreamt of a big house with a garden, like the Millner's. A few days later Henri Schoup drove me home and as he was about to leave Fiki walked up to him.

'Henri, can you drive me to Natalspruit?'

'When?' Henri said, looking at me inquiringly.

'When was it you wanted to go, sweetie?'

'Is Wednesday all right with you, Henri?' Fiki said.

'I suppose so,' Henri said, obviously uneasy. 'What time?'

'Any time in the afternoon.'

I walked Henri back to his car, feeling, and probably looking, stupid.

'Will it be all right, Henri?'

'But my dear chap, of course.'

I did not say another word to Fiki until she left, and all the way to and from Natalspruit I pretended a casualness, playing with Chris. Back in Sophiatown I crawled into my little room, into the loneliness which I dreaded so much; I began to cancel Fiki from my life, if she did not exist then she could not hurt me; she was crossing the street, jay-walking across Victoria Road, then suddenly this bus, this green bus with the enormous wheels, knocked Fiki down; someone screamed and I started with that numb pain of death in my stomach. I switched on the lights and played records very loud. I was in a sweat.

I dismantled Chris's cot and pushed it under the bed; my mother, who must have sensed the breakdown I was undergoing, came in to sit and talk to me; I could never fool her, she knew all my moods, the sensitive spots, the insecurities, but remained my constant friend; right or wrong, she was publicly on my side and when I was wrong she privately disapproved, when I was uncertain and wanted blind allegiance or sympathy she would be there.

'You mustn't let them visit too long.'

We had tea and I played all her favourite records, the Frank

Sinatra and Bing Crosby Christmas carols; we talked about everything except the problems of my home, laughed over the pranks of Chris, it was a long time before I could smile without the hint of pain but when she closed the door behind her I collapsed into the silence, the loneliness, the emptiness.

It was the same loneliness, the same emptiness which surrounded me in Milner Road as I searched from out of the silence the noises of Sophiatown, the noises of life. A horse neighed and sprinted about in the veld, but it was the wrong place to look for noise; I turned west at Gibson Street, shutting my eyes from the demolition, rejecting all associations with the houses, my eyes had looked long and seen too many deaths, I was hurrying away from the dirge; I wanted again to be a part of the living, a piece of the cycle of life, to pretend a larger, indestructible existence: the whistle of the wind among the branches, the birds of the sky, the worms of the earth, the animals that walk upon the land, the quiet sea, the shrill penny whistle, the voice of Miriam Makeba.

At Edward Road I jumped into a bus down to the terminus in Victoria Road, a few yards from Nobeni's shebeen, across the street from the shop which was a front for Sophiatown's biggest Fah Fee, numbers game, pool; there was life and noise, a man came out of the shop and removed his hat, returning it to his head, it was the signal for number nine, moon, and the number was signalled all along the street; I had seen this too often, knew that my mother would have picked up the signal, that people were nervously checking their betting slips, groaning or smiling, some nursing the slip of paper, others tearing it. There was a card game going at the corner of Miller Street, bus conductors and drivers gambling at a game called Five Cards, a kind of prestige Sophiatown game, the game of the Clevers or wide boys; but it was Monday, the boys' holiday, in the locations, and the Americans had probably paraded to the cinema dressed like models in *Esquire* magazine.

The well-dressed man about Sophiatown was exclusively styled with American and English labels unobtainable around the shops of Johannesburg; the boys were expensively dressed in a stunning ensemble of colour; 'Jewished' in their phraseology; in dress items described as 'can't gets'; clothes sent for from New York or London. Shoes from America—Florsheims, Winthrops, Bostonians, Saxone and Manfield from London; BVD's, Van Heusen, Arrow shirts; suits from Simpsons, Hector Powe, Robert Hall; Dobbs, Woodrow, Borsolino hats. The label was the thing.

I watched the gamblers for a while, the stakes were too high for me; across the road was a game of draughts, and there, too, the players were too advanced for me, the moves too complicated for me to follow, and although, in my own class, I was reasonably competent, people like William Dumba were in the major leagues. They were playing knock-out matches, six-game sets, and the games were exciting. I sat down to watch and cheer brilliant moves. Two hours later the Fah Fee runners came round to collect bets, William Dumba was an enthusiast, he staked about eight shillings and continued his winning streak on the draughtboard; the runners went to the empty lot on Gibson and Victoria Road to check their bettings which were handed to the pool man who collected the slip with the winning number and handed in the bag to Chung Fat.

Chapter Four

IT BEGAN to rise, the noise of Sophiatown, first in single battalions, a statement of the basic line, then like a cacophonous symphony, separate and different lines were added to the basic thematic noise. It began to fill my ears, to surround and intoxicate me; it came from the buses, the taxis, the people returning from work, the children chattering excitedly about the film; the noises came from everywhere, the reservoir had been switched open and the voices of the noise came gushing forward. A fraction of the noise rearranged itself into a children's fantasy, they were the hero of the film, *The Fastest Gun Alive*, each in his turn was Broderick Crawford, and in their mouths the name, Broderick, was blown into gigantic proportions; they invested the name with the image of the classical hero.

'O Broad-derick is de manne,' one of them said, imitating the bubbling speech of the actor. 'Did you hear him when he said: "I'm the fastest gun there is." Did you?'

'No, he was not standing like that,' another said. 'He was standing like this, with his legs apart; and, did you see his shooting hand? It was waving back and forward, like this, over the gun. Haikona man, serious.'

'And his cheeks, man,' the other said. 'Did you see his fat cheeks, bubbling up and down, like this? Very serious. And then . . .'

'And then: bang, bang, bang.'

'O Broad-derick is de real manne.'

'Okay, I'm Broad-derick.'

'Right, I'm Glenn Ford.'

They paced back away from each other, their shooting hands hovering over the imaginary gun in the imaginary holster, poised for the draw; the gun fighters stopped, measured each other, each searching for that nervous muscular twitch on the face, and, in the idiom of Westerns, for one of them it was going to be that last sunset; then they moved forward with the stereotype slow deliberateness, and stopped.

'My name is Broad-derick, the fastest gun there is,' one said. 'I hear you're fast; okay, let's see how fast.'

'I, I don't want to fight,' the other said, in that tortured, halting speech of Glenn Ford. 'I have no quarrel, no quarrel with you. I'm a peaceable man. No quarrel, no quarrel at all.'

'I hear you're a fast gun,' the Broderick Crawford one said. 'Therefore I have a quarrel with you.'

'I have no quarrel,' the Glenn Ford one said. 'Push—don't push me, Mista.'

'Mista Ford, I'm pushing.'

They draw their fingers and shoot with the mouth through the muzzle of the pointed fingers.

'You're dead, I got you.'

'I got you first.'

They argue animatedly, screaming over each other and out of hearing range, and in the distance they are grabbling in the dust in a fight that was like playing.

'That's how they start,' William Dumba said. 'Tomorrow they will be shooting real guns, not through their fingers.'

'Like the boy who killed Potoiki,' Moffat said, 'a mere snot-nose.'

'His case was last week, got three years.'

'The law is encouraging them.'

'Three years is cheap for a man's life.'

'Anyway, Potoiki got what he was looking for,' Lazarus said. 'If these tsotsis kill each other off like that Sophiatown can be a good place. The police are hopeless, they don't care.'

'The police are only interested in Passes and liquor,' Moffat said.

'Yah, but kill a white man,' William Dumba said, 'then you'll see our police turning the place upside down.'

'Kill a black man and it's three years,' Moffat said. 'They like it when the perkies, the monkeys, kill each other.'

'The man who killed my father got six months,' I said.

'Black life is nothing,' Dumba said. 'I've heard these boys say: I'll go and work for your life; that's all it is, a short stretch for a number at Croesus cemetery.'

The news of the sentence had filled me with a sense of personal shame; I had denied Joseph Modisane the mourning rites which he, as a father, deserved from his son, withheld the tears to wash away the blood from his face; I did not demonstrate a public love for him or swear allegiance to his cause, I had let him pass out of my life without protesting the pain inflicted upon his body, without public acknowledgement that his passing would leave a vacancy in my life; I had denied him my tears and seemingly my sympathy. He died a stranger, by the hand of a stranger I could not hate sufficiently to study the features of his face, which I could not commit together with other remembrances.

In 180 days he would be free, to gloat, perhaps, at his victory, to mock our bereavement, strutting in the twilight of our sorrow; my chest was puffing with the resounding sound of revenge. My father had been sneered at, I had been cheated; I owed it to myself to allow my father the tears I had denied him, and thus to vindicate myself I bound myself to revenge. I ravaged through my mind for the details of that face, gnawing at anything to bring back that face, the little things to piece it together, but all that I could remember were the manacled hands, the silhouette to which my indifference had failed to add detail.

The law as an arbiter had betrayed me, its justice unsatisfactory; I resolved to exact my own justice. What kind of law contained this kind of justice? Was this the justice of the white man? I was to learn that justice in South African law was tinted with skin colour; it is no growl of bitterness, but the statement of an impersonal fact, that had my father been white the black killer would have suffered a commensurate punishment. I was black, the law was indifferent to black crime against blacks, there was no reason to suppose the law would be more severe with me if I killed my father's killer. I vowed it on my masculinity to cut down the man, and for months I made oblique references about him but I could get nothing from my mother.

Somehow I am glad that I did not look at that face, never got to know the man's name; that I could have murdered him, the cold-blooded calculation of such an act, the total acceptance of responsibility for the snapping out of another's life, the budgeting for a token term of imprisonment, is something which would have destroyed me; I know today that my conscience would have failed to accommodate this thing. I am glad. In the communal culture of my ancestors which still governs our lives, we all share the same blood, and the taking of it, even in the execution of justice, is condemned as an uncivilised ritual. The question of my father's death is a matter of his individual conscience, I want no part of it. I may have met him begging in the streets for the bread to sustain his body, I like to think that I might have invested in his life, for he was the grave which entombed my father's life; as it is said that Moshoeshoe, the paramount chief of Basutoland, instead of raining his vengeance on the derelict army which had eaten his father, sent down from his mountain fortress a herd of cattle to the cannibal army with the message that he could not desecrate the graves of his father.

Perhaps it was for another reason, something beyond the comforts of rationalisations, the fact that I fear violence perhaps more than I hate it. Since the death of my father I have often looked upon death, at the violence contained in it, the bleak death mask; if I feared death, it was that its component, violence, horrified and intimidated me. I am saturated with violence, it was a piece of the noise that was Sophiatown, of the feverish intensity of Sophiatown life, it was, and is, the expression and the clarification of our society. All of us, black and white, are committed to violence, it is the background of the complex attitudes of our dichotomous society, the relationships complicated and standardised by the permeability of skin colour; it is the quality of the group attitudes, we are born into it, we live with it and we die of it, each unto his own race, in the sweat-house of our skins. We seldom report the death of a South African, we speak of a dead African, a dead Indian, a dead Coloured, a dead European. We are separated and segregated from the cradle to the grave.

Violence is often the term of reference in our relationships; it wears many and variable masks, our patterns of behaviour are functional, advantageous, we wear masks of submission and servility, of arrogance and of aggression; and because in South Africa every white man is every black man's boss we supplicate, we prostrate ourselves, wearing the mask of submission and servility for the purpose of blackmailing favours from the white masters, to skate around and out of trouble with the police. We transform into the traditional good Native, the respectful, non-cheeky Native who has been educated and conditioned into an acceptance of his inferiority.

There is a time to be brave and a time for common sense. Perhaps it was better articulated by Henry Nxumalo: 'I like nonsense some times, but I like common sense more. God knows the African has cause to strike out against the individual white man or against the hooligan police, but this is too easy, one of those futile gestures to bolster the morale of the Africans, to titillate the conscience of the world into making carefully-worded resolutions larded with polite criticisms of South Africa's racial policies, but nothing ever gets done; that, I suppose, is left to my devices. I do not care to protest against apartheid, the Security Council of the United Nations is far more eloquent; I am interested solely—as a human necessity—in ending the pigmentocracy of South Africa. Until I can do this, in my own terms, in my own time, I will accommodate the situation and allow myself the patronisation of those moved to pity by my condition.'

The shadow of apartheid spreads long over my life, I have to live with it, to come to terms with its reality and to arrange myself under the will of its authority. I have to be sane, calculating and ruthless in order to survive; I was sane that night as I walked from Lower Houghton to Sophiatown against curfew regulations in a restricted area for blacks. I realised my position and planned my strategy accordingly.

I had been confronted in the servant's quarters of a girl friend working as a domestic servant in Lower Houghton; she had smuggled me into her room, supposedly against the ruling of the white master. It was arranged for me to arrive during dinner, and whilst the white family was at the meal Esther came out through the kitchen door and signalled me through the back gate, past the refuse bins along a path lined with flower-beds.

'Take off your shoes,' Esther whispered, 'you'll trample the flowers of the missis.'

I removed my shoes, tippytoeing on, an impatient, panting open-eye of anticipation; I walked against an obstacle.

'Sh,' she said, ushering me into her room.

An hour later she brought me a bowl of soup, then a meat dish, steam pudding and coffee, all served in attractive china; it was the luxury we called 'dog's meat', from the stories told around the locations that kitchen girls served their boy friends dishes prepared from the rations for the dogs, which were fed more nutritiously than the children of the locations. And although some white employers pretended not to notice the traffic in the back-yards, they objected to their best china being used by Natives; I have worked for firms where separate cups were used by whites and by blacks, and I have seen a white typist break her own cup on the allegation that it had been used by a Native. A competent cook may be mollycoddled by being permitted to keep a 'husband' in the back-yard, but this is never extended to include the use of the china; Esther probably intended to impress me.

The radio was blaring throughout our conversation, and we were preparing to get into bed when there was a knock at the door. Esther motioned me behind the door as she slipped her nightie over her clothes.

'I'm sleeping, master,' she said, unlocking the door.

The door forced her back into the room; she gasped as a man walked in closing the door behind him. I felt stupid on being discovered behind the door.

'I'm sleeping, master,' he mimicked. 'I knew I would catch you one day.'

'This is my new boy friend,' she said, pointing at me. 'I told you I didn't want you any more.'

'Heit, bricade,' he said, 'this is my cheerie; take a walk, friend, this cheerie is a rubberneck—a real Delilah.'

'Why, friend,' I said, bluffing a man I knew by reputation as the knife terror of Alexandra Township. 'She's also my cheerie.'

'Don't get hot running, friend,' he said, removing his jacket. 'Take a walk, bricade.'

'You better go, Willie,' she said, 'I don't want trouble.'

'That's right, bricade.'

I took my hat and went out; it was after midnight, I did not have a special Pass, Native public transport had stopped three hours ago. My pride had been hurt and I was too snobbish to lock myself in the servant's outdoor lavatory and spend the night there; I determined to brave the police and the tsotsis, to walk the nine miles to Sophiatown. Two hours later, on the Jan Smuts Avenue, I was surprised by a police block.

'Nag Pass, kaffir,' the white constable said, shining a torch in my face. 'Night Special.'

I pulled my hat off and came to military attention; I squeezed a sob into my voice, shook my body with fear, trembling before the authority confronting me.

'My baas, my crown,' I said, in my textbook Afrikaans. 'I have a School Pass, my baas.'

'Skool kinders is almal aan die slaap,' he said.

'Yes, my baasie,' I said. 'I was very stupid tonight, I was nearly led into the ways of the devil. This kaffir meid, my baas, was trying to trick me into sleeping in her room, but I know it is against the law, my baasie; so I said to her: the law says I must not sleep on the property of the white master. I know I didn't have a Special Pass, but I said to myself, this is wrong, you must go. This is the truth, my baasie.'

'Jy's 'n goei kaffir,' he said, becoming sickeningly paternal, 'a very good kaffir. Let me see your Pass—you must be careful, these kaffir women are bad, very bad. You must learn good at school and be a good Native; don't run after these bad women and don't mix with the trouble-makers.'

'Hier is dit, my baas,' I said, 'the Pass.'

'Ek sien,' he said, looking at the Pass under the torch light. 'Now, tell the baas where you're going?'

'Sophiatown, my baas,' I said. 'I'm very sorry to be out so late, my baas; it's this kaffir meid, my baas, very bad; she delay me until it's too late for the buses, then she says I must sleep, but I say no, it's wrong; also I see, my baas, the clothes of a man, and I say to myself, trouble; but she try to stop me, say it belong to her brother, but I say she lie and I go home.'

'You must watch these meide,' the constable said, with fatherly concern. 'You watch out for them, they're the devil's work; now, listen here, weg is jy, gone with you.'

'Baie dankie, baasie,' I said, bowing my head several times, 'thank you very much, my baasie.'

'Don't let me catch you again,' he said, playfully kicking my bottom, but there was enough power behind it to make it playfully brutal.

'Thank you, my baasie.'

I was rubbing my hands over the spot where I was kicked, hopping forward and pretending a playful pain, all to the amusement of the white police constable and his African aides. Bloody swine, I mumbled through the laughing and the clowning. Two police blocks later, played with the same obsequiousness, I arrived home.

Violence exists in our day-to-day group relationships, the expression of the public conscience; it is contained in the law, the instrument of maintaining law and order. Our aggression is totally integrated, completely multi-racial. The African directs his aggression, perhaps more viciously, against his own group, particularly against the more successful Africans who are resented for being successful. The public image of South Africa is white, and white is the standard of civilisation; what is not white is black, and black is the badge of ignorance and savagery, and the (South) African searching for acceptance surrounds himself with the symbols and the values of white civilisation; thus the successful African is immediately identified with white.

Violence and death walk abroad in Sophiatown, striking out in revenge or for thrills or caprice; I have lived in my room trembling with fear, wondering when it would be my turn, sweating away the minutes whilst somebody was screaming for help, shouting against the violence which was claiming for death another victim. The screams would mount to a final resounding peal, then nothing but the calm of death.

During those frequent minutes, trembling up a heavy sweat on my bed, I lived my life on my nervous system, dreading and yet hoping and waiting for that final last-ditch scream when death would take over. Is it a friend out there whose blood is screaming forth through the multiple stab wounds? A relative, perhaps? Most definitely a stranger, the world is filled with people, it is like the beach, who is going to count the pebbles? But pebbles do not bleed, do not feel, do not think, they are not closely dependent one upon the other, like men; and there in my room I knew that after the facts have been examined, the motives analysed, the rationalisations equated, the truth will confront me with a sense of shame; I would admit that no man, no relative or friend or stranger deserves the death of a beast. It was Caesar's boast that 'the skies are painted with unnumber'd sparks, they are all fire and every one doth shine'; if I allowed one spark—no matter how distant and insignificant—to be extinguished, then by this, my fire too would forfeit the right to flicker, and be snuffed out.

The rationalisations, the comforts of unreason, prevailed momentarily upon me, but death would not let me forget, its avatars, the bodies, were everywhere, waiting for the Black Maria, on show as an emasculating commentary on my cowardice. I crawled out of my room, unable to cope with the uncertainty, it was imperative to know the identity of the body; there were others, those like myself who felt a personal guilt, and the uncommitted, curious spectators, crowding round the body, mumbling questions to each other.

Is he still alive?

Who is he?

Has anybody got matches?

We shuffled forward, each elbowing into a grand-stand bird's-eye view of the still face under the flickering glow of the match flame; and unashamedly, each to each other, we sighed in relief: I don't; do you know him? Then the man we had dehumanised with the label 'stranger' transformed into someone very dear, very close, usually to an old woman and two girls, perhaps a mother, a wife or sister; it was painful watching them falling on the body and raising a cry so piteous and despairing that I could have died in sympathy. Then I recognised the pain, heard the same wailing, remembered another time, another situation, and I felt very close to the bereaved; they were my relations, we were joined by the pain of death. At that point of identification I walked away. About four hours later I heard the voices of indignation, the Black Maria had arrived.

'If it was a white person the Black Maria would have been here in twenty minutes,' a voice said.

'It's like the ambulance,' another said, 'a man can die waiting for it. They don't care.'

Every time it happened I drenched with sweat in my room, vowing never to let it happen again, promising the dead that violence shall not claim another man without me responding to the call for help. It must never happen again, it need not happen if I, and others, were vigilant and prevented men from injuring one another. I had cowered in my room with the cushion over my head shutting out the summons for help, suffocating the sense of responsibility; if I was brave enough to watch, I stood aloof with those of my inclining whilst thugs battered and mutilated a man to death; looking on in horror and immobilised with fear.

The knives descended from all angles, three knives jabbing at a man flaying his hands, blocking off the knives, warding off the strikes coming down on his head, taking most of the stabs on the arms.

'Help me! Please, help me.'

'Yes, spy, call them,' one of the men said, stabbing on the rhythm of the words.

The warding-off hands became slower, unco-ordinated, the stabbers were striking at ease, at selective targets; then the hands became even slower, the victim began the fall, and soon it was over, but for the screaming and the streaming blood. The stabbers stopped and looked at the silhouettes against the walls and the fences, throwing out a challenge.

'Those who got a sting can come forward,' one stabber said. 'What? Not one. Who's got pluck? Who wants to see his mother?'

All along Victoria Road to Tucker Street they brandish their knives, clearing people out of their way, and when they are out of sight, we become unfrozen and rush forward to the man bleeding into the gutter, fumbling frantically to stop the wounds from bleeding the man to death.

'Somebody phone the police for an ambulance.'

'There isn't time, stop the first car.'

A car is flagged, we persuade the driver, bully him, threaten with violence if he is leaden and unresponsive, to rush the man to hospital; sometimes we got volunteers to accompany the wounded man to hospital, others would promise to inform the wounded man's relatives; with some luck and the diligence of the hospital staff an occasional victim would survive the assault, but there were those the attackers dragged into dark alleys, assaulted and left to die away from the notice of the mad crowds of Sophiatown; these we discovered in the morning, dead and stripped of their clothes, left to die in the dark passages, in the open drains, in the skeletons of the demolished houses.

And yet always there was this emasculating silence which, in itself, was for the gangsters their best insurance against arrest; they knew that none of us would have, as they say, the pluck, to give testimony against them, and our silence sprang from a foundation of fear, the corner-stone of the gangster rule of Sophiatown. We were all aware of the danger of sudden heroics, of being produced as a witness against them, it would be stupid and impractical since the law was lenient against them; so we made Sophiatown into a vacuum of necessary silence, embracing the wisdom of the three monkeys. With our silence, the indifference of the law, the strain of being black in South Africa, we produced men and boys with long records of murder and names picked up from the gallery of Hollywood films: Boston Blackie, Durango Kid, Lefty, Stiles, Gunner Martin.

I learned, there in Sophiatown, that one looked at the killing and never at the faces of the killers; one also knew that the law is white and justice casual, that it could not protect us against the knives of Sophiatown, so we tolerated the murders whilst the law encouraged them with its indifference. We laughed and made ribald comments when police commissioners complained publicly against the lack of co-operation with the police, against the accusations that the Natives did not recognise their responsibility as citizens, that we do not fly to the law's standard; perhaps we jibed and jeered because the commissioner had not been—on this very question—as eloquent as Thomas Jefferson in his inaugural speech: 'every man would meet the invasions of the public order as his own personal concern.'

The law is white, its legislators are white, its executive authority is white, and yet we were being criticised for not flying to the standard of the law; we who were black and therefore denied the responsibility of formulating this law or being ruled by consent. This was probably as amusing as the American and the British democratic principle that all men are born equal—except for Niggers and slaves; they are property. The pronouncements were larded with the usual assurances of police protection, but the inflexions were obvious, the emphasis insinuating on crimes directed against whites and their property. In Sophiatown we hooted at these appeals to patriotism and public duty, they contained conflicts of loyalty and a pragmatic contradiction; the standard function of law, the duty of the police, is a concern with the maintenance of law and order; but discrimination is contained in the law and the police are the instruments of black oppression, and if I had to choose between the tsotsis and the police my vote would be cast for the tsotsis. This is the morality of black South Africa.

I had hoped that after the first ten murders I would be able to live with death, that the screams in the night would become less personal, the intensity would burn itself out, but there was to be no compact with death; I began to anticipate the screams, to suffer in advance, to feel this pain of death gathering in my chest like a biliousness which I could not break simply by belching or vomiting. I was choking with it. There was little comfort in rushing forward when the man no longer needed me, the rationalisations confronted me with the view of the real problem: my life is valueless in the valley of the dead, only in the living can there be life; I am involved in the death of the living.

I was listening to noisy jazz on the record player when one of those interminable screams rose over the noise, it seemed to come from a few feet away, seeming to come from inside the yard; I rushed out of the room with a fighting stick in my hand, but it was out in the street and the woman was screaming the usual summons; I was not feeling particularly brave, I did not want to be savaged with knives, I did not want to die; I was afraid of being afraid. I walked out into the street, up to the man who was slapping the girl; the rescue attempt was easier than I could have hoped for, the would-be rapist was a boyhood playmate and persuading him, by the continence of our friendship, to employ gentler means of persuasion, was peacefully successful.

'Go home, my sister,' I said, 'and don't walk alone.'

Pieters and I were exchanging reminiscences, joking about the street fights we had, the territorial protection we paid when we passed through areas controlled by gangs on our way to Balanski's cinema, the bed-bug palace, which fed us on low-budget cowboy films and other tuppenny horribles we referred to as skiet en donner, the sound and fury thrillers from Republic Pictures. There was Buck Jones and his horse, Silver; the evil genius from the serial *The Drums of Fu Manchu*. We were recalling the titles of the chapters: 'Pendulum of Doom', 'Death Dials a Number', when suddenly I noticed the girl I had rescued advancing towards us with an impi of six armed men.

'It's them!'

There was no time to hold an indaba, the impi was in a fighting mood; Pieters and I broke off in different directions, we were back in the days of the gang wars, running in the face of odds, because he who runs from a fight lives to fight another day. I was Buck Jones racing Silver across the plains, pursued by the crooks, moving rapidly, thinking fast; I was running up Gold Street towards the dark passage running behind the Diggers Hall, I knew every turning in that passage. I lost them. I stopped for a while and listened, then I doubled back over the fence and into the yard of the hall, keeping in the shadows and listening, and back in Gold Street I looked both sides of the street before emerging from the shadows. I had stuffed my hat inside the shirt and was walking casually down the street when suddenly they pounced upon me; they had apparently anticipated me and were waiting.

I was struck with a stick on the head, the blow staggering me on to the street; blows descended on my body from all sides, most of them thudding on the head which I covered with my hands, my body crouching low, preferring the blows on the body. Throughout the assault I kept one single thought repeating in my head, a determination to be on my feet; the man who falls during an assault tumbles into his grave, because in Sophiatown a felled man gets kicked in the face and heavy boots crushed on the head.

It was my turn at the guillotine, Sophiatown was revenging herself on me, striking out against the overcrowding, the congestion of hate, the prejudice, the starvation, the frustrating life in a ghetto. They stood back, the people of Sophiatown, and allowed violence to satiate itself; I did not scream, I resigned myself up to my fate, the fate which was linking my destiny with that of my father; this was a communion with him, we would switch back our identities, my coffin would carry his name, as his had carried mine. The beating continued, they struck at my head through the shielding hands, my feet were beginning to weaken, they could not support my body; I was sinking and I surrendered myself to my father, committed my life into his hands. I was not afraid, there was a throbbing in my head but I had gone past the point of feeling pain; I was no longer struggling, I was back in that little mud pool, my hands groping for anything to hold me down, to stop the struggling and drown.

'Hamba, nja,' voices shouted. 'Go, dog.'

Then another voice began screaming in my head: Run, run! My body was wilting on my legs, but I willed it into motion; I was going home. I looped forward, charging on unco-ordinated legs, diving forward into the gravel, my face scratching on the ground, but I would not stay down; I hauled myself up, waltzed forward and dived down on to my face, rising and falling my way home where I collapsed into my mother's room, exhausted from the beating, with a headache which lasted a week.

'You must not do it again,' Mother said. 'I do not want another death in the house. Is he too, God, to die like his father?'

'You cannot protect all the screaming noises of Sophiatown,' Solly Godide said.

I could not explain it to Ma-Willie and to friends, perhaps not even to myself, but it was the only time when I had not been afraid; but the irony of it all is that, as it turned out, it was Sir Galahad, not the dragon, who was slain.

I did not learn, perhaps because of the influence of the Hollywood films, the daredevil hero complex of the American male; I wanted to be with the good boys against the bad boys, so we formed a street-corner gang: Philip, Spampu, Mannass, Ncali, Valance, Dwarf, Niff and I; we were the Target Kids, with targets drawn on the sides of the shop on Gold and Victoria Road. Target was for girls, and we wrote the names of the girls we wanted; but we were also a kind of vigilante group concerned with keeping our corner safe from the marauding gangs of Sophiatown; we were neither thieves nor thugs, and never carried knives, but we never hesitated to use violence against the tsotsis, the bull-catchers, who attacked, robbed and stripped people. We answered the tsotsis with violence, which was a kind of lingua franca, and, in effect, we too were tsotsis; legally we should have handed them over to the police, but we were black, the tsotsis were black and the law was white. We had no intention of being produced by whites as witnesses against blacks, this would have exposed us to the vengeance of the tsotsis, arranged us in the line of the knives and guns, and to the scorn of other Africans. The tsotsis were violent men, the force of violence was the only voice they respected; it was a comforting morality adequately masking the violence in us, we were little giants with power complexes, filled with acts of cruelty, injustice and oppression. We cleansed ourselves with rationalisations, armed in point with pious indulgences, like a Christian straight out of the confession box.

We grouped round our corner singing pop songs, making instrument sounds with the mouth, whistling wolf calls at the passing parade of girls, daring each other on. We bound ourselves to a code of ethics, impressment tactics were not permitted; but insinuated into our approach was an element of

67

emotional blackmail. We bull-chested to the rescue of the girls in trouble, then after a brief conference one of the heroes to the rescue gallantly offered to escort home the distressed lady, using the opportunity to charm her; it seldom occurred to us that a woman thus under stress would have to feel obligated. The pursuit of the girl was all a game, a test of ability, the power of persuasion, and we armed ourselves with velvets of seduction, memorising romantic passages from romances and poems. Philip Mothibedi loved Edgar Allen Poe's 'Annabel Lee' which never failed for him.

'She's mine,' Philip said, with professional nonchalance. 'I said to her, you are my Annabel Lee; then right there in the middle of the street I stopped her and pointed to the moon. By that time I had her eating out of my hand; I held her face in my hands, looking earnestly and passionately into her eyes:

For the moon never beams, without bringing me dreams
Of the beautiful Annabel Lee;
And the stars never rise, but I feel the bright eyes
Of the beautiful Annabel Lee.

'The quotation melted her, right into my arms.'
'And then?' we said. 'Then what?'
'I kissed her.'
'De real Casanova, man,' Stan Ncali Dondolo said. 'Just like Charles Boyer, man, actually, in *Hold Back the Dawn*; serious man—de real manne.'

It was Sunday night, Solly Godide, a friend outside the gang, was attacked by the bull-catchers, stabbing and robbing him of a watch and wallet; it was done with speed and precision, and by the time we were aware of it the bull-catchers were moving away in different directions; we selected our man and stayed with him along Victoria Road catching up with him in front of the A.M.E. Church, it was probably Philip who tripped him. We handled him with violent rudeness.

'Look, just give us the watch and the wallet.'

'I didn't take his watch,' he said, 'I was not there.'

We were little power moguls blind to justice and right, determined to beat the truth out of a stone if necessary, forgetting the sacred principle that without law there can be no crime and that without proof there can be no guilt; but I think we wanted a confession more than the wallet and the watch, seeking to justify the beating we were itching for. We decided to beat a confession out of him, we were possessed by the power of violence, it seemed to guide and direct our hands, to add force and viciousness to our blows. It was not until the energy of the violence had exhausted itself, when we were panting, that we stopped.

'Now, will you give us the things?'

Our victim collapsed into our hands, his face contorted with pain, the lips moving, trying to mouth words that had no sound. It was a piteous sight. We looked at each other, ashamed at what we saw in each other, beasts without human passion, then we began to panic; there was that look of death in his face which filled us with both fear and humanity, and with patient petition we got from him his address; we balanced him on our hands and carried him home, explained to his parents, and every day, for a week, we went to see him in a kind of appeasement of our conscience.

What if he had died? What possible justification could there have been for it? That he stole a watch and a wallet? Was that the equivalent of a life? I was horrified by the inhumanity, shutting my eyes and blacking out from my mind memories of my father; the equation was obvious, I could not pretend to hate violence and yet allow myself to be manœuvred by it in claiming death. We were not the police, we were not tsotsis, and yet we had come too close to becoming harbingers of death.

Chapter Five

WE FELL into a silence around the draughtboard, concentrating on the game; it was our way of pretending an existence without consciousness, an existence of accommodating the smell of insult, the assegai wound of humiliation, in which every hurt is pushed down—and banked—in the stomach, piling up until in the end every possible insult, humiliation, hurt has been documented, classified and filed, so that one can no longer feel anything except the consuming fear that only one violent eruption could release the cauldron; but the safety valves, the flash-bulb warning system is only as effective as the individual sense of restraint; my warning system is radar sensitive, I am on constant alert against anger, joy, love, getting drunk, becoming sick; I am afraid to vomit the accumulation in my stomach, the violence would be too great for me to control. So we fall into a silence, absorbed in the diversion of the game of draughts, but my chest was bloated almost to pain by that bilious feeling which death and remembrances of it always caused; the intricate moves on the board—calculatedly cunning, brilliant and treacherous —seemed to resemble somehow the temper of Sophiatown, a kaleidoscope of variable moods and passions, movingly beautiful one minute, the next, indescribably ugly and horrid. Our lives were the pieces on the board being manipulated by a man-made fate, children born into a social position and playing out a patterned destiny; I seemed to see us all, black and white, on the draughtboard, manœuvred into a trap, and devoured by South Africa, one colour against the other.

We are entrapped, this consciousness was never more vivid than on that July day when Chris was born, but I pretended to be distracted by the miracle of birth, actually happy as Dr Wolfson delivered Fiki; I was pacing outside the room, like the Hollywood cliché of the nervous husband, but I was not in a film and Fiki was not being delivered in antiseptic Hollywood hospital wards, she was in a rooming-house in Sophiatown, in a yard littered by the dog, by the droppings of pigeons and fowls, spiced with skokiaan fumes and the smells of the outdoor lavatory, the community centre which was impossible to keep sanitary, it was shared by six families. There was little reason for anxiety about complications, I had never known it in my parents, the chances of a successful birth out-balance the statistics of difficult birth, yet I could not resist miming the histrionics of the anxious white husband, as parodied—I hope —in Hollywood films; I was pacing in front of the door, affectedly nervous, chain smoking, stopping, listening, continuing the marathon, all to the amusement and delight of young brother Pancho and Suzan. Ma-Willie was assisting the doctor, rushing to the kitchen, returning with a pail of hot water; she stopped for a brief moment, her head following my pacing hither and thither, she shook her head, almost in despair and entered the maternity room.

A sharp cry came from the room, I stopped, listening nervously; Fiki was in pain, the birth was no longer a matter of easiness and clowning; I looked sharply at Pancho, he forced a boyish grin, I stepped on the cigarette—fear needs no props; then I heard it, the cry, the music of life and we laughed together, my sisters and brothers and I; it rose steadily, gaining strength and volume, the crying I was to describe as the Concerto for Sniffles and Sobs in C, Opus 1, No. 2. Fiki and I were already decided on a name, the baby was to be named after a family in California: Nevitt for a boy and Christine for a girl.

I had met Norman Cousins, editor of the *Saturday Review of Literature*, through a mutual friend, Dr Ellen Hellmann, when he visited South Africa in December, 1956; I took Norman round the locations, showing him the sights of apartheid, meeting and talking to some of the victims of the system which he hoped to write about in his magazine; in the course of discussions in my room—Fiki had gone to mother and therefore missed meeting him—I intimated a desire to take my family out of South Africa, possibly to Britain, Canada or the United States, to any place which could offer Fiki and I respite from the intolerance of South Africa. In his article, 'The Man Who Didn't Come to Dinner', Norman Cousins articulated my desire to emigrate from South Africa. On 23rd April, 1957, I received this letter:

Dear Mr Modisane,

We have just read Norman Cousins' article about the death of Nxumalo and the tragic situation in Johannesburg. We should like very much to sponsor your coming to this country.

My husband is Prof. of Psychology at the University of California and director of a research project at Vassar College, Poughkeepsie, New York. He could give you a job until you find something in your field. Since it would be necessary for you to have a job waiting, according to Immigration requirements, we could provide a job of editing manuscripts.

It would give us real pleasure to do this, and unless you have already arranged something else we hope you will send us the necessary forms to fill out.

Sincerely yours,
Christine Sanford.
(Mrs Nevitt Sanford)

PS. We can give you a loan for travel expenses if you need it. If you wish to study at the University of California, certainly that could be arranged.

Fiki and I were moved, surprised, devastated by the letter,

it did not seem real that there were still people like the Sanfords, we thought they had gone out of print; I was confused, I had been hurt by people so often I was not certain whether I could survive this kindness; I could not cope with the simple power, the human kindness of the Sanfords; I was disorientated by it; the suspicion of, my hatred for white people was betrayed, how could I isolate and hate them apart? Race hatred is a devastating avalanche, it cannot afford to classify, to pick and choose its subjects; I preferred the whites as prejudiced brutes I could hate at first sight, hate was the single human emotion which held me together, I leaned upon it gently, jealously, clutching desperately on to it, until I was sabotaged by that letter; South Africa was all around me, its attitudes were regulating my life, the violence of its hatred had forced upon me and those of my white friends a relationship of masks, in which every response is carefully selected and rehearsed. In the presence of South African friends I could wear a mask, be the eternal actor in a make-believe world of tinsel reality, revealing the face, the profile which photographed the best, but I was suddenly confronted with an unknown quantity before which I stood unmasked and naked. I was conditioned to dealing only with the symbols in which each of us in the different race groups saw each other, not as individuals, but as representative facsimiles of either a despised race or a privileged and hated group; a new assessment was being insinuated upon me by the letter, the Sanfords were white and white is the symbol of arrogant authority; it is less exacting to react to white itself, not the individual who is white, but the individual act of human kindness separated them and imposed upon me this distinction; I could not wear a mask in their presence, could I remove the mask in my relationship with South African whites? Were there Sanfords among them?

We were excited, Fiki and I, and settled down to answer their letter, to thank them for the gesture, to accept with gratitude; when our first child was on the way we wrote to them for permission to name our child for them.

'It's a baby girl,' Ma-Willie said, coming out of the maternity room.

'You can see your baby now,' Dr Wolfson said. 'She's a beautiful child.'

'Well, doctor,' I said, 'I mean, of course.'

'No, I'm not joking,' Dr Wolfson said, 'I've delivered many babies—at birth they're usually a mess, this child has well defined features.'

'Sweetie,' I said, to the exhausted but proudly beaming Fiki, 'this baby is sensational. Good show, sweetie.'

An hour later flash-bulbs were lighting the twitching, sensitive face, but that evening whilst Fiki was resting I sat in one corner of the room fondling Chris with the clumsy care of a nervous father; the enthusiasm, the excitement of the birth had settled into its proper place, there was a quiet dignity in the look of pride and satisfaction on Fiki's face, but for me it was also the moment of recognition: I was responsible for a life, the confrontation terrified and depressed me. I began to brood, as my father must have brooded over the future of his son.

I was a slave in the land of my ancestors, condemned to a life of servitude, into which life I had inadvertently committed my daughter; the life I held in my hands was my personal offering to the jackals of South Africa, my individual contribution placed at the foot of the master; it was my investment towards the maintenance and the continuance of the slave dynasty, I had added my share to the nourishment of the cosmic life of the slave.

Suddenly the features of her face began to blur, there was something undifferentiated about them, they were more red than black and the indefinition disturbed me; I was looking at a neutral face, possibly black, just a representative facsimile

74

of millions of faceless masks; those who had seen her remarked that she looked like me, implying that our features were similar, but I have no face, I have no name, my whole existence slithers behind a mask called Bloke. I became desperate, here was a mask of millions of black faces, but I determined that this was a face they shall not deface, I will define all its particularities.

I mumbled my decision: South Africa shall not have her; I will take my family out of Sophiatown, out of South Africa, to a place where Chris shall start out as a human being. I refused to commit her into slavery. Chris made me realise more sharply how urgently I hated South Africa, I saw us all, black and white, entrapped in this disgusting putridity.

I must protect you from the jackals, salvage you from out of the cesspool, away from the decomposition; you will breathe the air of the free. My daughter shall not learn the morality of the slave, that life is sustained by hatred, that the purpose of life is to outlast the master, to survive to the day of the beheading. The slave may be legally freed, but he shall never be emotionally and intellectually free until the symbol of his oppression shall be destroyed, as it was said that the French revolutionaries could not accept the victory of their cause until the head of the king rolled off the guillotine; it was perhaps more eloquently articulated by Hegel: 'to be truly free the slave must not only break the chain; he must also shatter the image in both his and his former master's mind.'

My daughter shall be told the truth, she shall not learn as I have learned; my parents were primarily concerned with developing an integrated human being, my father wanted me to grow up to be a good man; he educated me to respect and humble myself before people, even the ones Thomas Jefferson described as 'those who feel power and forget right, too high-minded to endure the degradation of the other'. I was educated into an acceptance that the white man is noble in reason and just, the impression was burned into my mind, until whiteness was invested with the symbol of purity and justice; but this reality was disorganised, the foundations of my faith broken up, when the lie exploded in my face, and in that moment I suffered a disorientation of values, a demolition of personality. The relevation was a traumatic experience, both shocking and cruel.

I will have to explain to my daughter the dichotomy of our social structure, and hope by telling her the truth to gain her respect even if perhaps all that I will deserve will be understanding; for such a truth will demand explanation and how could I possibly explain 300 years of slavery? That I am one of a despised and humiliated race into which I have delivered her; this confessional emasculation would be destroying, could possibly arouse in her a loathing for me, for our ancestors, for everything black, including herself; she will, as I have, develop a complicated ambivalence towards the white man, a strange mixture of hatred, fear and a snickering admiration for the race which has for so long and with such efficiency imposed its will over the destiny of the black South African.

If I lived in South Africa I would be forced to risk this danger, but that moment, holding her in my arms I knew, and perhaps understood why my father could not face the castration ceremony of the truth; I could not bring myself to face the reality of such a confrontation, for my soul I could not.

What had been a dream was now transformed into a possible reality by the letter of the Sanfords, the probability of Chris being transformed into the thing I am was reduced appreciably; for whatever the comforts, it is a heavy thing to be preserved in a tomb of hatred, to feel yourself suffocating and inextricably forced into a corner, snarling and scratching out in the vomit of one's own hatred the loud wail of despair; to free my soul I had to reject from the human race the jackals of South Africa, refusing to share with them the same humanity. I could destroy them with my hatred if I could deface them, erase the definition from their faces, so that I saw, not individuals, but faceless masks; it is difficult to savage human beings, one has to dehumanise them before exterminating them, like some people drown cats or poison rats, or the soldier who goes to war against the black peril, the yellow menace, the Communist threat.

I have no use for human feelings, I stripped myself of them that day I looked upon the battered remains of the man who was my father; I pushed down the pain, forced it down, refused to cry and never cried since; every pain, every hurt, every insult I pushed down and held down like vomit; I have graduated bloody well, I cannot feel anything, I have no emotional responses, I am incapable of being humiliated, I have long ceased to experience the sensation of feeling a hurt. I am a corpse. Even the hatred is a formal declaration.

Dreams? Hope? Faith? These are pillars of insecurity. My daughter will learn that there is no such thing as brotherhood; there are no neighbours, there are only enemies who carry Three-Star knives in the locations and Saracen armed trucks in the white camp. Maybe in another world, in another time, she may come to realise the humanity I could not pass on to her, that man is neither black nor white, wholly good or bad, that man is essentially a composite of vice and virtue; that virtue is not necessarily white and vice black; but that country cannot be white South Africa, for she will be smothered in the stench that will smell around the world the day South Africa's racial combustion breaks out in a colour-caste explosion of putridity.

Chapter Six

CHRIS shall not be let loose into the world as I was, a naïve, orphaned and awkward child going through junior high school, in a confusing, changing world which was celebrating the first anniversary of the Second World War. Hitler's army was goose-stepping over Europe and even the deceptively peaceful shores of South Africa were touched by complicated allegiances; there were those of us, black and white, who hoped for deliverance in a German victory, African mothers were naming their children after Hitler. Our hearts burnt with the memory of the sinking of the *Mendi*, the disillusionment of the Africans who fought in the First World War was still green in our memories.

As boys we were fired with the glory of war and deflated when the history teacher teased us about going to war to protect the privilege of being oppressed in South Africa.

'In any case, you'll not fight,' he said. 'Africans are not armed, they're ambulance drivers and stretcher-bearers.'

That destroyed the great fascination of the glory of war, we privately cheered the military advance of the armies of the Third Reich; it was not so much a question of admiring Hitler, but an emotional alliance with the enemy of South Africa, in the same sense that we cheered the victory of any visiting sport's team over the national teams. At football or rugby matches, in boxing stadiums, the non-European enclosure roars in loud praise and encouragement, our demonstration of black condemnation of South African policies, and for our trouble, usually at the defeat of the local team or idol, the white South Africans throw bottles at the black South Africans; the newspaper criticises the non-Europeans, accusing them of lacking in patriotism, with broad suggestions, in editorials and reader's letters, that non-Europeans should be banned from international sporting events.

It was also the age in my life when I was experiencing a kind of after-the-apple Garden of Eden illumination, I was becoming conscious of girls, of myself, I was embarrassed by the khaki shorts with seat-sized patches, the home-tailored shirts, the cloth braces, the bare feet; then there were the bandy legs which were a subject of ridicule and coarse comment.

'Hey, Willie, stop the ball,' they teased, as they passed the ball between my crooked legs. I was always left out of the school team. 'Pick him for the team? As what, goalie? The ball will pass between his legs.'

I fought several brawls in defence of my legs, shrinking into myself whenever I thought the girls were giggling at me; I developed a persecution complex, but later I learned to live with my legs, to cover the hurt behind a joke.

'Are you limping?'

'No, only on Wednesdays (whichever day of the week).'

There were certain things I could not even begin to joke about. Poverty was a real and present fact in my life and I became more conscious of it as a teenager living in affluent South Africa, exposed as I was to the opulence of the whites: the palatial homes with parks for gardens, the cars, the clothes, the sense of well-being; I was assaulted with hard-sell advertising campaigns in fashion magazines, newspapers, cinemas, spending hours filling in mail order coupons for food, warm clothes for the winter, lightweight suits and raincoats for the summer, clothes for the children, furniture, refrigerators, radios. I became obsessed with money, sent in entry forms to almost every cash prize contest I saw, did all kinds of odd jobs: selling newspapers, being the look-out at gambling schools, running errands, carrying parcels for people coming off the buses, gambling, anything, and every penny I made went to Ma-Willie who often gave me tuppence a day for school lunches. It broke my heart seeing her working so hard, running a shebeen, selling snuff, taking in washing; I needed money to ease the burden for her.

'One day I'll retire you, mama,' I promised her.

I was going through the period of puberty; I was embarrassed by the shabby clothes, the hand-me-downs, but it was unfair to expect my mother to provide me with clothes to my now more expensive taste; I had gone through junior high school when I made my first independent decision, I could not risk discussing it with her, so I accepted a position as a messenger at Vanguard Booksellers at forty-five shillings a week; she objected, but I had decided against short pants at high school. I would buy clothes and save enough for books and then return to school. Half of the salary went to Ma-William, the rest was spent on flashy American clothes; the idea of holding down a job gave me a sense of responsibility and the tight-bottomed pants, the long jackets, made me feel like a man, and for a while school was pushed out of my mind, at the end of the week I made money which I carried home. This seemed important.

At the time there seemed nothing wrong with the job, except that for the first time I came to find myself face to face with the social attitudes of our society; hitherto I had brushed with it at the hands of the police. Perhaps I should not have reacted, should have conditioned myself to an acceptance of it, but I was young and full of causes, I wanted to change the world. I expected things to be different.

My messenger errands took me to the swank white suburbs of Johannesburg, right up to the front doors; it gave me a juvenile thrill to walk to the front door, handle the door knobs or the attractive knockers; but always there was the harsh white face impatiently ordering me to the back door where the same face with somewhat mellower lines signed for the book.

I was seized with a compulsion to use the front door, but I invariably ended up at the back; I refused to accept this condition, I promised it to myself that some day I shall be accepted through the front door. The hostility was amusing, and there were times when I did it for the masochistic pleasure of seeing the look of indignation, then the complete transformation at the back door; most of them seemed to think that I had been taught a lesson or something.

I wanted to change the world with a smile, I was always polite during those back-door exchanges, but at the end I was frustrated and irritated; four years later I gave it up and went back to school to matriculate, I wanted to rise above the messenger bicycle and the back door; what I did not realise was that I would never, in South Africa, be able to rise above the limitations imposed upon me by my colour, more eloquently articulated by Dr Verwoerd: Natives should not be allowed to rise above certain levels of labour.

Going back to school was a practical decision, even the dream of becoming a doctor was resuscitated, but I did not earn a brilliant pass or win a scholarship or bursary; even if my father had lived he could not have managed the fees, but it was medicine or nothing, I saw little point in an arts or science degree, I did not desire a teaching post, the salary was not worth the time and effort; I could earn as much in industry or commerce, and it was time I faced my responsibility. I had got a girl in trouble and the pressure to marry was terrific, but I was under economic stresses which I managed to explain would only be aggravated by an early marriage; Maggie and I decided we should wait a couple of years, during which time I would save up for the lobola, bride price, and the wedding expenses. Our daughter, Honey, was born to become an integral part of the Motaung family, taking Maggie's family name.

I went back to the bookshop, into a white collar job, and

£16 a month seemed a lot of money, until it was divided between Ma-Willie and Honey; but the prospects were good, I held a responsible post in a pleasant atmosphere; the relationship between the black and the white staff was stimulated by Fanny Klenermann, the trigger-tempered owner; Fanny was a warm, responsive human being, a stimulating other-side of the usual white South African. She spoke with the temper and the rat-a-tat repartee of a sergeant-major, flared with the tantrums of a Hollywood film star, a fanatical perfectionist who became hysterical in the face of carelessness and ignorance; her knowledge of books was uncanny, her mind an index file of information and detail, and together with Joseph Moëd they managed Johannesburg's most efficient bookshop where assistants were trained with military impersonality.

'I can't work with this woman, Joe,' Fanny would say bouncing through the shop like an animated tank. 'She's impossible. She told a customer that *Arrow in the Blue* is a novel.'

Her temper was non-racial, it was zeroed at the staff irrespective of colour or sex, and those of us who made up the African staff loved and admired her sense of fair play. We cheerfully took our turn at the firing squad of her anger. I think she mothered me somewhat, and I loved her for what she did for me as a person, for making me feel and believe myself equal to the white staff. Fanny insisted on good human relations, and although the black staff were paid in accordance with the Government's official scale for Native wages, we worked in an atmosphere of equality; she was determined not to tolerate white attitudes in her business, we called each other by our first names, not the traditional 'baas' or 'missis'.

Familiarity can sometimes be a hard thing to learn, or perhaps more accurately, it is often difficult to unlearn a set of responses; it was not easy to call her Fanny, her age deserved— according to the teachings of our customs—a measure of respect which could never include the discourtesy of first names between elders and juniors. In fact the choice was mine to determine, not a command imposed upon me to show public respect to those I privately despised. I addressed Fanny as Miss Klenermann, in deference to her age and in courtesy, and perhaps in appreciation for breaking down my inferiority complex.

But it was an exacting experience, outside the shop I was confronted by the real attitudes of South Africa; thus Vanguard Booksellers became a private world where Miss Karpolovsky was Lela, Mr Malan was D.G., Mr Stein was Philip, but out in the street they became the formal whites I addressed as Miss or Missis, Mister or Baas; but Cynthia, Lela and Philip were the friends I knew would not flinch with embarrassment, with just that slight muscular twitch in the face if I should call them by their first names, out of the shop, in the company of their friends. Ordinarily one did not greet them in the street, I was hurt by the slight of those who looked ahead and did not respond, either by design or accident. And yet we circled, like vultures, over the friendships we made in the shop, waiting to tear into the flesh of those we judged as insincere; we dared not entrust our friendship to whites whose fidelity had not been tested.

'You know, George, the new assistant is a phony,' I said, to George Gaboo, the African graduate who was the head of the stock room. 'She pretended she didn't see me when I greeted her outside Belfast.'

'Okay, we'll fix her.'

Fixing her implied the assistant would receive very little help from us, that customers would be kept waiting whilst she fumbled with trying to find the customer's book; most of them were lazy and unintelligent, depending on help from the stock room, and for every impatient customer who walked out the assistant would face the firing squad temper of Fanny. This was our recourse, we ganged up against assistants with masked white attitudes, forcing their mistakes to the notice of Fanny, who would rather dismiss an assistant than lose a disgruntled customer. There were, of course, the assistants who objected, privately to us, against being addressed by their first names, like the Afrikaner who corrected the enthusiasm of my familiarity.

'I'm Baas Jan.'

Baas Jan was an unpleasant Afrikaner with white-man-boss attitudes, this especially in contrast to D. G. Malan, who had in my estimation, because of the informality of his manner, ceased to be an Afrikaner. D.G. was human. When I first joined the staff I was intimidated by his name which I could not help associating with that of Dr Daniel Malan, then the moving spirit behind the fanatical racialism gaining impetus in the South Africa of 1947. Baas Jan made it possible for me to dislike him as a man and despise him because he was an Afrikaner. I began to assemble my trap; I was courteous towards him, which was part of the snare waiting to close in around him, for it was important not to show public animosity toward him; then my opportunity presented itself.

'Excuse me, Baas Jan,' I said, when I was sure Fanny could not help hearing me. 'We haven't got it in stock, but I think there may be a copy in the shop.'

'Where?'

I walked over to the shelf and got the book out, but by this time the customer had left.

'Why didn't you tell me where it was on the phone?'

'Because I thought you had looked,' I said. 'It was in the right section.'

'William,' Miss Klenermann said, 'come up here, please.'

'Yes, Miss Klenermann.'

'Why did you call him Baas Jan?'

'He told me to, Miss Klenermann.'

Baas Jan had a ten-minute—very loud and rough—session with Fanny, all the assistants and customers alike heard the exchanges, and Baas Jan could have died with embarrasment and anger, that he—a white man, Afrikaner—was being humiliated, with Natives listening in, for having done the right and proper thing—putting a Native in his place—according to well-established South African practice; Baas Jan did not stay with us too long after that episode.

Miss Klenermann and Joe Moëd were not the usual liberals of South Africa, they were progressive in their attitudes, their reactions were not determined by colour, and under their guidance I became less conscious of it, less dominated by it; even the viciousness of the police who swore at my mother as they pushed her into the kwela-kwela, of the thugs who elbowed me off the sidewalks, the snot-nose police constables who destroyed my father's pride, seemed far less important than they were accepted to be against the human dynamism of Fanny and Joe.

It was at the bookshop where I made my first transcolour friendship; Philip Stein and I were the same age, he had been to university, was a poet and completely non-political. He was without the affectations and the pretensions of the usual young university types who seemed to present the impression of 'look ma, no race prejudice'. Philip and I spoke together like men, even though I realised that his regard sprang from a sense of pity, and at times I thought he had committed himself to easing for me the burden of being black; I did not want to be pitied, but I accommodated this because I valued his friendship, perhaps for the selfish reason that he was my best hope for acceptance as a black man, as an equal. Philip's friendship was free, there was no question of nursing the sensibilities of the poor, under-privileged Native; I need not have read Plato or understood, and appreciated, art, music and drama, to be recognised by him as an intelligent Native.

But we did have literature in common, each hoped for a far richer and more satisfying triumph in writing, and a result more fundamental and astounding; he wrote poetry and I tried my hand at prose. Philip sensed the storming strain of the problems which troubled my soul, the frustrations of struggling to articulate, more eloquently through my writing, the ulcer of our society; he introduced me to the world of the Russian and the French literary masters, men who extracted from their own troubled times the flowering of genius which sparked sharp criticism against the social condition of man; I resolved to make literary criticisms, as they had done, against the injustice of our society, to lay bare the inhuman breast for the world to stare at; to do this without personal bitterness. Through knowing Philip I came to realise more sharply that man's smallness is a state of mind, not necessarily his heritage.

But I was too personally involved in the dynamics of being black in South Africa, I could not intellectually shrug off the oppression, the cruelty, the injustice, as though it were a careless trifle; I lived with it twenty-four hours a day, every day of my life, I could not be an uncommitted and disinterested spectator; yet I knew Philip was right, knew that I had to re-educate myself into believing in myself, into an acceptance of the objectivity of art, the inalienable persuasion of philosophy, the principles of freedom and equality. Subjectivism was, however, emotionally far more persuasive: oppression, poverty and personal humiliation cannot be wholly experienced vicariously, or something one can be intellectual about; one can perhaps only sympathise, nothing more. There are very few things which can be as irritating as the smug understanding of those jokers who profess to know what it would be like to be black in South Africa; it is an arrogant understatement to presume, in the drawing-rooms of their public library homes, to understand the suffocating life in one room. I submit, respectfully, that it is beyond academic comprehension.

I made an honest effort at being intellectual about my oppression, shut its reality from out of my mind, walking with shut eyes through many worlds of hate, hop-skipping round, over and about the affrontery of black degradation; I began crawling into small corners, making excuses, a rather incongruous black apologist, talking in intellectual negativisms: I don't like it, but after all, nothing is perfect, not even the American concept of democracy, denying, as it does, equality to twenty millions of its negro citizens.

I persuaded myself into becoming a leisurely committed theorist sliming about in search of respectability; it was easy during the United Party Government of General J. C. Smuts; semi-educated and responsible Africans were encouraged to feel less black than their uneducated brothers; they were issued with Exemption Certificates, a Pass which exempted them from carrying a Pass, but most important, they were formed into an exclusive and effective middle class, not white enough to be European and too respectable to be black. The Exemption Certificate became a symbol of snobocracy.

I became attracted to this class, embracing all its bourgeois values, perhaps the most important of which was that a gentleman does not raise his voice in loud protest: he persuades, makes accommodations, accepts compromises, binds himself to the honour of a gentleman's agreement. Acceptance into this class became a driving motive, but I was a nobody's son, brought up in a shebeen; there was no kudos attached to my name, my father had been a messenger at Jimmy's Market, Von Weilligh Street; my mother had far better relations, her brother, J. K. Mrupe, was a man of property with vast holdings in Alexandra Township, but it was, primarily, an uneducated family.

I was rejected by this world, the white world rejected me;

I was appalled to find the black middle class as snobbish and as sectionary as the world of the whites, except that the pain was more concentrated because of the physical nearness of this black class; white rejection was a social force in another social environment, almost in another world. I found myself a displaced person, caught between and rejected by the two worlds with which I presumed a mental level; it was perhaps this single factor which has contributed to the strong feeling of rejection which is apparent in my reactions, but more constructively it forced upon me the realisation and the acceptance of my condition; I became cynical about my colour and the reaction to it.

I directed my energy to my writing, determined to use it as the weapon for gate-crashing into the worlds which rejected me; my writing showed a studied omission of commitment, the histrionics of tight-fisted protest, and in my first published short story, *The Dignity of Begging*, I created a satirical situation in which I sat back and laughed at the worlds which rejected. I projected myself into the character of Nathaniel Mokgomare, an educated African capable in any society of earning himself an independent living, but handicapped by being black in a society which has determined that black is the condition of being dependent on white charity, in the same sense that a cripple is dependent for his existence on public charity; but the beggar needs to be horribly deformed to arouse sympathetic patronage, and the African is disqualified by his colour from earning an independent living, hopelessly helpless in his incapacity to overcome the burden of his colour.

To the handicap of being black I added physical deformity, investing my character with a kind of double indemnity, then confronted him with the realisation of his condition, complete with the stereotyped destiny determined for him; Nathaniel accepts the challenge, deciding that if he is condemned to be a beggar he would become a professional one, with the strict observance of the ethics of the profession. He exploits his deformity, assuming a quality which transfers his demerits to where they finally belong, on the conscience of the over-privileged white public; his eyes plead for human kindness, but sneer behind every 'thank you, baas; God bless you, baas'.

The Dignity of Begging is the reflection of the only possible life—with dignity and sanity—which the African could accept in order to accommodate South Africans; perhaps one of the explanations responsible, among sensitive Africans, for the existence of that phenomenon identified and classified as The Native Mind, a subject which engrosses the attention of the anthropologists, sociologists and psychologists, who have given us such memorable quotes as: The Natives are always smiling, they're a happy people; how can anybody say they're oppressed and miserable?

Why not? Even in Shakespeare's time people have been known to 'smile and murder whilst they smile'. The Native has to survive his oppressors, he knows that time is on his side, history is on his side, and with time, God will be on his side; the smile policy is one of careless ease, its convenience is contained in the fact that the African cannot at this moment afford to lose his temper, so he must joke about the things which give him most pain. On the main Johannesburg–Orlando road there is a traffic sign on which some African humourist has added a 'very' between the words 'native' and 'cross'.

| very |
| NATIVES / CROSS HERE |

Until the African loses his sense of humour, he will smile; the Government has not as yet legislated against smiling, in

89

any case, everything else is either treasonable or seditious; if I criticise the Government's racial policies or speak trouble-making lunacies about freedom, liberty, equality and fraternity for the black races, I will be named a Communist; if I should become recalcitrant and angry, lawless and violent, I would be certified as Bestial, Savage and Barbaric. There seems very little left which could be considered appropriate, or safe, except the policy to smile and smile; smiling has its advantages, it has for some time now been discovered that Natives have good healthy teeth, and so white, which is rather baffling when one considers that malnutrition is rampant among them; but it is a proverbial fact that a flashing smile will turn away wrath.

Africans have discovered—and this by way of self-protection—that the white South African is hopelessly and fanatically susceptible to flattery, a weapon which the Africans use with vicious enthusiasm to express their sincerest contempt.

The South African police force attracts into its ranks young Afrikaners recruited from the Platteland, rural areas, for it is perhaps the only employment agency which requires, as a qualification, a minimum of intelligence; I do not, of course, wish it to be understood that the force is crawling with country idiots, there are a few urban idiots, not too many intelligent ones and a few English-speaking strays usually to be found in administrative posts; but the police constable on the beat is invariably Afrikaans, with strong cultural and language ties, stuttering with the historical hatred and fear which the Afrikaner bears the African, yet an African could almost be forgiven anything if he is obsequiously respectful, bowing with servility and speaking in Afrikaans; but heaven help the English-speaking African, because if there is anything the Afrikaner hates more than the English, and the Jews, and the Indians, it is a black Englishman. I would never attempt talking in English to an Afrikaner police constable, not if I know that with

Afrikaans I could get him to waive even his prejudice.

The African needs to be a master in the art of chicanery, for only the simple and the very proud are arrested on trifling offences, but there is always present the danger of not knowing where to draw the line; white liberals scream their criticisms against Africans, that we bring upon ourselves—by the very nature of our obsequious behaviour—the contempt of the whites, that the canvas smile and the yes-baas mentality is sickening. They possibly have a case, but it is a known fact that most people laugh at the baas's joke; in any case, how many of them could take a 'go to hell' from an African?

Chapter Seven

I OBSERVED Philip Stein all the time, the geiger counter of my senses probing, receiving, analysing his reactions, and at the end when the raging tempest of my suspicions had been exhausted I discovered we could exchange nuances with creative relish without his face going red, without him compromising his whiteness; and when my complexes showed he criticised me without sounding superior.

In accepting my invitation and coming to my room in Sophiatown he became the first white person to be received socially, and he was perhaps aware of this; he smiled as the startled neighbours paraded outside the door, staring at what must have been an unusual sight; we had tea, and to them—it was possibly as much of a surprise to me—the sight of a white man sitting down to tea in a black house, drinking out of a cup which had been used by an African, shocked them visibly even more than I; I introduced him to my mother, who pretended a calm, I presume for the benefit of the neighbours, but I could sense a conflict in her, she was unable to decide on the correct form of address, but finally her training prevailed, and she called him Baas Philip. I decided to let her work it out for herself, and it took a long time to accustom herself to calling my white friends by their first names; yet I still observe the subtlety with which she feels her way around their names, mouthing them on first meetings, almost as if to protect herself against any possible unpleasantness.

When I visited Philip's home the reaction was similar, but different also; his parents received me with courtesy and kindness, apparently it was the first time for them too, they were pointedly careful not to embarrass me by word or deed, and that in itself—possibly because they were efficient at it—made me feel uncomfortable; Philip invited me into his room to look at his books, we talked for a while and he left me, and I was sitting in there pretending to read when he returned with a tray of food; he lunched with his parents, and yet I did not feel slighted, the ordeal would have been unbearable for all concerned; it is perhaps significant that I was not made to sit in the back-yard or the kitchen, which would have been the South African thing to do. Philip's parents belonged to another generation, perhaps not as flexible as to throw over their behaviour patterns overnight; I understood this and I think Philip knew.

All of us in South Africa have been conditioned to the attitudes and the prejudices of our society, we are educated into an acceptance that racially we are different, that the white man has advanced to such a high degree of civilisation that it will take the Native 2,000 years to attain that degree; this single fact exists as a premise in the minds of people who may otherwise not themselves be necessarily prejudiced. I was a dinner guest at the home of Dr Ellen Hellmann in Houghton, after dinner we retired to the living-room for coffee whilst listening to European classical music; I suppose I must have visibly seemed to be enjoying and recognising the music.

'Do you like this music?' Dr Bodo Koch said.

'Yes.'

'I thought you people like only jazz,' Dr Koch said. 'Jazz has no meaning for me, I think it's all noise.'

'I like both,' I said.

'I can't understand that,' he said, 'I've been surrounded by this music all my life—it was the first sound I ever heard; I don't suppose it may have been the same for you.'

Dr Bodo Koch is above race prejudice, even though it may not seem so within the implications of what he said, but he and I are products—and perhaps victims—of the attitudes

93

of our society; it was a case of genuine reconcilement, very unlike the unmistakable attitudes of the woman who said:

'You speak very good English, tell me, do you think in your mother tongue and translate into English?'

'No, I think in English and then translate—or interpret, as you like—in my mother tongue,' I said, much to her annoyance. 'This accounts for speaking with an accent.'

There is a resentment—almost as deep-rooted as the prejudice itself—against the educated African, not so much because he is allegedly cheeky, but that he fails to conform to the stereotype image of the black man sanctified and cherished with jealous intensity by the white man; such a Native must—as a desperate necessity—be humiliated into submission. The educated African is resented equally by the blacks because he speaks English, which is one of the symbols of white supremacy, he is resentfully called a Situation, something not belonging to either, but tactfully situated between white oppression and black rebellion. The English regard him as a curio, they listen to him with critical attention to detail as regard to accent, usage and syntax; when they have taken a decision they pronounce, with almost divine tolerance and Christian charity, that the African speaks English beautifully; the more naïve listen with unmasked agony whilst the African is struggling with syntax to communicate his thoughts; they suffer patiently between interruptions to request the African to articulate with precision, but these self-same King's English enthusiasts will listen with enthralment to a continental accent.

The Afrikaners are almost psychotic in their reaction to the English-speaking African, whom they accuse of talking back with insolence and aping the white man; the devices of humiliating into submission the arrogant African are various, and most of them are embarrassingly unintelligent. When Philip bought his own business he asked me to join him in reconstructing a bookshop which had gone bankrupt, and one of the left-over staff was an African messenger called Aaron who was scheming to set up for himself an independent live-lihood; he had a new idea almost every week, and one morn-ing he came into the office effervescent with the idea of purchasing a light van; he was shuffling and fidgety, ambling and mumbling all morning, then finally approached Philip for a loan to make a down payment, he had no collateral to offer, nothing but his labour, and Philip was concerned about the loan, it was a bad investment for him and for Aaron; but Aaron was enthusiastic, he pleaded with his eyes and begged with his manner, unable to understand that it was not so much a question of not wanting to let him have the money.

While Philip employed all his graces to discourage Aaron's entreaties, for some reason Aaron believed that it was only a matter of finding the right argument to persuade Philip to his way of thinking, until in the end I could no longer bear the self-emasculation; I told him, in an African dialect, to think about the matter more carefully and at all times to conduct his business deals as a matter between man and man; but it interested me to note that I was more embarrassed than Aaron, because as an African I felt embarrassment, not so much for Aaron but for an African emasculating himself, and in that embarrassment I saw myself reflected and involved. I was annoyed by the unmanly indignity of his pleas.

'What did you just say to him?' Philip said.

'I told him to stop being so obsequious.'

There was an unnecessary heaviness in the shop, Philip was embarrassed for Aaron, but the bookkeeper, Mrs Stanger, was embarrassed into irritation by the insolence of my course; her reaction was typical, it was necessary for me to be humi-liated.

'Can he spell obsequious?' Mrs Stanger said, perhaps it was meant to be a witticism.

Shop assistants hold perhaps championship records in the

art of humiliating the allegedly cheeky African customer, particularly that rare piece of Africana, the neo-sophisticate who has developed a palate for European foods; I remember that once I confronted a shop assistant with a list of items I wanted: a jar of stuffed olives, a tin of asparagus, a quarter of smoked salmon, a half-pound of chopped chicken liver, a piece of Esrom cheese; and with every item I called out she reacted with jerky motions of looking at me in bewilderment, and throughout all this I was faintly amused.

'Is this for you?' she said, unable to contain herself, and somewhat confused that I seemed to be picking the items at random.

'Yes.'

'Do you eat these things?' she said, placing a peculiar emphasis on the word 'eat'.

'Yes.'

She shook her head with incredulity, and I extracted as much as I could from the situation, playing it strictly for shocks for the benefit of the waiting white customers, and just to add —as they say—injury to insult, I enquired about Russian caviar; I did not particularly want caviar, I could not afford it anyway, but I could not deny myself the luxury of watching them react, it was priceless; I do not especially like caviar, it is a pretentious luxury, a bourgeois symbol of social affectation and palatal sophistication, its nutritious value cannot bridge the gap between starvation and health; I could feed my family for two days on the price of eight ounces of caviar. Perhaps it is sour grapes, but I do not like it, in the same sense that some people do not like strong cheeses; but if I admitted as much in those frightfully smart dinner parties I would immediately be classified as unsophisticated and uncivilised, possibly with rude remarks made about my race.

'It's a lot of money,' the bewildered assistant said.

I handed her—for the sake of effect—a five-pound note.

Her concern was understandable, and in effect, justified, the wage scales laid down for Natives are determined—by design —not to encourage them to develop luxury taste buds, and politically, not to make them economically self-sufficient; the Native must be enslaved to a dependency on white charity, at my salary it was an act of criminal irresponsibility to have bought those items; the reasons and excuses are irrelevant when seen against the background of the fact that my sister, Marguerite, had recently lost her baby suffering from malnutrition; it is perhaps ironic that I was buying those items to entertain white friends that evening, and in my usual extravagance I had spent the equivalent of a week's wages; this is perhaps the reason why I am constantly being accused of living above my means, which may be true, but I believe the point is an arguable one. I submit, respectfully, that my means have always been below my standard of living.

This argument reminds me of what can only be described as a dirty joke; the high incidence of malnutrition and tuberculosis among the Africans is attributed to their eating habits, and their staple diet of mealie meal porridge; why don't they eat more vegetable and fruit? It rather reminds one of the Marie Antoinette classic: Why don't they eat cake? The reasons are uncomfortably, if not blatantly, simple. In Johannesburg the minimum wage required to sustain a family of five is estimated at £33 per month, the average unskilled wage is £16 per month, which means that 80 per cent of the African families in Johannesburg live below the poverty datum line. Statistics can be very cold and inhuman, but the stark horror of what they mean cannot be ignored: African children between one and four years old are dying at twenty-five times the rate of white children. The figures for the Cape are equally disturbing, especially when one remembers that the natural resources allow a standard of living for the whites in South Africa second only to that of North America, and perhaps even more frustrating when confronted with the fact that South Africa is a land of plenty; it was Dr Nkomo who said that South Africa is rich enough to satisfy all our needs, but not enough for all our greed.

According to the statistics of the Medical Officer of Health, Dr J. A. Richter, 48 per cent of the children born in the Port Elizabeth area die before they are one year old, that the mortality rate has risen in one year from 244·4 per thousand in 1960 to 481·9 per thousand in 1961; that is, in the year 1960–61 nearly half the children born died before they were four years old. The figures amount to an even more dreadful picture and moral indictment when seen in a country which in one year destroyed 370,000 gallons of skim milk in the Transvaal alone, estimated as enough to have saved 80 per cent of the children who died of kwashiorkor in the same year. In the eight main urban centres 10,000 children die every year from the protein-deficiency disease of kwashiorkor, 66 per cent of non-white children in the Cape suffer from iron-deficiency anaemia, and 30 per cent from rickets.

Yet each year huge surpluses of fruit are either left rotting or dumped into the sea or ploughed back into the earth; millions of bags of maize are exported at cut prices.

I do not claim to understand statistics, but I do know that in my family there were six children, two of whom died from malnutrition; I am not asking for charity, but I do demand that the fruits of my labour shall not be taken from out of my mouth.

The African male over eighteen pays a compulsory, and discriminatory, poll tax, which is forced upon him irrespective of whether he hàs an income; the other race groups pay an income tax calculated on a graduation scale, a white worker has to earn above a certain figure before he can be taxed. This system of taxation is designed to force the rural African to migrate to the city, into the mines and domestic service, leaving the land to be worked, inefficiently and uneconomically, by women and old men; the system is successful because the land cannot support even the bare minimum needs of the people who work it.

A man who lives below the poverty datum line is expected to provide his starving children with milk, butter, eggs, vegetable and fruit; he is criticised, and this by way of accusation, for cutting down on those foods which are considered essential to the health of his children. These critics are deliberately blind to the fat fact staring them in the eye that when poverty holds dominion over a family the essentials of life are the first things to be cut down upon; for what else is there to cut down upon but food? A house to live in, fires for heating, these are the things which cannot go; thus milk can be sacrificed, butter becomes a luxury, eggs a dish for kings, and these essentials for nourishment and life are the first to be cut down upon. A family which cannot live within its means is suddenly discovered to be living above its means, this being the criticism white employers level at the members of their African staff who are always borrowing money against their wages around Tuesday and Wednesday.

The fact that 80 per cent of urban African families live below the poverty datum line is rationalised by such pronouncements that 'the Govenment is doing a lot for its Natives' who have a higher standard of living than anywhere else on the African continent. Look at those modern-equipped hospitals which cost a million pounds. It is this rationalisation which inspire cabinet ministers, Government supporters and other do-gooders to go into ecstatics in extolling the virtues of the Government, almost to the point where it begins to seem that the Government is doing more than enough for the black workers of South Africa. I assert, emphatically, that it is the duty of any modern, and prosperous, government to provide—as a right, not as a Christian charity—a decent standard of living for its workers, health services, equal and compulsory education, adequate housing; this is the reason for which people pay taxes. For all the piracy and pillage of African labour, the exploitation and the profits of a fruitful country, the Government deserves to do a whole lot more. The million-pound hospitals are not enough, the people need food.

I took a visiting British journalist on a guided tour of the locations, he had obviously been reading one of those State Information Office pamphlets; he wanted to see the positive side of apartheid, the things the Government was doing by way of social services for the Natives—he even spoke in the vernacular of those pamphlets: Africans were Natives, hospitals were Native hospitals. I showed him the rosier side of South Africa, the model housing schemes of Dube, Meadowlands and certain parts of Orlando; then I showed him Newclare, Shantytown, Sophiatown, ending the tour at Coronation Hospital with its fancy face-bricks, modern installations and the efficient matron, who began a phonograph record sing-song about the humanitarian dedication of the Government medical services to the suffering black masses; and with a kind of nervous-energy enthusiasm she took us on a tour of the theatres, the wards, round the beds with the usual chit chat with patients, and eventually the tour led into the children's ward, the precise place I wanted the journalist tourist to see.

We were immediately challenged by the blast-furnace screaming of children in various advanced stages of malnutrition; children with dome-like heads, top-heavy wobbling gnomes balancing precariously on reedy legs; others with grotesquely ballooned stomachs flanked by a tattoo of ribs; they seemed like mutants from another's nightmare, staring at us with glassy eyes bulging like blisters, and all around us— on beds huddled together, two deep and all along the aisles— were intravenous tubes futilely pumping the life-giving nourishment into the faded bodies of those ghastly wide-eyed screaming children who would only return to the same conditions on leaving that had brought them into the hospital in the first place. That colony of children faced death because they were the victims of starvation, children sacrificed at the altar of the greed and comfort of white South Africa.

Even my cynicism could not accommodate the horror; I had thought to have persuaded upon myself the character of a tough dare-devil with a concrete reinforced stomach. After all, I had seen my first murder at fourteen and by twenty-one I had hoped to be a veteran, but the sight of those children made me feel sick; my journalist friend suddenly began wilting on his legs, the matron rushed a chair up to him, on to which he collapsed; she scuttled about and brought him a sedative. It took him fifteen minutes to recover sufficiently to want to turn his back on it all; we all wanted to leave the nightmare behind us, to turn our backs and forget.

And yet all too frequently I am forced to realise that behind the structure of the Native wages, the discriminatory poll tax, is the arrogant dirty joke that Africans should be taught correct dieting habits, and over this I am confronted with the Christian charity of a Christian Government which exposes people to starvation and then boasts of a million-pound hospital, to treat malnutrition cases.

Chapter Eight

FOR A FEW hours I had been engrossed in the game of draughts, by the vicious intelligence guiding the bony fingers of William Dumba, the intense, almost spell-binding concentration wrinkling his brow; and through it all my mind was sifting through the sewer of remembrances. The game, like our promiscuous love, excessive drinking, blind drunkenness, the compulsive joyousness of our nice-times, the singing, the dancing, the violence and the killing, had entranced me, a kind of diversion from the grim reality of Sophiatown, the grip of poverty and starvation. All around us children were dying of malnutrition because our poverty had to classify as accessories food items like eggs, butter, milk, fruit and vegetable; these and clothing were the first things to be sacrificed because everything else like rent, heating and fares were fixed and unavoidable. They cried from starvation in the dirty yards, the beriberi children of Sophiatown, and with them whined their dogs, and as their mothers fed them on starch concentrates, because they were filling, the hungry children shared this with their hungry dogs.

Members of the South African S.P.C.A. were shocked by the condition of the animals in the locations; it was cruel, a case of criminal negligence that dogs are starved, they said. Have these people no human feeling? They petitioned support in the press, describing with disturbing detail the physical state of the dogs of Sophiatown, lobbying for support to pressure the City Council into proclaiming restrictions against Africans keeping pets. It did not succeed though. It was easy for them to be publicly appalled, they did not have to live with it, they did not, as did the Africans, have to hate themselves for being unable to feed both the children and their dogs. I have seen dogs nibbling into the buckets of outdoor lavatories, seen the difficulty with which people tried to keep them away, and in the end—because they could not do better than what was in the buckets—they pretended not to notice them. The children were sick, the dogs were sick.

Suddenly I was irritated by the game of draughts, by the futility, the utter boredom of allowing my energy to respond to symptoms, rather than causes; we took up arms against the advance of poverty and starvation when the real enemy was the economic structure of South Africa; we lost the struggle to protect Sophiatown against the bulldozers because we concerned ourselves with the morality of the scheme, re-acting to the principle that Natives should not be encouraged to develop a sense of permanency in the urban areas; all these instead of challenging the structure of the Government's Native policy; every time it happened we concerned ourselves with treating the symptoms instead of attacking the causes.

The Government is unyielding in its Native policy, the tentacles of discrimination spread their grip over every aspect of our lives, right into the very houses we live in; nothing belongs to us as an inviolable right, not our lives, our labour or the occupancy of our homes. The legislature is emphatic and unequivocal. With the Natives (Urban Areas) Act of 1945, the Minister stipulates that accommodation must be provided for the reasonable labour requirements of the area; in human terms, this means that only those employed in the municipal district of any urban area are permitted to reside in that area. If the breadwinner in the family dies, in this case mainly the male into whose Reference Book the permit for the house is stamped, his widow and children must vacate the premises in favour of an able-bodied man who will earn his right to that house by virtue of being employed, in say, the municipal district of Johannesburg. Into the Pass or Reference

Book of every adult African male are stamped two permits under the section: Labour Bureau, Efflux and Influx Control and Registration:

1. Permitted to seek work in the proclaimed area of Johannesburg until (dated), and remain therein for duration of contract of service entered during this period.
2. Permitted to remain in the proclaimed area of Johannesburg until present contract of service is terminated.

The superintendent in a municipal location issues a permit against the house occupied by the African worker, which permit will expire the moment the African loses his employment and cancelled if unable to secure approved employment within three weeks; such an African worker will be endorsed out of the municipal area. No work, no permit; no permit, no house. All municipal locations are rigidly controlled with regulations and restrictions; permits for visiting friends and relations who may wish to stay for a few days; entry permits for friends who belong to another race group; permits for one's own children to continue residing in one's own house once they attain the majority age.

According to the Government Notice No. 804 of 1958, any policeman is entitled to enter and search, without warrant, at any reasonable time of day and night, the premises in a town in which he has reason to believe or suspect that an African boy, eighteen years of age, is committing the criminal offence of residing with his father without having the necessary permission to do so.

Yet, even more drastic than the regulations and restrictions is the system of ethnic grouping, the breaking up of people into tribal units, docketing them into the Mnguni group; Zulus zoned from the Xhosas, the Ndebele and the Swazi;

the Sotho group; Basutos from the Pedi, the Tswana, the Shangaan and the Venda. The ethnic groups then become tied by language, ethnic custom and culture, practice and petty jealousies and suspicion; they are encouraged to live, think, react as an ethnic group with ethnic interests. We raised a loud protest against this classification, pointing out all the dangers, which were, in part, proved valid by the internecine strife at the model townships of Daveyton, Dube and Meadowlands where Zulu impis clashed with Basuto factions in the bloodiest faction fights in South African history since the Tshaka wars. The Government and the race relationalists have been, almost deliberately, blind as to the causes of those faction fights; and repeatedly the cause has been put down to the savagery of the Natives.

It was against these regulations and restrictions, the pedigreeing of people, that we in Sophiatown resisted the removal and the resettlement scheme; whatever else Sophiatown was, there were no controls and prohibitions, we held freehold rights to our properties. We objected to resettlement at Meadowlands which, practically, was a sanitary improvement on Sophiatown; Meadowlands provided proper housing to thousands of families who had hitherto lived in rooming houses; but physically, Meadowlands is soul-destroying, a depressing monotony, the houses look like thousands of mushrooms on a hillside, small unit detached houses dispatched without love or propriety, monolithic monsters from the architect's boards of the National Building Research Institute. The only people who are lyrical about Meadowlands are the whites, in reply to whom Peter Raboroko, Secretary of Education in the Pan-Africanist Congress Shadow Government, said: I am pleased the Europeans love Meadowlands, that's where they will be settled when South Africa becomes black. They have since ceased being publicly ecstatic about Meadowlands.

Some Africans have come to accept Meadowlands as a practical advantage, a four-roomed house with a little garden has physical comfort and social privacy; it was Eduard 'Dwarf' Tiro who summed up the virtues of Meadowlands as against Sophiatown where one had to queue outside at the communal lavatories.

'You don't have to greet your neighbour at the lavatory,' he said.

The resettlement scheme came under immediate fire from the African National Congress, we cheered the speakers at the protest meetings and adopted long-winded resolutions; every Sunday morning we assembled at Freedom Square, Morris and Victoria Road, to be stampeded into orgiastic reverberations of resounding slogans by thumb-raising politicians trading on mob passions, and one after the other they mounted the platform almost in an effort to outdo each other by the sheer volume of noise.

'Maye buye!' the politician shouted, his thumb raised in the A.N.C. sign.

'Afrika!' we shouted.

'Maye buye!'

'Afrika!'

'Afrika!' the politician said.

'Maye buye!' we chorused.

'Afrika!'

'Maye buye!' Our voices resounding a mile away.

This chant never failed to work us up into a frenzy of enthusiasm, filling some with a sense of fervour, and others with hysteria; its primary significance was to rouse the rally into a noisy passion which released some of the anger bottled up inside us. It usually left us exhausted and limp at the end of the meeting. After a calculated pause the speaker, attended by two interpreters, began a tirade against the Government, invariably intended for the Special Branch taking notes, and to impress the meeting with the speaker's bravado and fear-lessness. It seldom failed to seem like a satirist's show, at which the comedian is concerned that none of his material is lost; I have heard speakers request an interpreter into English.

'Our friends may not be understanding Xhosa.'

The audience loved the circus, nodding their approval at the courtesy, and as they joked, playing at politics, we laughed at the jokes, at the police, often losing sight of the danger to our homes or the seriousness of the purpose for which we had assembled; and as we laughed and shouted slogans, the police took notes and at times they, too, enjoyed the wholesome jokes; but they were never deterred from their purpose, they prepared for their task of the removal of Sophiatown even in the face of violent defiance, and documented a case against 154 people who were to be later indicted for treason.

Then the nature and the temper of the resistance against the removal scheme changed in pace and colour, we flexed our rebellion for a physical showdown; it began to be rumoured around the protest meetings, in and about Sophiatown, that we would resist, by force if necessary, the will of the Govern-ment; a campaign with a top secret plan was whispered in the wind, the hush-hush M-plan which would be implemented on the night before the day of the first removals; the top secret plan was of such priority in secrecy that there was found no one who knew any details about it, except that it would spring into effective action on the night before the removal day. Perhaps we expected too much, placed too heavy a responsibility on the African National Congress, but this did not stop us from being enthusiastic; I was particularly excited by the prospect that in Sophiatown the revolution for which we all conspired in our impatient anger might be sparked off; there was going to be a secret issue of arms which would finally resolve the imbalance of political power, but then I saw the revolution itself only as it affected Sophiatown. I waited with the others of my inclining for the signal to arms and the details of the M-plan.

The sudden importance of Sophiatown, as the strategic trigger point, was accentuated by the announced personal appearance of Chief Albert Luthuli, President-General of the A.N.C., who would address the meeting in Sophiatown's Freedom Square; it was impossible to underscore the importance of the Sophiatown campaign of protest, and the honour of the attendance of the Chief in the presence of our cause. But the moment the Chief landed at Jan Smuts Airport he was served with a banning order restricting him from attending and addressing meetings; we were infuriated by the arrogance of Mr C. R. Swart, then Minister of Justice, whom we dared in our anger to arrest the Chief whilst addressing our meeting. We hoped Chief Luthuli would defy the ban and address our meeting, and we were encouraged by a rumour that he would, and throughout the meeting we expected to see him march defiantly up to the platform; there was excitement over the news that the Chief was in a house some fifty yards away, then it was said he would address the meeting from a house in Morris Street through an address system connected to the meeting.

We were deeply disappointed, for some reason it had become important to us for our leader to have defied the ban and involved himself in our purpose to the point of going to jail; Mr Swart had, by the use of force and the machinery of the law, won another victory against us.

Two thousand police armed with rifles, revolvers and sten guns threw a security veil round Sophiatown; one policeman every fifty yards along Main Road, Toby Street and Johannes Street. Throughout the night before the removal day A.N.C. volunteers moved families from the zones specified for clearance; there were those people who refused to be removed, and defiantly moved into the centre of Sophiatown. Special

Branch men and the press drove round the township measuring the temper of the people; Anthony Sampson, then editor of *Drum*, is reported to have met Major Spengler, head of the Johannesburg Special Branch, and asked him if the police were expecting trouble.

'No,' Major Spengler is reported to have replied. 'Are you?'

There was a heaviness over Sophiatown during that raining night as we expected the explosion which we had hoped would persuade the Government into reconsidering its policy of removing Sophiatown; but the policy was pursued, the first families were moved through a cordon of police lining the route almost all the way from Sophiatown to Meadowlands; the politicians continued a feeble protest, the people of Sophiatown raged their frustration with little schemes like moving out of the troubled zones, crowding into the centre of the township, refusing to sell their properties and heckling about details; but the move was carried out and the top secret M-plan remained locked in a file classified as top secret. The spirit of the protest was broken, some faced the reality and reconciled themselves to the will of the Government.

But there were those of us, like myself, who hoped for a miracle; I refused the offer of a house from the representative of the re-dumping board, euphemistically called the Resettlement Board, thereby releasing the board from the responsibility of rehousing me; this in the full knowledge that the day my landlord, Mr Nanabhai, was forced to sell or face expropriation, I would have nowhere to go, with seventy-two hours to get there; I placed the responsibility of finding alternative accommodation upon myself, and also the danger of being endorsed out of the proclaimed area of Johannesburg. I resolved to stay on in Sophiatown up to the last moment, to the day Mr Nanabhai sold and the day my permit to remain in Sophiatown would be cancelled.

The permit system was introduced to Sophiatown when the

Resettlement Board took over the administration of the Western Areas: Martindale, Sophiatown and Newclare; system was implemented with the intention to protect the legal residents of Sophiatown in their legitimate right to a house in Meadowlands, to protect them against the poaching pirates from other areas—people not entitled to be rehoused—seeking to be settled in the model township set aside for rightful residents of Sophiatown. To earn the right to be protected against the poachers, the people of the Western Areas were required to apply to a board which would examine and investigate the claim of the applicants. The conditions were simple, the people had to establish fifteen years of unbroken residence in these areas, and to prove this the applicants were called upon to place and identify a variety of Sophiatown landmarks. This set off a vigorous know-your-township campaign, and some of the questions alleged to have been put to applicants were brought to the attention of *Drum* magazine.

Who is the fattest woman in Sophiatown?
Who is Sophiatown's oldest Chinese woman?
Where is the biggest rock in Sophiatown?
Who operates the biggest fah-fee pool in Sophiatown?

My editor, Sylvester Stein, assigned me to investigate these allegations, in an effort to prove that the questions were in fact unfair and prejudicial. Get the permit story, I was told; so I went to the interrogation room in the Pass Office down Market Street, Johannesburg. I found a queue of people nervously waiting to face the inquisition; they were tense, mouthing each to himself questions and answers most likely to be asked, questions and answers compiled from the experiences of those who had faced the inquisition. It was like watching a terrible nightmare, listening to bits of the audible fragments of monologues they were mumbling, names of streets, the postal addresses of Sophiatown's prosperous people, the names of the various missions of the Lutheran Church, the names and surgeries of medical practitioners. It was both comical and tragical.

I interviewed the white interrogator flanked by his African assistant rubber stampers, who were, in tone and attitude, more impatient and flamboyantly vicious than even he was; I produced my police card, explained my assignment and confronted them with the allegations.

'The questions we ask are fair,' the white interrogator said. 'You will find that people who live in the Western Areas will agree.'

'But there are these allegations,' I said.

'Find out for yourself,' he said, 'why don't you sit down, listen to the questions, see how the interview is conducted, then judge for yourself.'

'I live in Sophiatown,' I said, 'I would like to submit myself to the questions.'

It was perhaps an unfair advantage, but in my private capacity I was a resident of Sophiatown needing a permit as desperately as the sweating men waiting outside; ethics were out of the question, we were taking advantage of each other, and no trick, no matter how vile, was left unexploited. I intended to exploit the human propensity for justice and fair play in the face of a challenge, knowing that by this I would be blackmailing them to pretend a willingness of being just and fair, and have a permit stamped into my Pass. Some twenty questions later we both won; they proved their point and I got a permit:

Resident of Sophiatown, in terms of Section 10 (1) (b) of Act 25 of 1945 as amended. (Signed by the Influx Control Officer, Native Resettlement Board, 8-8-1956.)

I accepted to be present during the questioning of a few applicants; the questions were reasonable and fair, people walked out smiling, seemingly unable to understand why they could have submitted themselves to such unnecessary tensions. I knew that the soft-pedalling questions were intended for my benefit, and that the Board did not particularly mind letting off six people in order to fool the Press; but it was a fortunate experience for the six people, and a seized opportunity for me. The story was spiked.

To weed out the pirates who had no legitimate right to be in Sophiatown, the police launched into a vigorous campaign, entire families were arrested for not having permits; but these offenders were released on an admission-of-guilt fine and allowed to return to their homes, only to be raided again a few nights later.

It was shortly before Fiki left me when we were raided; it was 2.30 in the morning when we were roused by a violent pounding on the door; they banged so hard and long it seemed the intention was to break the door down. My immediate reaction was that it was a night raid by the tsotsis who forced their way into people's homes and carried off all the furniture; I trembled with fear out of bed, annoyed that I had on several occasions resisted to buy a gun, for fear that during one of those all-too-frequent provocations I might discard the processes of persuasion and permit myself the anger to use it; I fumbled in the dark for a weapon to defend my family, being afraid to open the door and hoping that if it was the tsotsis the noise, continued long enough, would attract the police, but I also knew the door could not withstand the force of the banging long enough; the police have the notorious habit of not being on the spot when they are needed.

'Who is it?' I ventured, keeping clear of the door; I and the tsotsis had seen too many films at which people have been shot through the door.

'Police! Open up!'

I pretended to be struggling with the locks, waiting for some sign that it was the police and not tsotsis; there was very little difference in the tactics of both the police and the tsotsis, both would kick and bang at the door. I could not be sure, the banging was so violent that it woke Chris and she started crying, and it was then that I summoned up the courage to face the danger threatening us. I opened the door and stood aside as the torches flashed into my face.

'Who's in the room with you?' the constable said, in the usual authoritative Afrikaans voice of the police.

'My wife and child,' I said, not altogether certain which of the terrors I would have preferred.

They flashed their torches on the bed, full blast on Fiki cowering behind the sheet she was clutching over her breasts. I took Chris out of the cot, pressing her against my body, reassuring her with the security and the warmth of a familiar body; it was important to make her feel she was not alone during that violent experience, and through the bullying and the unnecessary brutality I managed to pacify her.

'Pass,' the constable said.

'We are going to Diepkloof, baas,' I said, 'as soon as our house is ready.'

'Have you bought a house?'

'Yes, my baas.'

Diepkloof was the middle-class development scheme where Africans of means put down a deposit and selected from about four architect's models the house of their choice. There was no possible way of disproving my story, many of the houses in Diepkloof were still under construction; besides, there was a snob thing about Africans who selected to live in Diepkloof, these were the educated Africans, the professional people who could afford the trappings and trinkets of middle-class existence.

'Have you got a permit?'

'Ja, my baas.'

They were satisfied, and justly too, in that, although I was one of those hated educated Natives I knew my place, was respectful and spoke reasonably well in the other official language; I could not swear to it, but I remember that one of them actually wished me a good night. I followed them into the yard, explaining that mother was sleeping in the next room, together with three sisters; in the third, the kitchen, two young brothers of school-going age; but I could not possibly have relatives in all the rooms in the yard, so three of my neighbours were arrested.

The dawn patrol moved out of our yard, with their prisoners, into the one across the street; the doors of most of the rooms were wide open, deserted by the people who had fled the raid. When the police drove off in the kwela-kwela people emerged from out of the dark yards, out of the ruins of the demolished houses, out of dark alleys; they were dressed in scanty garments: blankets, bed sheets, towels, table spreads, in almost anything which was handy at the time of fleeing. Men, women and children thronged the streets, and I realised for perhaps the first time what the protective permit system did, in human terms, to the people who for some reason had not been issued with permits or had had them cancelled on expiry; people were turned into cunning law-breakers, apprehensive and ready to flee from their homes to evade the processes of the law which required them to have permission in order to live in the peace and security of their homes.

I appreciated the good fortune of having had the permit stamped into my Pass, but the protection—allowed me by the circumstance of luck—would not extend to more than two months, at the end of which I would have either to move out of Sophiatown or start paying admission-of-guilt fines; I could of course have moved to Diepkloof where I could buy a house, but never the land; and besides, I did not have the £190 required as a down payment. I did have two months to raise it, but then I was not particularly willing. I had developed a sense of frigid indecisiveness, a purposelessness of existence in which nothing was of importance adequate in content to involve myself with; I felt little, if any, enthusiasm, refused to respond beyond the sterility of today. There was a presence of doom about me, my mind was impotent with obsessions of death—my own death; I explored the various permutations by which death would overtake my life. I had myself shot through the head, crushed to a dough on the concrete pavement below a ten-storey building, mangled by a bus or a train; but throughout these murder plots against myself there was a calculated avoidance of death by stabbing, or being beaten or kicked to a pulp; my unconscious mind rejected the mutilation of my body by another, but every moment of life in the Sophiatown which was dying seemed as a tearing at my flesh, a feast of vultures, which left of my body the gaping holes of a skeleton.

I was dissatisfied by the prospect of bonding over twenty years of my labour, it seemed an interminable period, but it was the endlessness of it which terrified me more; I elected to accept the gamesmanship of living on the fringe of police arrests for as long as I could.

But the people of Sophiatown were taunted into the cul-de-sac of their patience; thousands of us marched to the staccato of anger to protest to the mayor in the City Hall of Johannesburg, to be received in courtesy in his chambers by Mr Max Goodman, who received our delegates; he explained, with regret, that there was very little he could do about the permit raids, except that he would bring to the attention of the Commissioner of Police the volume of the protest. It was not from a lack of appreciation for the flower-beds—although some quarters implied as much—that in our angry thousands we spread across and into the lawn, trampling the flowers.

There was a momentary break in the permit raids and we joked that the revenue from the raids was something not to be easily sneezed at; predicted a return to the reign of terror.

A few weeks later the police revived hostilities, began a fresh offensive with a vengeful efficiency; doors which were not opened promptly were forced with crowbars and offenders were dragged out without adequate time to dress properly; a young woman appeared in the Native Commissioner's Court in Fordsburg with a rug covering her petticoat, and a court clerk was overheard to remark: 'Has she got a dress? I know these people, I've been dealing with them for years.' There was that know-all expression on his face, the arrogant dogmatism of the professional racialist.

Around the bullying and victimisation is the cynical explanation that the permit system was intended to protect the legitimate right of the people of Sophiatown to a house in Meadowlands; except that somebody must have overlooked the necessity of explaining that the issue of the permits would be complicated by the power complex of the interrogator, and by the further hazard that the permits could expire by the arbitrary discretion of the raiding police or the agents of the board. It was a peculiar kind of protection, its amount of justice seemed reflected in the situation of those without permits, who were arrested and fined, then went back to their homes in Sophiatown only to be arrested and fined again some days later, never forced or able to move out. This process was repeated every few days at £3 a time.

Sophiatown was destroyed in a determination to bring it and the other areas where Africans still held freehold rights under the influence of the Government's general policy that no African is entitled to acquire freehold title to land anywhere in South Africa, nor is it the intention of the present Nationalist Government ever to grant such right to the African, even in his own reserves; this is contained in the Natives (Urban Areas Consolidation) Act No. 25 of 1945. For our freehold title we were offered leasehold tenure. As more pressure was applied, the more unbearable it became, until the people of Sophiatown surrendered up their resistance and grudgingly sold their properties to the Resettlement Board at prices assessed by devaluators of the board; and as they were moved, so their homes fell before the bulldozers.

Chapter Nine

NOTHING in my life seemed to have any meaning, all around me there was the futility and the apathy, the dying of the children, the empty gestures of the life reflected in the seemingly meaningless destruction of that life, the demolition of Sophiatown; my life is like the penny whistle music spinning on eternally with the same repetitive persistency; it is deceptively happy, but all this is on the surface, like the melodic and the harmonic lines of the kwela played by the penny whistle, or the voice of Miriam Makeba, which bristle with a propelling joyousness. But contained in it is the sharp hint of pain—almost enjoyed in a sense—as is at times heard in the alto sax of Paul Desmond, the desperation of a man in search of God; beneath all this is the heavy storm-trooping rhythmic line, a jazzy knell tolling a structure of sadness into a pyramid of monotony; the sadness is a rhythm unchanging in its thematic structure, oppressive, dominating and regulating the tonality of the laughter and the joy. My life, like the kwela, has grown out of the gutters of the slums, from among the swelling smells of the open drains, out of the pressure of political stress and the endlessness of frustration.

But there is always the kwela and the nice-time when we surround ourselves with people, screaming noises almost as if to convince ourselves of our existence, in a glorification of our living at a feverish pitch, on our nervous system; at our nice-times, to the orgiastic rhythms of the kwela we conglomerate into an incestuous society where sex becomes promiscuous and friendship explodes into murderous hatred. The penny whistle band picks up a tune—a rhythm, to be exact—and the music swells, the emotions rise and the imagination waxes, then suddenly—for a brief moment only—the noise is stilled, then another kind of noise rises, first tentatively, then swells until the music can no longer be heard; it is a noise which is a mixture of Hollywood films and the sounds which are not words, but moods of the feeling required to transport us into an existence where white South Africa is another planet in another galaxy and apartheid becomes a sound in a nightmare.

Stuik uit.

Hop, man.

Shangri-La.

Veza.

Jika, rubber.

Heaven can wait.

Our bodies become obsessed and possessed by the rhythms; time is frozen, memory is obliterated as we enter into a cosmic existence; the dance becomes loaded with sex symbols, the suggestions in the gyrations become more explicit, the body surrenders to the music, to the nice-time, to the sensuous; still the rhythms multiply with a compulsiveness which enslaves the body, a mask-like trance encases the face, and we become dizzy; the gyrations become gymnastics, the body contorting spectral patterns which respond only to the noise. Then suddenly the music stops, the link with the spiritual world is broken; the real becomes present, and anger and revulsion break loose, we want to strike at something, the nearest thing.

You pushed me, spy.

So what, tsotsi?

You want to see your mother?

Make me dead, man. Kill me.

A woman screams and the people throw themselves against the walls, they fall silent; the musicians are packing their instruments, pretending a casualness. Three men walk slowly up to the bandstand.

Play!

It's two o'clock, the dance is over.

Play.

We are tired, friend.

Your mother's your friend. Play.

The musicians unpack their instruments, the mouthpiece is adjusted, the leader stamps the beat with the foot and the music rises, the dreams swirl and the nice-time continues.

This strange mixture of sadness and joy is perhaps the real heartbeat—the song of Sophiatown, whose destruction had shocked and angered me so profoundly in the course of one day; the Sophiatown which brought back so many memories on that Monday in July, and with them mainly the sadness.

I was back in the noise, having run from the screaming silence which surrounded me in Millner Road; I was again a piece in the human traffic, a part flowing into the whole. Victoria Road was writhing with the smell of human bodies as I walked back to my room behind the corrugated iron fence. My sister, Daisy, brought a cup of tea and placed it on the dresser, she revolved her body around the waist without moving her legs, throwing around feelers and sizing my mood; her eyes were furtively shooting glances at me and around the room, and I pretended not to notice that she was debating a decision as to the moment most appropriate to present her case, but she must have decided against it.

'It's dark,' she said, drawing the curtains to let in more light, and left.

I fought against the loneliness of being alone, I wanted to call her back and ask her what it was she wanted, but it was her game and I had to let her play it her own way; I wanted Fiki and Chris back with me, but the things which threw us apart were still real and present, perhaps during one of those moods of justification I preferred to believe that she did not understand the things which pumped and drove me on. I was trying to reconstruct the pieces, to find some sense, some meaning, some purpose, and all that I could find was the nagging monosyllabic Why? I could not frame the question, there was no single answer which could encompass the scope of the question; there was a moment of transference of guilt. It was nobody's fault, the whole thing was bigger than all of us. It was not my father's fault, nor that of his ancestors; it was not Fiki's fault, it was not the fault of any one single being. So the 'why?' was invalidated.

When?

The landing of Van Riebeek was inevitable, the conflict of interests was inevitable, the clash of arms and the conquest of Africa was inevitable; the Act of Union in 1910 was inevitable, even the betrayal of the rights of the Africans was inevitable, the group attitudes and the discrimination was inevitable; and yet somewhere the question has to be asked. Why? When? Perhaps an amalgam of the two will some day be necessary in the construction of a question which might be written in blood.

Why did I mutate into a hollow man? I hoped, there in my room, the white man would perfect his ultimate weapon and blow himself and his prejudice into the hell he has subjected me to; if he should fail, then I, who hate and fear violence, will be forced to appeal to the arbitrament of violence. What is it that will change men into beasts of destruction? I do not as a principle or a psychology hate the white man, but I do hate to see the death of children from causes which have been willed by man's greed; that these children shall not continue to die so horribly I must coolly and calculatedly force myself into acting out within myself the contradiction in the dilemma of the whole of modern man, who builds up an arsenal of weapons of absolute destruction on the moral of defending peace. I believe that no one single life is more important or merited than another, and in a determination to save one life I may have to destroy the life endangering it. I want life for all South Africa, and if the greater safety of one life shall be purchased at the price of another, then I will take it. This morality is as pretentious as the biblical fact that with the help of God—the same God that both white and black South Africa worships—Moses closed the Red Sea over the pursuing army of Egypt. The white man in South Africa functions on the same principle, except perhaps arguing from the point that a black life deserves less; but I argue on the side of Abraham Lincoln: 'It seems strange that any men should dare to ask a just God's assistance in wringing their bread from the sweat of other men's faces.'

I am disgusted by the men who have left me no other choice than to kill; I am not even sure that I sincerely want to kill them—perhaps if I could divest them of the power to injure others—but this is the precise point at which we are in conflict; the white man would rather destroy the perfect harmony of the whole country than surrender the power which strikes at children, and I would accept to destroy him rather than accommodate the murder of children of whatever colour.

Colour is fundamental in South African thinking, is the dominant factor in the making of our mores; but it goes even deeper than is normally realised. Perhaps Nadine Gordimer came closest to understanding this when she wrote that 'it is far more than a question or a matter of prejudice or discrimination or conflict of loyalties—we have built a morality on it. We have even gone deeper; we have built our own sense of sin, and our own form of tragedy. We have added hazards of our own to man's fate, and to save his soul he must wrestle not only with the usual lust, greed and pride, but also with a set of demons marked: Made in South Africa.'

It is impossible to be South African and without some shade of race attitudes, conveniently known as race prejudice, and the favourite question liberal South Africans love to answer is: Are you race prejudiced? Whereupon the answer is: I have no race prejudice at all. At this point we become noble and conforming and purged. Against the background of South Africa this question and answer is a bigoted over-simplication, and almost as loaded as: Would you like your daughter to marry a Native? The question which should be but never is asked, is: How race prejudiced are you?

I am not suggesting there was no prejudice prior to the South Africa of 1948, but it was around then that the white man in South Africa decided to recognise the portentous presence of the black peril threatening his existence as a white man; it was that moment in history when he decided to rally round the flag of apartheid in defence of Christian principles, democratic ideals and Western civilization; the black peril was made to become synonymous with Communist infiltration.

Whilst the freedom-loving nations of the world, including the Government of South Africa, deliberated in New York to entrench the rights of man, to reaffirm for all time the dignity of man and to banish from the face of the earth the Hiroshima of wars, one single word was invading the imagination of South Africa; and whilst the free-world nations were smacking their lips over the eloquence of the Declaration of Human Rights, one word—with no specific dictionary meaning—changed the South African scene overnight, and won the general election for the Nationalist Party; one word, three-syllabled, charged with an emotional intensity which suited the general temper of white South Africa; a one-word ideology which inflated the political life of Dr Daniel François Malan and punctured that of General Jan Christian Smuts, and unleashed the race monster of our age.

Apartheid, the one-word onslaught on the human dignity which the men in New York were so lyrical over, became a parliamentary joke the opposition members of the United Party made undergraduate witticisms about, whilst it entrenched white supremacy and relegated the Native to his place; and as they did this the non-white races were dehumanised and defaced. The pigeon-hole philosophy of apartheid manifested itself when the segregation notices went up everywhere, particularly in Johannesburg: 'Europeans Only' and 'Non-European', but I noticed a peculiar—if not subtle— omission of the 'only' on the Non-European signs.

I was soon to find myself being forced—by the letter of the law—to use separate entrances into the post offices, banks, railway stations, public buildings; it became a criminal offence for me to use the amenities set aside for the whites, who were either indifferent or satisfied with this arrangement. There was no massive white indignation at this insult on the dignity of the black races. I found myself unable to use the Eloff Street entrance into Park Station, a habit I had cultivated over the years; I became resentful, it was a pleasing-to-the-eye entrance, there were flower-beds, a water fountain and other details I have not seen for so long that I have forgotten them; and, of course, the Non-European entrance, then still under construction, was dismal and bleak, and because I have been educated into an acceptance of the primacy of law and order I accommodated, rather than defied, this effrontery. Everywhere I turned there were these prohibitions taunting me, defying my manhood with their arrogance, their challenge was driving me out of my mind; but I am only a man, afraid and apprehensive, perhaps even a coward. I should have walked past the notices and registered, to myself, a protest against that which offended my manhood, but I was afraid to go to prison, rationalising that it would have been a futile gesture. Dear, dear God.

It got to a point where I became insensitive to the oppression around me; I accommodated the carrying of a Pass because it was the law; I sweated in the black igloo that was Sophiatown because it was the law; I walked through the 'Non-European' entrance, used the 'Natives and Goods' lifts, jogged from foot to foot at the 'Native Counter' in the banks and post offices, waited patiently for the green 'For Coloured Persons' buses; I permitted my labour to be exploited, accepted the discrimination against my colour, cowered under the will of the Immorality Act of 1957, which lays down that sexual acts between black and white are illegal, un-Christian and immoral, and was instead excited by the juvenile satisfaction of outsmarting the law by mating illegally, drinking behind locked doors. All these I did because I respected the law, because I was law-abiding. In the name of law and order I accommodated a variety of humiliations. I permitted sidewalk bullies to push me about, to poke their fingers into my nostrils, spitting insults into my eyes, and because I had arranged myself under the will of the law I permitted other men—armed by the letter of the law and under the protection of the law—to castrate me.

And because the Afrikaners were such unintelligent oppressors they disturbed the perfect tranquility of the African middle class, mingled them with the commonality; the old guard, the masters of consultations and concessions and compromises found themselves without a protector, commingled with the common dust; then out of expedience, rather than loyalty, they looked for recognition in that instrument of rebellion, the African National Congress, and were disturbed to find that there had emerged, inside this body, a clique of nationalists under the leadership of Anton Lembede, Peter Mda, Walter Sisulu, Nelson Mandela, with support from dissentionists like Robert Sobukwe and P. K. Leballo, who were challenging the respectable politics of the old guard; these young rebels had formed themselves into the Youth League, with visions which spread beyond the borders of South Africa and a trouble-making slogan: Afrika for Africans.

Theirs was the language of the young, one which I could understand; they called to Africans to depend on their own resources in the struggle for liberation, preaching nationalism, exalting the dream of an African nation, supreme and independent; they advocated a strategy founded on militancy, boycott was to be the weapon of mass action and political education. They explained the realism of the African's struggle, exploded the myth that white South Africa would voluntarily undergo a Christian change of heart, underlining the fact that Africans should not expect mercy at the hands of the whites in the event of a showdown.

I found myself responding to their call; we hailed them in Sophiatown as the messiahs of African liberation, insinuating our own interpretations into the things they said; Afrika for Africans came to mean the same thing as: Drive the whites into the sea. For me they were the realists who loved freedom with a desperation which aimed to do something about it, rather than resolutions and memorandums; these nationalists were prepared to employ their revolutionary right in the securement of that freedom. I had become fanatical over the question of asserting my dignity as a man, threw aside the mellowing influences of peaceful negotiations, which in my opinion divides effects; I resolved that revolution was the only way out of the dilemma. Moral protest had failed, constitutional means—which were a farce since Africans did not have the vote—had failed, and white South Africa would not be swayed by persuasion; and since no action, however drastic, is not justified in the defence of freedom, I joined them. I shouted as loud as their shrillest chorus: Afrika for Africans. Drive the white man into the sea. It was not so much a question of anti-whitism, I was merely restating the anxiety and the anger of Patrick Henry: 'Sir, we have done everything that could be done to avert the storm which is now coming on. We have petitioned; we have remonstrated; we have supplicated; we have prostrated ourselves before the tyrannical hand of the Ministry of Parliament.' I felt that Africans have for far too long been at the business end of the sjambok, I wanted to feel the handle of the whip.

Congress leaders were no longer being shouted down as sell-outs, and throughout the township we were celebrating the fact that they had finally come to realise that 'if we mean to be free, if we mean not basely to abandon the noble struggle in which we have so long engaged and which we have pledged ourselves never to abandon until the glorious object of our contest shall be attained, we must fight! An appeal to arms and the God of hosts is all that is left to us.' The old guard, the responsible leaders of the African National Congress, were disturbed by this rebel-rousing sentiment; they preferred the round-table conferences, the pomp of consultations and the nobility of gentlemen's agreements.

I despised their dotering, wanted to shout through their bickering to remind them of the mine workers' strike of 1946, to extract a lesson from it; but an old fool is less than a child which needs but one experience of fire, the old man believes that one burn does not make a traumatic experience. One would have liked to think that that would be a year of awakening for them, since it was at the height of their conflict with General Smuts over the body politic of the Natives Representative Council.

In 1946 the Communist Party organised through the Mine Workers' Union 60,000 African mine workers to go on strike for a basic wage of ten shillings a day instead of the two shillings and fourpence per shift; the strike stretched into the fourth day when General Smuts, realising the threat to the country's economy, acted with brute efficiency; the police made a baton charge against the demonstrating miners, forcing them into the compounds and on to their job sites, and in the riot which broke out nine Africans were killed.

The African National Congress had declined to endorse the miners' strike on the grounds that it had been organised by the Communists. Anton Lembede and the Youth League fiercely attacked Dr A. B. Xuma, then President-General of the A.N.C., for not calling a general strike in support of the miners' claims; and his refusal, particularly since the ruthlessness with which General Smuts crushed the strike had shocked Africans everywhere, proved the claim of the Youth League that Africans could expect very little mercy in the hands of even the self-styled 'liberal' Government of the Congress Alliance.

By 1949 the Youth League had lost its patience with the cautious policies of Dr Xuma and at the presidential elections they put up the name of Dr James S. Moroka as their choice in direct opposition to Dr Xuma, who suffered a landslide defeat. The delegates at the Bloemfontein conference voted for what has come to be known as the 1949 Line of Action, which advocated militancy—boycotts against dummy institutions like the Natives Representative Council, the Advisory Boards, the Bunga: Let us not be the instruments of our own oppression, they resolved.

Factions formed over the strategy of boycott, those of the old guard who served on these institutions still solaced themselves with the fond hope of peaceful negotiations and were convinced in the power of persuasion; they fervently believed that some good may yet have come out of their policy, forcing thereby a compromise. Final decision was deferred to the next conference twelve months later, but the deadlock was never resolved and the Youth League lost their advantage. I was livid, for as long as the whites could get at us through these moderating influences, for so long will our agitation be ineffectual. The responsible leaders engaged in secret indabas with Government officials and liberal groups in an effort which was like extracting water from a stone, and with every empty promise they were made they pulled out the fangs of the Youth League, which had lost its guiding star in the death of Anton Lembede.

In 1950 apartheid became something more than prohibition notices in public places, it became invested with the respectability of law and order, the standard Western men revere above justice and life; I realised then that cruelty and injustice will be accommodated the moment they become the will of the law. White South Africa was indifferent to the acts of law which Dr D. F. Malan's Government was introducing in the House; the Acts were intended for the Africans, designed towards the safety, maintenance and entrenchment of the white man, not only in the South but throughout the continent of Africa. It was significant that the Afrikaner nationalists introduced their policy of repression with the Suppression of Communism Act which initially outlawed the Communist Party, but also wrote into Communism a definition to include all protest, moral or otherwise, against the peace and security of the State; to speak out against the oppression of the non-white groups, to demand the right of the share of responsibility for the determination of the laws of the country, these were documented as acts of Communism.

Mr Charles Robberts Swart, the then Minister of Justice, who sired the Act is a far more brilliant strategist than is normally conceded. It was around the time when the free world was shouting denunciations against Communism and arming to defend peace against the Red peril; what Mr C. R. Swart did was to exploit this psychosis, thereby blackmailing the otherwise unwilling democracies of Britain and America into nodding acquiescence. But his greatest single victory was over the South Africans—black and white—who were paranoid about Communism. The whole campaign of discouraging liberal whites from taking a stand on the side of Africans was brilliant in concept, so that in the end only those who had already been named Communists and the few who did not mind the association anyway, joined the Africans in their struggle against apartheid.

Mr Swart began his smear campaign by naming as Communists the known card-holding members of the Party, then forced them to resign their jobs and restricted their movements; the purpose of the Act was to hamshackle African political organisations, to remove from them the 'organisational' talents of whites; to amputate the effect of trade unionism among Africans, and to free the white Garment Worker's Union from the control of Communists like the named Emil Solly Sachs, who was forced to resign as its secretary; it was vicious and vindictive since Solly Sachs had been expelled from the Party in 1930 for right deviationism.

The Honourable Mr Swart used the Suppression of Communism Act to liquidate political opponents like Sam Kahn and Brian Bunting by forcing them to resign their seats in Parliament; and in his usual arrogance he announced in Parliament that 'systematically, the Government has acted against trade union officials', that by 21st July, 1953, the names of fifty-three trade union leaders were on the liquidator's list; by 18th September, thirty-three of these had been removed from their posts, and soon after, a further fifteen were removed. The back benchers applauded.

The leisurely uncommitted white South Africans were far more concerned with revenging themselves on Communism; those who cared were divided by their prejudices and separated by their set of complicated loyalties; it was Father Trevor Huddleston who realised the dilemma of the white South African: 'the Suppression of Communism Act is peculiarly effective as a deterrent to those white South Africans who, liberal in their sympathies, dread the consequences of being identified in any way with Communism. It is also effective in silencing those Africans whose terribly limited freedom can vanish immediately they are involved in a police raid.' And yet in the universities, particularly at Witwatersrand and Cape Town, the young students who could not accommodate South African thinking found themselves—in sheer desperation—following causes aligned with Communism, the only cause standing on a progressive platform; and it is for this single reason that the young university students—although continuing to belong to the privileged class and maintained from the profits made on the sweat of Africans' faces—were drawn into Communism and learned their liberalism from reading Lenin.

Like the white electorate I resisted the moral implications contained in the Suppression of Communism Act, arguing that it did not affect me personally; I am an African nationalist as much concerned about white supremacy as about Communist domination, enunciating the same clichés about the fear of falling into the tentacle embrace of the Russian bear. I resolved that the Communists should look after themselves, bury their own dead. The struggle for African liberation must be the direct responsibility of the Africans, that the ultimate victory must be for the Africans and not for Russia. I allowed myself to be diverted from the simple truth: an assault on the liberties of any group in a society is an assault against the whole society. I was played, as on a chess board, basically because of my reaction to Communism, into a prejudice, into underwriting this grotesque intolerance.

During the same year I was to be again puppeted into a similar reaction by the passage of the Group Areas Act of Mr Theophilus Ebenhaezer Donges, the Minister of the Interior, who assured that it was designed to protect the interest of the separate race groups, particularly the non-whites, from unfair competition. I joined the racialists, white and black, in howling against the Indian traders in the townships, who drove round in the latest American cars. It was particularly unfortunate that the Indians held most of the trading rights in Sophiatown, that some of them were penny-pinching vampires who built their fortune on the blackmarket during the war. The political manipulator, trading on our base emotions, persuaded us into believing that zoned in racial igloos the Africans would have a fighting chance in the trading jungle. It is painful to admit, seen in retrospect, that there was some truth in what they said; African business in the townships is a fiscal enterprise, even though it has been at the expense of the Indians. Where does justice and fair play begin? What is the margin of difference between greed and ruthless enterprise? I often wondered at the Minister's assurance that 'the Act would be applied with fairness and justice'.

But there was contained in this the real implications of the Act, the fact which the Minister had somehow neglected to mention—the fact that the assurances and guarantees were intended for the white voters. The voters of Westdene, the white suburb adjacent to Sophiatown, complained about the black spot on their door-step, and so Sophiatown was declared a white area. The claims of the people of Sophiatown were ignored; they were not voters. The same pattern decided against the Coloureds of Sparks Estate in Durban, except for the fact that the Coloureds were voters and this presented a slight problem. The more powerful white voters of Sherwood appealed to the Group Arcas Board, complaining that the houses of the Coloureds were visible from their back-yards; to placate the whites of Sherwood a buffer strip of trees and shrubs has now been erected and the Coloureds' houses are no longer growing-weeds which can be seen from the back-yards of the whites. In Kliptown, just outside Johannesburg, the whites wanted to move out because of the proximity of the black location; but the Minister ignored their wishes and re-zoned the area for whites. The blacks were removed.

When whites complained to the Group Areas Board against black proximity, the blacks were removed; when the blacks complained against white encroachment, the blacks were removed.

But the reaction of the Africans against the Indians required very little activation from the Government; the Indians, like the Chinese, were on a higher level of under-privilege, existing in a vacuum removed from the aspirations of the Africans, but the Group Areas Act—which threatened the cornerstone of their security—and the Asiatic Land Tenure Act of 1946—which prohibited the further sale of land to them in Natal—shook them out of their apathy. The South African Indian Congress, which had been a kind of social club financed by the Indian merchant class, began on a policy of alignment with the struggle of the Africans; and at presidential level an alliance with the African National Congress was concluded. It was an alliance which was to cause uneasiness and a split in the ranks of the A.N.C.

On the day-to-day personal relationships there was no real friendship nor were there bonds of brotherhood which united them in a common and equal misery; the Indians constituted a peculiar and powerful economic interest the Africans feared as a potential force which could lean to the side of the whites. They were not subject to the Pass laws and as such enjoyed labour benefits. The Government, in its design to part the Indians from the agitation of the Africans, endowed them with conditional privileges whose enjoyment depended on the Indians retaining their racial identity both socially and politically. Government policy and legislation made it unlikely that apartheid measures would be such as to unite the Indians, Coloureds and Chinese in a common hole of desperation. Since because of their religious practices the Indians are riddled with taboos and a vicious intolerance which divides them from each other, their intolerance towards the Africans is understandable. Thus it is that the social relationship between the Africans and the Indians is not so different from that between black and white; far less different than is supposed by the politicians. There is very little social contact, except on the master and servant level. The Indians reject and segregate against the Africans, who are refused attention—or at best tolerated—in the swank Indian-owned milk bars, restaurants and cinemas; where the Indian patrons refuse to share tables and seating arrangements. In the cinemas, particularly in Johannesburg and Durban, African patrons are humiliated, treated with impatience and relegated to inferior seats. If there is a big Indian, Coloured and Chinese crowd at the box-office, the house-full sign goes up for Africans.

It was easy for me to rationalise this humiliation, I was a cinema fan—the cinema being the only cultural recreation for the Africans—where I could take a date over the week-end for a two-hour escape from the physical reality of South Africa. The Indian-owned cinemas were more pleasant than the bug palace mud-house cinemas of the locations and screened the better films. Every Saturday afternoon, for more than ten years, I cringed and crawled, smiled and begged for small favours; forged friendships with the cinema managers as a protection against personal discrimination; I exacted favours like being seated in the fifth row instead of the first three from the screen. I hated every greasy smile which greeted my attempts and despised myself for it, and in an effort to raise my feeble flag of self-respect I mumbled determinations never again to submit myself to it, but I would be back the following week-end.

Perhaps it is true the black South African is a master at accommodating injustice and humiliation; but once in a while this violation touches too deeply and unleashes a savage hatred which strikes out with barbaric violence; this is a fact which has ceased to surprise us, our country's annual calendar has so many race riots.

Such a time was in the Durban of 1949 when Africans were incensed almost to madness by a seemingly trivial incident which was to result in the death of 190 people. Zulus burnt

Indian-owned property, men were clubbed to death with knobkerries, Indian women and girls were outraged, in an orgy of arson, rape, looting and killing.

The commission of enquiry reported in its findings that the cause of the rioting was an assault on a fourteen-year-old African boy by an Indian adult, that in the tussle the boy's head struck against the glass of a shop window, and in withdrawing it the boy received multiple cuts which caused a flow of blood. This assault—which could possibly have been punishment for a boyish mischief—took place at the Victoria Street bus terminus around the peak hour when people were waiting for transportation home, and that which in any other circumstance would, and should, have been dismissed as common assault, assumed an aspect of importance which placed it on a level of a national incident. Indians responded to the African's dissatisfaction over the incident by mobilising a concerted attack on Africans; word spread that Indians were killing Africans on sight, and in the locations the Zulu formed themselves into an impi which determined to rid themselves permanently of the attitudes of the Indians. They chalked up all the wrongs—real and imagined—which they had suffered at the hands of the Indians. They resolved to humiliate the Indians, to violate the sanctity of their women, to act out their indignation against the unilateral sex bar the Indians imposed on their women. Indian men were forced to witness the outrage on their women and children.

The military and the naval reinforcements called out to restore law and order were themselves touched by the violence of the killing, and in the end more people had died from bullet wounds than from the actual rioting. The casualty figures stood at 142 dead and 1,087 injured, of which 48 subsequently died.

But the real tragedy to come out of the massacre is the awful fact that in the locations of Johannesburg the Africans were shouting: 'Serve those bloody Indians right.' And in Durban, up to this day, the Africans still harbour a simmering hatred for the Indians and their attitudes. Indian restaurants and cinemas in Durban still discriminate against Africans, and accommodate them when in the company of white friends or those Africans of achievement. During subsequent riots in Sophiatown, Newclare and Alexandra Township, Indian-owned shops were broken into and looted.

Yet none of us have learned from this waste of human life; not the Europeans, nor the Indians nor the Africans.

The non-white politicians hoped for an easy solution in their campaign against the anti-Indian feeling in the locations or in the Indian mansions, they became astoundingly intellectual about this urgently vital property; argument became their chief reliance, pointing out that for all their prejudice the Indians were companion victims of discrimination, that given the same advantage the Africans would probably behave similarly. It was an intellectual concept not easily equated with the fact that the discrimination suffered at the hands of the Indians was far more intimate than that from the whites, with whom contact was confined to eight working hours, that the rest of the time was spent in the neighbourhood of Indians who resented violently any form of social mobility with Africans. Even intellectually I could not rationalise the discrimination of the Indians, it made nonsense of our fight against white attitudes.

But the African and the Indian politicians concluded the alliance, gambling to chance the burning issue of inter-group relations; in the locations we shouted down the alliance, accusing the Indians of having both feet in India and only their greed in South Africa. We feared that in the event of a real showdown the Indians would desert the Struggle and wait to negotiate with the winner or avail themselves of the Government's repatriation scheme. We joked, rather nastily, that if the Government were to relax the repression against them they would ally their fortunes with the whites; but what I found even more suspect was the Indian Government's interminable motions at the United Nations on the treatment of people of Indian origin in South Africa; the people of Indian origin are not the only oppressed people in that country.

From out of the alliance came the Congress Alliance which included the white Congress of Democrats, the South African Coloured People's Organisation, the Trade Union Congress. From this moment in history every campaign against white domination had to be fought on a platform of combined racial interests; each organisation selected a particular Act which touched the interests of the different race groups. The Defiance Campaign in 1952 was a splendid demonstration of the multi-racial unity; it was a six-point campaign with something in it for everybody: the Separate Representation of Voter's Act, for the Coloureds; the Suppression of Communism Act, for the white Congress of Democrats; the Group Areas Act, especially for the Indians; the Pass Laws and the culling of cattle, for the Africans.

The Congress Alliance despatched a communiqué to Dr Malan's Government requesting the repeal, by 29th February, 1952, of the six Acts; the request was as polite as perhaps only Africans could make it, and contained such profundities as, 'by constitutional means', 'legitimate demands' and 'our inherent rights'.

Dr Malan's reply was professional: 'the Government will make full use of the machinery at its disposal to quell any disturbance and, thereafter, deal adequately with those responsible for inciting subversive activities of any nature whatsoever'.

The campaign was a staggering success, it rallied a massive support to the cause of the African National Congress, Africans in their thousands rushed in to become card-holding members; it fired the imagination of those liberal whites who had been

136

searching for some way to demonstrate a sympathy for the cause of the Africans. People were arrested in their thousands for entering locations without permits, for using the 'For Europeans Only' amenities: sitting on European benches in parks, demanding service at European counters in post offices, using European entrances into railway stations and other public buildings. And as they were shepherded in the kwela-kwelas and driven off to the police stations they sang, in perfect harmony, the protest songs of the A.N.C. Thus, not too soon, the campaign assumed the pomp and splendour of a carnival, and some were drawn into it by the sheer compulsion and sweep of it.

The campaign failed to impress me for reasons altogether personal. We were again responding to symptoms, not the cause; except perhaps for the Pass laws, whose repeal would disturb the economic balance of the country, the repeal of the submitted Acts would have brought little reconstruction; the entire structure must be challenged and destroyed, and with it will fall the body politic of apartheid. I submit that apartheid is not the leaves of the branches, it is the tree itself.

Others too had misgivings, the older politicians—in their usual caution—pontificated that nothing constructive could come out of so foolhardy a scheme, arguing that passive resistance was an alien concept to the Africans, that the campaign was Indian controlled. The matured Youth League leaders—who had since gone respectable—argued that it was in line with their programme of action, to educate and prepare the Africans for future action. All the arguments for it, the justifications, were fraudulent. I thought it inconceivable that it could have any effect, it was not as if they were dealing with the humane British Government which could, at times, be persuaded by the conscience of its public's opinion. Mahatma Gandhi's passive resistance was successful in India because of a variety of persuasions; the British were ready to get out of

India; and there was, of course, also the discretion to frustrate Communist infiltration. It required very little effort to predict that the Nationalist Government would not be swayed by the moral principle of the campaign; the prospect of people volunteering to go to prison must have amused them, since white farmers were screaming for labour.

The United Party and its English-language press saw in the campaign an advantage which might return them to power, interpreting it as a challenge to the Government to relent and be realistic—to accept the United Party's forward looking policy of segregation with, in realisation that their policy of apartheid was administered too harshly, justice and Christian benevolence. For the Government and its Afrikaans press the campaign was a threat to the Afrikaner nationalism, a threat against the folk, the Afrikaner nation; they identified it as another Blood River danger threatening and directed, personally, at the Afrikaner nation, and they came out to meet the danger like wild, frightened children. The Congress leaders were indicted on charges under the Suppression of Communism Act. The townships reacted with excitement, this was the confrontation we had been waiting for; according to the principles of the campaign, there was to be no defence, no appeal and no payment of fines, everybody was to accept terms of imprisonment. The leaders were on trial in the court of our suspicion. I was cynical about the sincerity and the commitment of our leaders to the cause of African liberation. Dr Moroka had said at a meeting in Fordsburg: 'I cannot go out alone to get your freedom for you.' Would he himself go to prison for that which he told us to go, into the hell that is South African prisons?

President-General Dr James S. Moroka employed separate counsel to conduct his personal defence, to submit a plea in mitigation to his case; that the doctor was a friend of the Afrikaner people, had co-operated with Government

138

institutions, that he had subsidised—from personal funds—the education of European children; the doctor then made the final assertion that he did not believe in racial equality.

Even I was shocked, I had not hoped for as much. I burned my Youth League membership card and retreated into a political wilderness. I was disillusioned beyond reconciliation, and decided to separate my life and interests from politics, until there shall rise from out of the slum of African politics a new and more professional liberation movement. I assumed a mask of political innocence and established a reputation for being apolitical. I turned again to my writing, but this time there was a broad omission of the commitment to fight against the prejudice against my skin, to speak out against injustice and wrong. I wrote innocuous short stories, escapist trash, about boxers with domestic problems, respectable pickpockets, hole-in-the-wall housebreakers, private detectives and other cardboard images of romanticism, and yet even against this background my escapist hero was seldom, if ever, on the side of formal law and order. Like me, my characters were invested with a contempt for the law, their efforts were directed towards a flaunting of the law; my heroes were social maladjusts in a society where heroism is measured by acts of defiance against law and order. I did not then recognise the sociological significance of what I was doing, that with a central idea behind them I could use my stories as a reflection or a study of our society.

But the yellow African magazines encouraged and paid for short stories which presented an image of the African as an uncomplicated sentimentalist with an addiction for pin-ups, nice-times, violence in love and temper; which made one wonder whether the Africans lived in a candy floss of vulgarity, in the make-up for their women, their advertised hair straighteners and skin lotions.

Chapter Ten

BUT I AM black, because I am black I was a piece of the ugliness of Sophiatown and a victim of the violence of white South Africa; I became an unwilling agitator trapped in the blackness of my skin, and because I am black I was forced to become a piece of the decisions, a part of black resistance. I wanted to be both black and unconcerned with the games at politics, but a non-committed African is the same black as a committed Native. Intellectually I resisted involvement with political parties, rejected attempts to be drawn into political discussions, yet my physical being became a tool of the decisions of the African National Congress. There was no choice, during riots the police shot their rifles and sten guns at anything which was black.

After every riot there were the usual stories that the police had been provoked beyond human endurance, that in self-defence they had been compelled to open fire at the rioters. I have seen people who had been shot by the police, some I have seen just before they died; seen the glint in their eyes, then the forced, but brave smile and then nothing. I suppose it was brave to die like that, definitely courageous to face police guns with stones in their hands; yet it was so futile. But it happened every time there was a riot. My mind screamed to them against this futility, that theirs was a useless way of dying, but how does one tell a dying man that his death is meaningless? I have never seen a dead policeman.

I have lived through many riots, I have looked upon death too many times. I know the stark horror of South African riots. The police have their excitement and are initiated into manhood; the politicians are provided with a few more martyrs to hang on their glib tongues, but it is the people in the locations who know the full concentrated meaning of the strikes which the politicians call for in their best platform showmanship.

Such a call came forth in 1951 when the politicians called for a one-day strike on May Day; it was another of those political adventurisms, people were instructed to stay home, away from work, in protest against some legislation. I cannot remember which, possibly the Suppression of Communism Act; it was somehow not explained why I should protest, I was not a Communist, and when I did become a part of the protest I could not explain it to myself, except that the politicians thought I ought to. I doubt if it would have made any difference if they had explained, but I believe a code of etiquette ought to have been considered; if a man is asked to die he deserves the decency of an explanation.

People died in that stay-at-home strike, laid down their lives without question or even a promise for a better tomorrow for their children; there still has to be a national relief fund for the families of these martyrs, and since there is at least one such adventure a year this fund is urgent.

The May Day riots, as I saw them, were the bloodiest on record, even for Sophiatown. I saw it happen, could smell the pungency of death, tasted the salt in my mouth, brushed shoulders with it and stared at it full face, as I had seen it on the battered face of my father; but the canvas was larger and the sight of blood and the taste of death did not revolt me. Rather the sight and the smell filled me with maniacal hatred for the police, something which made me understand why oppressed peoples go on a murder rampage after a successful revolution.

I saw the police rehearsing their roles in the drama of murder unfolding before us; it was a cool, calculated, cold-blooded dress rehearsal. It was around ten in the morning when it all began. The impressive parade began in earnest in Victoria Road spreading along the area covering Gibson to Good Street; mounted patrols, marching detachments and military convoys in a resplendent show of arms; it was a magnificent sight, an august show, dazzling in military ritual. Brass buttons and military drill never fail to draw a crowd.

We lined the street to watch, with silent awe, the spectral parade, we did not cheer or wave flags; we stood there spell-bound, transfixed as by a stately, slow and solemn funeral train. There was a promise of death and we could sense the horror in that promise, and yet we could not turn our faces aside, turn our backs to it. Then suddenly, as if in fulfilment of that promise, an order was shouted through the loudspeaker. The people were given three minutes to disperse, but the people mumbled and shuffled their three minutes away.

'Disperse the crowds!' the order boomed through the loudspeaker, and the South African police went into the kind of action for which they deserve, and win, medals.

The mounted police steered their horses into the crowds, galloping into men and women, charging into mothers with children strapped on their backs; screaming women and children were running from one horse and baton into another; men were collapsing under baton wallops, falling to the ground before the galloping horses. I saw a mounted policeman charging in the direction of a woman running for shelter, heard her terrified scream as she fell under the horse, the rider almost falling off his mount from the sheer force of the blow. He had meant to cudgel her but had missed.

I was insane with anger; I shrieked and swore, but was too petrified with fear to move from behind the corrugated-iron fence which girded in our yard. I stood peering over the fence, swearing and afraid. It is inhuman to even suggest that I thought the police were enjoying themselves, like a man at a duck shooting. There were these two mounted contestants racing for a black figure, two polo players swinging together at the ball, both missing the strike, their horses in near collision; swinging the mounts round and charging again. I was ashamed in my coma of cowardice. I wanted to step outside, and with my bare hands strangle each one of them in turn. But I was afraid.

Then it happened, I mean the action which has caused the death of many people in countless riots; it is not an act of bravery, of reckless courage, nor definitely one of stupidity. It is an action which shows man as a complicated set of responses capable—under normal circumstances—of reactions within a limited range of experiences, but beyond a certain limit of endurance of loosing control of his rationale, shouting like Laertes:

> To hell, allegiance! vows, to the blackest devil!
> Conscience and grace, to the profoundest pit!
> I dare damnation:—to this point I stand,—
> That both the worlds I give to negligence,
> Let come what comes; only I'll be revenged. . . .

I believe that white South Africa—to preserve its privileged existence—is gambling on this very explosive probability, to push the black South African beyond the endurance limit, and then under the justification of self-defence, the preservation of law and order, and in protection of Western civilization, to completely crush the African, to obliterate him from the face of South Africa. They are committed to accomplish this before the Africans can organise themselves into a striking or a retaliatory force. This eagerness can be seen in the streets when the bullies bait an African into a temper.

On that day in May the police succeeded in their efforts; except for a few minor bruises, there was no real danger to them. Someone threw a stone and it bounced off the shoulder of a mounted policeman, then there was another, and another, until the stones seemed to drop from out of the fleecy, solitary clouds drifting by unconcernedly, as if to emphasise their non-alignment. It seemed the police had not expected to be attacked, for a moment they were open-mouthed, withholding belief, like a bully struck by the local coward. Like clots of sweat panic began gathering on their faces, I saw it mounting in their ranks, the restlessness, the creeping fear. In vain they flayed their truncheons about, parrying the stones with the butts of their rifles. From behind the fence I threw a stone, my single contribution, unconcerned with its effectiveness. With it I had my say. I returned to my post. I was encouraged to discover they were human after all; the superman cloak had fallen off, stripped of the sense of authority. They started running, even though their bodies may not have moved more than three feet; it was the mind which was running. They were holding their rifles high in the air, scampering about in a confused retreat. They may not have been supermen, but they were not men either; and although their mind was running, the bodies would not follow until they had been ordered to. We were throwing stones at a machine fitted with discipline. It was a victory to us, we had brought out the flaw in the mechanism, the human element of fear.

It was a brief, empty victory, but it was a glorious brief moment, almost worth dying for. The order to open fire disciplined them into juggernauts of death; from that moment on there was no excitement, only death. The rifles and the sten guns were crackling death, spitting at anything which moved—anything black. The police selected their targets at random with persistent accuracy; watching through a crack through the corrugated iron I saw a policeman support himself against a pillar, the muzzle of his rifle panning slowly across and then crack. The shooting, the screaming, the dying, continued for what seemed like the whole day, and the snap staccato of the guns echoed from all around Sophiatown; and the smell and the decay of death spread over the township, over the burning cinders and the smog.

And the night spread its darkness over the darkness of those who had died, over those who huddled behind locked doors, and the women and the children under the beds; but it also brought an uneasy quiet, a respite from dying, a time to count the dead and a time to be angry. The police had retired to the Newlands Police Station presumably for fresh supplies and a deserved rest. Too many of us saw too much death that evening, until we were physically exhausted by the sight of death. And in our anger we prepared and waited for the next encounter. We laid the battleground. We smashed the bulbs of the electric standards, switching Sophiatown into the darkness which made all things equal.

A small patrol was treading up Gold Street without the shaving of a moon to light their steps, and for once it seemed God was on our side; at least the colour of our skin served us in a way that was purposeful. In the dark the police reacted to footsteps they could not see in their gun sights, and we followed the towering bravery of their course up the street. Then we started the game of nerves. I was in a group detailed to beat out signals on the electric standards, and with a stone I beat out a rhythm signalling the concentration of our forces in Gold Street; the group was assigned to cover the area between Good and Tucker Street. I struck the rhythmic tattoo three times, the sound coming from behind the police. When the patrol reached Victoria Road the signals for attack were sounded, the sharp peals rose from all round the police; we were shouting as the attacking Red Indians did in the films. It was a hideous noise.

We crushed our stones, almost point-blank, at them; they were shooting blind at imaginary targets. The shots were erratic and we pelted them, piling on the pressure from an arsenal which we had stockpiled in the yards all along the street. We shrieked and screamed as the stones harrassed them. Darkness had made the contest equal; though the police were at a tactical disadvantage, they had guns. We pelted them until we heard them running down the street towards Main Road, and along their retreat they collided with more stones. Some were knocked down, rising without bothering about their police caps, others dropped their rifles which disappeared into the yards. It made me feel good, and in a sense restored my masculinity, vindicating the sense of cowardice and shame which I had felt during the day; it made all of us feel proud that we had routed the law enforcement officers of the State. We had struck a blow, not at the police, but against the entire system, and I wished that those who had died could have been looking on at our moment of triumph, perhaps it might have filled them with a sense of purpose; that perhaps they did not die in vain, that although their death did not win anything, at least they were revenged most thoroughly for their pain.

The next morning—as the police were conducting reprisal raids, under the excuse of rounding up the lawless elements and searching for dangerous weapons, in fact dragging people out of their homes and assaulting them—the white newspapers carried banner-headline stories describing the remarkable restraint of the police, who in great danger to their person, were forced to open fire on the rioters. There has always been a margin of difference which, because of my limited education, I have been unable to appreciate: the police do not shoot at the Natives, casualties arise following a clash with the police. Reading the account of the riot in the *Rand Daily Mail* the next morning made me feel a great admiration for the police, and if I had not been directly involved in the riots I would have argued the case for the police. It was white justification speaking out. In Sophiatown the figure stood at eighteen Africans dead; one did not have to look for the casualty list of the police, and even when the newspapers reported the dangerous situation of the police being fired at by the Natives, the police were never hit; either the police wore bullet proofing or the Africans were using water pistols.

The leader pages of the newspapers usually carried editorials commending the police and blaming the rioting on the lawless element, the irresponsible tsotsis; this was all that white South Africa required to satisfy its conscience, to rationalise the death of eighteen people.

Blame it on the tsotsis, the parasitic layabouts who prey on both the whites and the responsible law-abiding Africans; blame it on the African National Congress, the irresponsible Communist agitators in the Congress; blame it on those who died; blame it on the overcrowding conditions of the slums. Then the responsible leaders in the African National Congress, intent on demonstrating their moderation, would dissociate themselves and the Congress from the rioting, from the violence, disowning those who had died; the Congress leaders would re-emphasise: 'Our struggle is a non-violent one.'

When everybody has blamed it on somebody else—and the more charitable have blamed it on history—the police would feel justified to launch the reprisal raids; hundreds of Africans would be rounded up on infringements of the Pass regulations and other minor technicalities. Of course the papers will explain that the raids are a new and vigorous police drive against illegal firearms and illicit brews; just routine raids aimed at protecting the Africans against the tsotsis.

The routine raids are routine only in their consistency of vengeance and brutality, but the hooliganism of the police is something which never gets into the newspapers; except for the very enthusiastic and unfortunate police constable who occasionally finds himself in court facing an assault charge brought against him by an African. But here, too, the free and courageous white press is—especially on matters of colour

147

—more white than free and courageous; and the white-owned black press is more yellow than black.

I have found the reprisal raids more terrifying than the actual riots. They do not mourn at the home of a coward, says an African proverb; I am either a coward or very careful. I have been stabbed only once, and it was a flesh wound. I have not been hit by a police bullet nor battered by police batons, and for someone born in Sophiatown that is a record. It is unbelievable that I have never been arrested for any crime or contravention of any of the thousands of Pass Regulations for which more than a million Africans are imprisoned each year, I suppose luck has had something to do with it, but I did spend a week-end in a place of detention for juvenile delinquents.

There is no set prescription for safety in a reprisal raid; during the reprisal raids following the 'Stay-at-Home' campaign of 1958, I escaped police assault by the providence of chance. In April, 1958, the white electorate went to the polls to decide between the uncompromising apartheid policy of the Nationalist Government and the watered-down segregation policy of the United Party, with its tongue-in-cheek policy of integration. The Congress Alliance decided on a campaign of mass witholding of African labour, a protest against the policies of both white parties. The Congress Alliance hoped the stay-at-home, if successful, would be a threat to the country's economic stability and shock the country into a recognition of the existence and the political demands of twelve million non-white races who are denied the vote.

The pro-United Party English press used the campaign as a bogey to frighten the voters into returning their cancerous United Party; much play was made of its moderate policy of integration (possible), partnership (ultimate) and trusteeship (permanent)—eloquent quibbles for baasskap and apartheid. The English press, the United Party and other hopefuls actually believed this would be the effect. I heard argument that under the United Party Government there would be a 'steady' return to better black-white relations. Integration was the new toy. Some Africanists saw in the campaign another Communist adventure. Mr Potlako Leballo said: 'We are against the campaign because it's left-wing inspired.' Fire-eating Joasia Madzynya, the Alexandra Township strong man, openly defied Alfred Luthuli's call for the branches to endorse the campaign; but in spite of the dissensions Sophiatown responded to a greater extent than the other areas, and therefore suffered the most.

On the first day of the stay-at-home the police were omnipresent, armed with the routine paraphernalia, but acted—surprisingly—with patience and restraint. Their commanding officer must have read to them the editorial in the *Sunday Times*: 'The police will earn high praise if, by their patience and restraint, they succeed in carrying out their duty with a minimum of force.'

The police did just that, until sunset.

By sunset the Africans who had sneaked off to work were assaulted by pickets as they got off the buses. This gave the police the justification they needed to throw off their 'patience and restraint'. The police interpretation of the situation was simple: These Natives are molesting law-abiding Africans, let's go get them. But since a law-abiding African is as black as a lawless Native, the police were liberal in their punitive action; every Native in the streets was a Congress agitator interfering with the rights of law-abiding Africans, so every African on the streets was assaulted.

The police hooliganism sparked off a few minor clashes at various points in Sophiatown; nothing serious, the casualty list was moderate. But the following morning it was very serious. The uniformed hooligans came in lorry loads, charging into the yards and houses dragging out people—who because

149

they had not gone to work were therefore A.N.C. agitators—assaulting and throwing them into the kwela-kwelas. It was dangerous to be caught out in the streets, the home—man's proverbial castle—was the most dangerous place to be trapped in; no place was safe. By nine o'clock that morning there was not a single man in Sophiatown; they had run into the surrounding white areas, disappearing behind the kopie outside Sophiatown into Linden.

I was caught in the centre of the vengeance of the police, not because I was black and lived in Sophiatown, but because I was a working journalist on *Golden City Post*. Six journalists and photographers were assigned to cover Sophiatown for the three days of the stay-at-home, and because the newspaper —as a matter of commercial policy—traded in battered corpses, fractured skulls, rape, murder, sex perversions and salacious confessions, our assignment was to bring back photographs of the police in action. We had been trained to a point of being disappointed if nothing dramatic happened. We followed the police vans round Sophiatown with cameras cocked, note books and cheap biros ready; every time the police rushed a man we clicked our shutters and Peter Magubane, famous for his reckless chances and outstanding photographs, abandoned the security of the press car for greater mobility with his camera.

Understandably the police did not wish to be identified from newspaper photographs bashing in skulls of agitators, so twice they warned Peter Magubane off, shouting at us to 'Fock off '. But we dared not report back to the office without scoop pictures of bleeding heads; we spent hours following the police and being warned off and we were desperate for a front-page picture. We decided to divide into three parties and because I took my own photographs I was left on my own at Ray Street. Without the protection of the press car I rated the same as any African on the streets, which means I had to keep a respectable distance from the police and still bring back reasonable pictures. A reporter of the *Bantu World* who was alone and on foot was later found with his head covered with blood after being battered by the police. I was not Peter Magubane. Nothing was happening around Ray Street, and except for an occasional excitement and average pictures of police jumping out of the vans and chasing an African into a yard, it was a dead beat. After an hour of uneventfulness I decided to move towards the bus terminus where most of the action was concentrated. At the corner of Meyer Street the police dropped out of the kwela-kwela to chase a man in my direction; there was little point in risking assault for a photograph of a police chase, the office files are filled with them. I disappeared into the nearest yard, scaled a fence into Gibson Street, across the street into another yard, over the fence into Miller and on to Tucker Street and one more yard and fence and I was home.

There was a crucial moment when the police stormed into the yard where I lived and discovered me re-loading my camera, but before they could pounce on me I confronted them with my press card, the impressive police seal and the signature of the deputy commissioner of police saved me from the storm troopers of law and order.

That evening we made a check of the hospitals, there were the usual caualties with police gun wounds, fractured skulls and broken limbs.

Then a rumour came through that the campaign was called off, it was reported that the announcement had been made over the radio, that it had been called off by Oliver Tambo; some said that the full text of the announcement would be in the morning papers. And because it came from those sources of mass communications controlled by the whites, the signal was dismissed as white propaganda intended at breaking the strike. The people of Sophiatown had a feeling of distrust towards the message, but it was authentic. It had been signed by the

National Secretary of the African National Congress. The signal had annoyed the youth of Sophiatown who were shooting questions at me: What right had Oliver Tambo to sign that document? I was sympathetic with their cause. In his comfortable home, away from the police batons and the guns, he had arrogated to himself the pretension to sign such a document; people were dying in Sophiatown when he was signing that document. I supported the view that the campaign should have been allowed to continue for the scheduled three days, whatever the consequences, which the A.N.C. should have realised before calling the strike.

Another campaign had failed, yet another blot on the African's determination for national liberation; another failure for the same reason the others before had failed. It was a misadventure in the political game played by amateurs.

The same editorial in the *Sunday Times* of the week-end before the campaign had stressed that 'it will be of immense benefit to race relations, and to the increasingly sympathetic interest which many Europeans in commerce and industry are taking in the problems of the urban Native workers, if it (the campaign) is conducted in a strictly orderly manner and is brought to an end as quickly as possible without serious incidents.'

Because of the stay-at-home campaign the Nationalist Government imposed a ban on all meetings and gatherings at which more than ten Natives were present; the ban remained enforced long after the usefulness of it had passed, and was not lifted 'as soon as possible'.

Chapter Eleven

My young mind was unable to understand the apathy of the white South Africans, the intensification of oppressive legislation against the Africans, the brutality of the police, all the injustice committed in the name of apartheid did not seem to concern them or violate their sense of justice and right. I was staggered by the complacent ignorance about the condition of my life in the slum yards which smelt of urine, by the fact that my human rights were disregarded by the body politic. Like the ostrich they accepted—with self-satisfied casualness—the grotesque distortions the newspapers printed about the riots. There had been a time when they had been incensed into silent indignation; and yet now, because they had been educated into an acceptance of the primacy of law and order, they did not—as their reflections in the Southern States of America—mob themselves into a lynching pack; perhaps it was that they held a dependable reliance on the banditry of the law to adequately proximate their murderous anger.

The police had been on a routine raid for dagga, marijuana, in the Northern Transvaal, when—according to newspaper reports—they were attacked by a fierce, prancing, savage horde of tribesmen, and in the skirmish five policemen—two white and three black—were barbarously butchered and mutilated. In the round-up of the murderers twenty-two Africans were arrested, charged, tried before the court of the land, found guilty and sentenced to pay the supreme penalty. About forty-eight hours before the execution the energy of a Johannesburg newspaper presented documented evidence that one of the twenty-two men had not, in fact, been anywhere within fifty miles of the scene of the clash with the police. An injunction was granted and the innocent man released.

After the hearing of the case had gone through the preparatory stage in the Magistrate's Court, the twenty-two were committed for trial in the High Court where the case was heard and the men condemned; and yet all through this process designed to protect the innocent from a possible error in law, an innocent man—together with the 'guilty'—had been condemned to death by hanging. Admittedly every country, at some moment of national anger, will be obsessed by a hanging mania, particularly after the murder of a national hero or the killing of a policeman, but even accepting this mass hysteria, a similar instance, in another place, would have raised doubts as to the individual guilt of the remaining twenty-one men. The newspaper was satisfied with its Boy Scout accomplishment and overlooked the enormity of the morality it had exposed. I thought that it was reasonable to suppose that the innocence of that one man was sufficient to intrude an element of doubt; the law specifies that guilt must be proved beyond any possible shadow of a doubt.

But South Africa, black and white, wanted a hanging: the whites, from an enraged sense of vengeance, and the blacks, to dissociate themselves from the barbarism of the act. Twenty-one lives for five. But then, of course, the Biblical meaning of an eye for an eye, one eye for one eye, has seldom been understood, far be it from being realised.

It became a mounting difficulty for me—even with all my own imperfections—to continue living in the same world with these people. We could not look at the same thing together. I found it disjoint. Yet my arrogance could not persuade me into a state of accepting that I alone was right, even if everybody else was so obviously wrong. Those of my friends who listened to me recount the events of the riots responded rather to the hurt I felt; I found none who realised the moral I was intending, but I understood that they could not do this without focusing upon themselves the guilt which they knew in the final analysis belonged in the conscience of every individual white man. A very respected friend confronted me with the moral principle of civilised man: the law is the law, which I understood to mean that all of us must arrange ourselves under the will of the law; and I remembered Jefferson stressing that 'for that will to be rightful, it must be just.' I refuse to accept the concept of the infallibility of the law; the law is the will of man in his status as the majority, but man is fallible and this fallibility is inherent in his efforts. When man seeks to evade responsibility for his actions, he invests the law with portentous infallibility.

'What about me, Bloke?' my friends have charged. 'You can't condemn whites without including me. I have no race prejudice, I don't believe in it. Am I to be condemned with the Afrikaners? What about me?'

Precisely. What about you? Where were you when they crucified my Lord? It was once a gospel chant, but it has a relevance for every individual man in the locations who has stood aside whilst the tsotsis desecrated the body of a man; in the over-developed white unconsciousness of police hooliganism against the Africans. I may very well pose the questions: Why should I personally be relegated to inferior positions? I do not believe in racial discrimination.

I prefer to believe that this dishonesty is intentional, perhaps a purposeful invention intended to mask the feeling of consciousness of guilt; but I refuse to accept them as being insensitive; they are white, they enjoy the rewards of being white even though they may be resisting responsibility for it. Custom and the statute has reserved for them all the key positions in our economy and polity; they own the land, the industries, the finances and the ways and means of earning a living. And even those of the ordinary working class are secured into the privileged class by a system of legislation and customary divides which transfer upon them prestige and all the symbols of authority, by virtue of being white. It is unnecessary for me to look upon a white man and be in doubt over his status in our society. By his colour I will know his class. It is dishonest to pretend otherwise; they are white and I am black.

The public image of South Africa is white, and this single factor is dramatically illuminated by the white hoboes in the street; they have to reach a certain depth of depravity before they can confront an African for alms, because the Africans —in the eyes of the upper white caste—are lower than the lowest white man. I was accosted by a white hobo in Jeppe Street. She was as poor as a black, and, some would say, dirty black; she was carrying a thin, dirty, hungry child. I know the look of hunger too well.

'Please, my boy,' she said, devastated by humiliation. 'Give a sixpence for coffee.'

This scene, her obvious sense of superiority, catalysed a complicated system of responses. Since poverty is black, she and I were locked into a common humanity, something which she would not acknowledge; she was white, a member of the privileged class, and I was black, the traditional divides had to be maintained. For me it immediately became a crack in the myth of white supremacy, I was instead in a position of superiority, possessed by an authority complex; this was invested upon me by her privation. The simple act of a human being appealing for assistance exaggerated into an historic episode almost worthy of the complicated set of human relationships of our society. I gave her a shilling.

Even in this I was emphasising my superiority over her, and yet it was interesting to note that even in her destitute moment she did not lose sight of the fact that I must be reminded that she was a member of the superior race group;

this fact she impressed by addressing me as 'boy'. She and I, in our moment of battle for superiority, were victims responding to race prejudice which is notorious for employing a scapegoat psychology; we were working out our frustrations on each other—the less fortunate members of our society— thus saving ourselves the trouble of facing up to the real causes of our condition.

And it is this single fact, this pattern of behaviour, which is responsible for our ostrich mentality. This apathy is in all of us. It is most sophisticated in the professional liberals, who are afflicted with a morbid sense of vicarious suffering with the Africans. They are the ones who are most psychotic about being condemned together with the honest racialists, and when I reply that I am oppressed in spite of their best efforts, they are offended and I am made to feel uncharitable. The fact is, the individual white South African—because of his moral impotence—has become increasingly powerless against the forces of apartheid; and because of this initial apathy I hold each one of them responsible for the South Africa we know today. They are the voters, they hold the power in their hands to have done something about it, but because apartheid held the promise of advantage for them they have accommodated. I have looked among them for a John Brown, for one man to stand up and say: 'It (the New Testament) teaches me, further, to remember, them that are in bonds as bound with me.'

There may be those who will accuse me of asking for too much; that is exactly what I am doing, asking for too much. I prefer to dispense with eloquent quibbles: the Africans are the most brutally oppressed of all the victims of apartheid, and I will single out from responsibility for this only those white South Africans who, because of an honest concern for right, will act on the simple fact that South Africa is an affront to man's conscience. I have looked among them for those who will die on the cross proclaiming the dignity of the concept of principle. Jesus went into the valley of the lepers. John Brown, under the shadow of the hangman's knot, made a point which I submit as a reference to those liberals with good intentions.

Now, if it is deemed necessary that I should forfeit my life for the furtherance of the ends of justice, and mingle my blood further with the blood of my children and with the blood of millions in this slave country whose rights are disregarded by wicked, cruel and unjust enactments, I say, let it be done.

Among these liberals are included personal friends I respect in their private capacity as individuals, but in the public image they are white, they live in white privilege; they have not rejected the fruits of being white; they live in 'Europeans Only' suburbs, they eat in 'Europeans Only' restaurants, recreate themselves in 'Europeans Only' cinemas, theatres, bars, art galleries and other public places. I have yet to listen to a white South African objecting to and rejecting the privileged condition of his lot; some have complained about my poverty, the slum conditions, but never about their inflated opulence.

I am instead insulted with multi-racial tea parties where we wear our different racial masks and become synthetically polite to each other, in a kind of masquerade where Africans are being educated into an acceptance of their inferior position. The masks in the charade are promiscuously polite, courtesy becomes a plague and gradually—by the rules of the game— the African is persuaded to understand that he must be humble if he is not to antagonise 'the growing number of Europeans who are taking an interest in African affairs and welfare'. I have smiled benignly, spoken in undertones and assumed a charm in personality as I sipped my tea with an observance of the social graces of the upper classes. But since it was a charade it was not desperately important if my manner was slightly incongruous and incompatible with my colour. I said the right things, echoed the appropriately eloquent justification for my social inequality; but the elegance of the occasions, their propensity for opulence seldom failed to emphasise the poverty and the squalor of my life. Every time I returned from these things Sophiatown became all the more depressing.

I remember that I used to become overpowered by a sense of self-consciousness, I felt that I was a curiosity at most of those tea parties. I was a piece of rare Africana; subjected to such illuminations like; 'I've never met an intelligent African before—I mean an African who is actually articulate.' Most of them were visibly struggling with the word 'African' which was almost always one beat too late. It was amusing to watch them struggling with the problem of whether I should be addressed as 'Mister' or 'African' or the standard 'Native', which came easier than the rest. Invariably the 'Native' would slip through and there would be the appropriate embarrassment masked with well-bred social courtesy; and at some point there would be the interminable references to the house servants who were blandly referred to as 'boy' or 'girl.' It was interesting to observe that all the training in social etiquette failed to have had any influence, because, although they were careful not to call me 'boy' or 'Native', this courtesy did not extend to their house servants. It was important for me to keep a straight-face detachment lest I should be seen willing to associate myself with house servants.

My relations with house servants have invariably been complicated; in some of the white homes I have come up against silent resentment from Africans who felt the indignity of having to wait upon another African; some African servants are proud of the snobbery of the families for which they work, and any lowering of standards is resented, and since I am black my presence at table was a serious depreciation of standard.

Others seemed to resent an extension of a privilege which was denied to them, and sometimes I was looked at with suspicion; I had arranged myself on the side of the whites, a potential traitor to their cause. In others there was a feeling of pride, one of them had arrived, was in effect accepted as good enough to sit at table with whites. It was all terribly complicated.

But essentially I was a curiosity, a main attraction, the added inducement in most invitations to a party: 'Bloke is coming.' When distinguished visitors from America or Britain were entertained, the 'smart' thing to do would be to have intelligent Africans with responsible ideas; there was a small circle of articulate Africans selected for their ability to assume an intellectual disinterest in party politics; then there was another circle of African politicians favoured for their liberalism, those who were passionately committed to multi-racialism —and spoke loudly, albeit dishonestly, about it being a great experiment in human relations, the only realistic policy for a sane South Africa. They were preferred by recovered racialists, professional liberals, campaigning Communists and practising leftists in campus jeans.

They tell a delightful story of the African being prompted with a finger in his back by a fashionable woman in mink: 'Come on, don't be shy. Tell the gentleman what the police did to you last week.'

The more intellectual African is invited to symposiums to read papers on such abstractions as 'The Psychology of Race Prejudice' or 'The Native Mind', and in this my good friend, Nimrod Mkele, who holds a Master's degree in psychology, goes into these intellectual pursuits with relish, to deliver scathing papers in which he debunks all the sacred cows of South Africa. Can Temba uses the opportunity to dazzle the white audience with his vital mind; he is cynical almost to a point of self-destruction, but it never fails to intrigue white women into wanting to mother him away from his philosophy of nihilism. Can Temba has realised that a woman will seek to patronise a man even into bed.

There is apathy among the Afrikaners too, who are struggling under the moral obligation to justify their cause by shouting down criticism from the English, the Jews, and the whole world; they see themselves maligned and persecuted by people who fail to understand the finer details of their unique problems. They are the chosen people whom God has seen fit to place in authority, government and guidance over the black races, to which God—in His infinite wisdom—has damned them beyond redemption, from which they cannot be saved even by the dying of Christ on the cross. The Afrikaners know for a fact that the Africans are happy in their condition, that the fermentation of rebellion is the work of Communist agitators, the jingo English press, and the meddling of Britain and America in what is essentially a domestic problem of South Africa. The question of the relation between the Afrikaner and the African, they maintain, is wholly and solely the responsibility of the Afrikaner; a matter between him and the God of Calvinism. They are genuinely concerned that the whites in the rest of the world are neglecting this sacred duty by criticising them; the Afrikaners see themselves as the last defenders of white civilization, and are so convinced in the rightness of their course that they are arming to fight with their backs against the wall.

The Afrikaner, they submit, understands the Native mind and is, moreover, best suited to guide the African to a greater realisation of his happiness. A reasonably intelligent Afrikaner woman, in absolute sincerity and regard for the Africans in her employment, said to me: 'We are not really bad, you know. Take me and my husband, we treat our Natives very well. And they like us. You know how they are always short of money; well, me and my husband are always ready to help them. We lend them money almost every day.'

I was not exactly sure what it was she was illustrating, but I restrained myself from insinuating a slight correction; my duty was to listen, to observe, to analyse—without comment—the different characters which made up our society. But she did overlook that if they paid their Natives a living wage the situation she described would have arisen less frequently.

I concede that the Afrikaner family was not conscious that it was upholding the policy of keeping Africans as perpetual dependants who have to work for the white man if they are to earn a living, that on their earnings the Africans cannot hope to gain economic independence from the white man. Economic independence is something the African will never be permitted, for the economy of South Africa and the continued prosperity of the white man are consolidated on the structure of Native wages. The wisdom of this was explained by a delegate at the 1958 Congress of the Association of Chambers of Commerce. During the discussion on Native wages, the delegate said: 'We have an opportunity that no other nation has. We are the only country that should never have a depression. Other Commonwealth countries have a uniformly high standard of living. They have little room for development. But in South Africa we have three-quarters of the population living on the breadline.'

It is an absolute necessity for the maintenance of white supremacy that the perpetuity of the structure of Native wages must be standardised at its present level so that the African is denied the potential power of economic independence which might presume upon him an equality with the white man. The necessary body of Africans required as black teachers, doctors, priests, nurses, should be discouraged from argument that since they perform services equal in academic qualifications to that of the whites, they should therefore be entitled to social equality. This is achieved by paying them on a lower scale than that of the whites.

South Africa is guided by a single paramount concern, and it is perhaps fitting that the country's most respected statesman should have articulated it. General Jan Christian Smuts said: 'There are certain things about which all South Africans are agreed, all parties and all sections, except those who are quite mad. The first is that it is a fixed policy to maintain white supremacy in South Africa.' It is comforting that even 'those who are quite mad' are at least sane about one other paramount issue: Native wages. The most articulate critics are the liberals whose remarkable campaign has been matched only by their cause; they compiled statistics which showed a gloomy picture of the poverty of the Africans, but in their own back-yards their house servants were not paid much better. But then, of course, conscience is like sleeping with a prostitute, one is filled with revulsion only after the act.

It has never failed to amuse me, watching the progress of this conscience at work. At the time it was nothing more than just an innocent joke; cruel, perhaps, because as it turned out we derived very little enjoyment from it. Lewis Nkosi and I realised the comic situation and could not resist it; perhaps it was another one of those things described as an African joke.

During and immediately following the 1957 bus boycott in Johannesburg, there was an activity of talk in the Chamber of Commerce; a discovery was made that Africans were in actual fact living—it was reported to be either on or below, I cannot remember—the breadline; but there was also this talk about inquiry, with a view of raising the level of Native wages. The *Golden City Post* praised in an enthusiastic editorial the realistic stand of the Chamber of Commerce on Native wages which that body was rightly examining. It was a brilliant editorial, at least Lewis and I thought it was; we were hopeful that, inspired by the courageous vision of the Chamber of Commerce, brighter things would result in our own back-yard, if the tone of the editorial was anything to judge by.

Lewis winked at me as he shuffled, lanky and jogging, into the office of the editor, and although I shared his enthusiasm I was not keen to thus embarrass the editor by the continence of our friendship. Lewis congratulated him on a brilliant and far-reaching editorial; touched and awkward with modesty, he thanked the young reporter, and nodding at me, he re-affirmed his hopes that something of value would result from the influence of the Chamber of Commerce. The genuine sincerity with which he expressed this hope detracted from the quality of humour which we had seen into the incident. We were embarrassed and uncomfortable when the editor ambled out and summoned Lewis into the office. The tension was disturbing. He had come to realise the implication contained in Lewis Nkosi's enthusiasm.

Lewis got a rise two weeks later.

I cannot detract from the almost simple sincerity of the Afrikaner woman, and although it is possible there are Afrikaners who might have a concern for the Africans, there is also the fact that their vote is responsible for the apartheid rule of the Nationalist Government.

There is apathy also among the Africans and the other non-white groups; they are waiting for a Moses to lead them out of slavery. To some this Moses is Red, he is White to others and Black only to a few. From the President-General of the African National Congress to the howlers at the protest meetings there is a fervent hope that the whites will undergo a voluntary change of heart, and among these are those who believe the United Nations will march into South Africa. It is fortunate that Great Britain's filibuster tactics in the United Nations will prevent this, the South African militia can repulse and rout the United Nations troops. None of the A.N.C. conferences has explored, contemplated or voted on the issue of an armed revolt, not even in jest; the African has not stirred to cancel his captivity. They are waiting for Moses;

there have been, of course, small ripples here and there. We are still concerned with mouthy resolutions, sing-songs, petty quarrels for leadership and pathetic slogans like, 'freedom in our life time'.

It is fashionable for intellectuals to be casually committed and with garbled phrases declare themselves above the banalities of politics. Others propound philosophies—which are derived from those of the white man—to explain the subjugation of the Africans, the situation of inferiority imposed upon him, his subservient position, as being a historical sequence, inevitable under the circumstances. The converted insist that the African has sinned, offended God as the heathens, disregarding his commandments; they see the unfortunate position of the African as having been willed by God in His infinite wisdom, the dispensation of divine wrath which shall descend 'even unto the third and the fourth generation'. Apartheid is God's punishment for their sins.

In the same tone the traditionalists pontificate about the African's abandonment of the ways of our ancestors, that the acceptance of an alien culture has emasculated us, that the gods of our ancestors have cast their shadow on us; they claim that the prophets of Africa had warned against this calamity. The Messianic myth persists strongly among them. The black Christians, the orthodox faithfuls, are atoning and have become holier than the saints; they are waiting for the redemption of the Second Coming. They accept their unfortunate position as the will of a terrible, vengeful God, hoping that perhaps with enough prayer the African may yet be redeemed.

I was bewildered by all this apathy, particularly as I was passing through a transitional period which for the sake of convenience I shall refer to as the age of bewilderment. From that day when I watched young, white police constables humiliate my father I swore I would restore his honour, restore—in my own estimation—his manhood. I wanted to fight, but there were none to share my enthusiasm; I was bewildered to find those who believed in the strength of peace, and the disillusionment had a strange effect on me. Perhaps there was another way of fighting. I was young, I was looking for a philosophy, searching for a morality.

I sought the friendship of those who were older than I, and in Solly Godide and Willie Boyce I found two who were enviably uncommitted; they had no politics and seemingly were without complicated experiences. We formed into a kind of three musketeers, concerned ourselves in each other's problems, mediating in strained affairs with girls. We were later joined by Simon, who with Solly and I became insatiable readers of detective stories, in particular those of Leslie Charteris. We were enchanted by 'The Saint', and the author could not write them fast enough for us; in between we filled in with Raphael Sabatini and Alexander Dumas, and our habit was to exhaust an author, then spend hours discussing the books.

But Simon Templar was to become more than 'The Saint', that infallible, that incorrigible braggart; he became, in fact, a real living influence, the escape image of our frustrations. His philosophy, his morality, persuaded itself upon us; 'The Saint' suited the temper of my life, served as a cushion against the pangs of a discriminating society. I adopted his carefree attitudes, and behind the shell of these nothing could touch my life: not the police raids, the violence of Sophiatown, not the injustice and the humiliation of being black in white South Africa; I could defy South Africa by flashing on that cynical 'Saintly' smile.

'The Saint' fought on the side of the good Blokes against the bad Blokes, and every man—saint or devil—was called Bloke, and this depersonalisation appealed to me, and thus Solly, Simon and I slid into calling each other Bloke, a label which increasingly found its way into our conversation. Of course everybody around us was also called Bloke, and thus it happened that Solly and Simon managed to crowd this label around me; people around us began to assume the label for my name, and gradually this label became a part of me I could not discourage; it began to overwhelm me, to become a piece of me, to impose a life of its own upon me; finally I was to accept it for a far deeper significance than I at the time realised. It did not occur to me that in accepting this label I was to obliterate my legal name, but so completely that people are surprised that I do have another name, something as ordinary as William; and because African mothers are known by the names of their first-born children my mother has since—and shall henceforth—come to be known as Ma-Bloke.

Of course I attempted to protect my legal name, insisted on writing it before Bloke, but people rejected and pushed the William aside, and the invasion has been so successful and complete that today my name is Bloke Modisane. The substitution of Bloke for my legal name had to be rationalised, and the older I became the more sophisticated became the shield against the thing I was. It suited the make-believe world of fantasy I was erecting around myself, this was a way of insinuating myself closer to 'The Saint'. I intruded myself into his world, fought in his suburb against the ungodly; our adventures were crusades against the evil in man, dispensing terror to the ungodly under the standard of justice. In this way I imposed myself upon the world which was rejecting me, challenging their attitude against the colour of my skin, which they held up to my face as an exhibit of the stain against my person; I qualified the challenge with the submission that the quality of the service I was performing to the State cannot continue to be ignored, that it more than adequately compensated for the 'vices in my blood'. I argued the case that my worth cries out for recognition, even in place of acceptance, as it was said that Othello was respected and recognised but not accepted into Venetian society. Roderigo describes Othello as a 'wheeling stranger of here and every where,' and Brabantio, in a fit of racial expectoration, says:

> *Whether a maid so tender, fair and happy,*
> *Would ever have to incur a general mock,*
> *Run from her guardage to the sooty bosom*
> *Of such a thing as thou, to fear, not to delight.*

I resolved that if I could not delight and be loved by white South Africa, at least I should be feared. I kept the wrath of my anger sliming behind every painting of a smile. 'The Saint' and everything which I read served only to resuscitate the loneliness I felt; I wanted more from life than I got back in return. It was easier in my teens, I could dream of the life I expected and thought I deserved, but growing up brought expectations and hopes of fulfilment. The confinement of South Africa, the endlessness, the tedium of life in the location bloated in me the desire for change; to find something new, another way of life, to look upon another culture, to satisfy a desperate hope that there must exist in this world other people different from the white South African. Like Lot I wandered in desperation searching for ten people in the Sodom and Gomorrah that was South Africa; because in spite of everything that was doctrinated into me, in spite of my colour, I believed that I belonged to the enormous family of man.

I became screamingly lonely as I sat through those travelogues in the cinema; they were invariably in colour, usually some island seemingly away from the prejudice of man. Every cinema ticket I bought was a few hours away from South Africa, and the urgency for this peace was so great that I was literally raised inside the cinema. Every characterisation I saw on the screen seemed to leave its mark on me; the performances of Spencer Tracy, in particular, filled me with a special kind of nobility; there was something Christ-like in the very way he looked, in every character he portrayed, he seemed to represent, for me, the spirit of man; the pure concept of goodness, defenceless against the connivance of evil. I felt that as a man Spencer Tracy is good.

My waking life has never been at ease since the Tuesday night, long ago, when I saw Ronald Colman in *Lost Horizon*; tears of anger blurred my vision as the film emphasised with sober detail the desperate need for a Shangri-la, and for months the thoughts depressed me to the verge of suicide. I am not certain I have survived that feeling. From that moment my life became acutely dominated by the lust to wander, to follow the dust until I am one with the grains of the dust in a Shangri-La away from the smallness of man.

After seeing James Hilton's idyllic story on the screen I became emotionally restless, to feel more sharply the futility of being black in a white man's world. I made enquiries about joining the Merchant Navy, I wanted to lose myself in the vast, flowing, deceptive calm of the sea; but the liberal Government of General J. C. Smuts would not allow me even that.

My detractors have selected to interpret the desire to lose myself as a cowardly flight from apartheid in the hope of finding a milder political climate; it was pointless to explain that I hate people and it was from them that I was running. Friends confronted me with the physical fact of my colour, that I will never be free of it or escape the prejudice against it. I would find it in England, America, Russia, India, everywhere.

'What will you do?' they said. 'Will you run all your life?'

I wanted to shut my eyes and scream: Yes! I will die searching. A man must bear the infirmities of his friends. I can barely understand this thing which will not let me be, I cannot sink my taproots anywhere; perhaps it is true that I am seeking for a cosmic existence, that in tangible terms this search is unreal, that even my needs and desires are inconstant. Perhaps some day I will come to learn to live with my colour, to harness the motor of the thing which pumps and drives me on; until then I will be generated along this lonely road which I scream noises into, and the loneliness echoes the screams back at me. Along this road I must walk alone; the screaming and shouting—the monologue in C sharp—is too frightening and personal. The line between fantasy and reality becomes less and less distinct; I cannot tell my friends from my enemies, everything is fading into dust. As the coffin of my father with my name on it had disappeared into the dust.

I am frightened by the eternity of endlessness; I hate long journeys, death terrifies me; and when the Native Commissioner spoke the marriage vows the dread of 'till death do you part' was suffocating. I wanted to run. But Fiki seemed like my best hope in the search for peace and stability, and because of the selfishness of my purpose I committed a mortal sin against her; in disregard of her safety, sanity and right as an individual human being I rushed her into marriage. I had been concerned, primarily, with the salvation of Bloke Modisane, and succeeded in destroying her, splintering her comfortable, uncomplicated life; she wanted a husband, a home and children, I wanted to run because there was no such thing as a normal existence for the children of Ham.

The confinement of the marriage became another of those chains which the Government was riveting on me, and in reacting against South Africa I found myself reacting against our marriage. It was an irritation I began to resent, I was disgusted with myself for the confinement of the marriage. I could not discuss it with Fiki, it was difficult to explain that although I hated the implications of our marriage I loved her; she was ecstatic with happiness, it seemed a shame to disturb that tranquillity. Then more and more with time I became demonic with envy. What right had she to happiness? What right has any black coon to happiness? How uncomplicated was life for her; why not for me? Perhaps if I tried. Desperately. To forget, to pretend. But I could not pretend the blackness from my hand.

I was conscious of the subtle manifestation of frustration, that it breeds in the homes of people who fill their houses with children; but it left me impotent. I persuaded myself that no man has the right to commit a woman to him if he cannot guarantee for her and his children a life of dignity; it was cruel and hideous to the children, particularly African children, who must for ever remain as nothing more than rented fixtures in the South African bazaar.

But there was sanctuary in the cinema, and even though I was segregated in the Indian-owned cinemas I managed to lose myself into the darkness, and in the dark I could not see my hand.

Chapter Twelve

IF HOLLYWOOD had intended to influence the development of a particular kind of person, I am that product; the tinsel morality, the repressed violence, the technicolor dreams, these are the things I absorbed in the name of culture. They were available. The theatres and galleries discriminated against me; I am well into my thirties and I have yet to see a full production of ballet or opera, even though South Africa has ballet and opera seasons to which the world's best talent is invited. I have stood in front of the His Majesty's Theatre in Commissioner Street looking at stills of the Italian Opera Company, the Sadler's Wells Ballet Company, the Old Vic, and then rush to read the reviews. When Julius Katchen and Campoli came to perform with the Johannesburg Symphony Orchestra I went out to buy recordings of the works they were going to perform, and through Roy Carter, a friend working at Recordia, I met both artists and had them autograph my records to me personally. In a sense this made up for the frustration of not seeing them in a live performance.

When John Osborne's *Look Back In Anger* came to South Africa Mr Carr, chairman of the Non-European Affairs, in his unfettered arrogance as the guardian of the morals of nine million Africans, decided against a special staging of the play for us because the play was too immoral. I had read the play. Jeanne and Malcolm Hart introduced me to Alan Dobie, the British actor invited to play Jimmy Porter. Alan Dobie negotiated an arrangement for me to watch the play through a hole at the back of the auditorium, and with due respects to Mr Carr my morals survived the play. I gained far more, culturally, than I lost morally. Alan Dobie's performance was something that nobody has the right to deny to anybody.

The Union of Southern African Artists and the Arts Federation, the two non-racial bodies founded in Johannesburg for the free dissemination of culture between the black and the white races, a kind of domestic cultural exchange, took up the issue with Equity, requesting that visiting British actors and musicians should be acquainted with South Africa's policy of discrimination in the arts; the two bodies succeeded in persuading Equity members to insist on a clause, in contract, that at least one in every six shows should be to a non-white audience. The limitations of this generous arrangement were exposed by Tommy Steele, Britain's golden boy of the big beat musical anarchy, who claimed that since he was not a member of Equity he was, therefore, not bound to the ruling.

Tommy Steele's recalcitrance particularly satisfied traditional white opinion which had already become concerned over the spectacle of white teenagers following black pennywhistle troupes to the zoo lake in Johannesburg and dancing side by side with black teenagers; the racialists saw the pennywhistle kwela music as an evil threatening to disrupt the South African way of life when in 1958 a Johannesburg newspaper published a reader's letter which ended with:

'. . . the white and the black youth are beginning to understand each other. Although they play and dance apart, there was no hate.'

Although the Union of Southern African Artists and the Arts Federation realised that they could not persuade theatre managers to open their doors to non-white audiences—the managements claimed that they were bound by regulations to construct separate entrances and separate amenities such as lavatories if they are to admit black audiences—Equity was requested to explain to its members that special performances for black audiences would have to be on non-contract days. The limitations of such an arrangement could not be realised

173

in London; managements argued, persuasively, that it was hazardous to dismantle, transport and erect sets in another theatre for one performance only, and then reverse the process to the original theatre. It was a difficult problem sometimes solved at the end of the run; but the managements usually crowded the contracted period so closely that the only free opportunity for a special non-white show would fall after the contracted period.

Yehudi Menuhin, the best-loved musician among black audiences, realising this tactic of the booking managements sacrificed his Sundays and spent them giving solo recitals to us—the white musicians of the Johannesburg Symphony Orchestra were not persuaded by the moral stand of Equity. During the Johannesburg Festival the programme of the London Symphony Orchestra was so crowded that the only appearance available before a black audience was a Saturday morning rehearsal. I was present to listen to a full-blown tuning of an orchestra, I had never realised what a noisy job it was. It was my first experience in the presence of a live symphony orchestra, but as it turned out, it was also the most irritating; after the tuning up the orchestra rehearsed bits of movements which were repeated over and over until in the end I walked out in disgust.

It was also during the festival that I almost saw my first ballet ever, but the nearest I got to realising this dream was to watch Dame Margot Fonteyn, in tight jeans, rehearsing sequences of the ballet she was going to dance before the exclusive white audience. At least the loosening-up exercises were varied.

When I became music critic for *Golden City Post* my column declared hostilities against managements and artists who lacked the moral integrity of Yehudi Menuhin. In a boxed item under the head: WE DIDN'T SEE—WHY NOT? I campaigned against every show which came to Johannesburg for which a date had not been announced for us; and with the co-operation of British Equity, the artists and the vigilant energy of the Union of Southern African Artists and the Arts Federation, we saw a complete performance of *The Pyjama Game*, and this after a prolonged nagging at the management; but it was Tommy Steele who posed perhaps the most unpleasant confrontation; I attacked him in my column in a story under the headline, THE HIGH PRICE OF STEELE, when after a two-week siege Mr Steele announced a performance for us at a guaranteed fee of £2,000. My column protested by submitting that a thousand Africans would have to pay two guineas each to meet his demand, and in my appeal—larded with principles and importuning his sense of justice—I drew his attention to the scale of Native wages, that two guineas represented more than three-quarters of the wages of most Africans. The Union of Southern African Artists, which is starved for funds, assumed responsibility and came out of it with a large deficit.

Alma Cogan subjected us to the same condition, and that night I took Chris with us to the concert at the Lyric Cinema, which has been awarded bouquets for modern ideas in planning and installations. Miss Cogan sang about six songs before retiring with the announcement that she was being overpowered by the heat; and in return for fees which were as high as two pounds we were treated to four community sing-songs at which we were invited to sing along and a few that she sang on her own.

The visits to South Africa of American jazz musicians: Tony Scott in 1957 and the Bud Shank Quartet in 1958, marked the most striking advance in the new deal for Africans. The rebellious disposition of Tony Scott amounted to what can only be described—in South African terms—as cultural subversion; he challenged the morality of apartheid by making a public announcement, on discovering that his concert was before an all-white audience, threatening, if necessary, to break his contract if it meant playing to segregated audiences. He consented to appear before an all-black audience, which, as he explained, would 'even up the score'. Then he confronted the promoters of the show with the demand to play only to integrated audiences. The venue for his third Johannesburg appearance was the Witwatersrand University great hall where mixed audiences were permitted provided the promoters satisfied the condition of segregated seating arrangements.

That night, on stage, Tony Scott defied another of those unwritten South African laws by introducing Kippie Moeketsi, the African alto saxophone player, and Johannesburg must have gasped as perhaps for the first time in that city black and white stood side by side on stage in a public hall. Those of us in the hall waited, with sweating palms, for developments, but what in South Africa had been built up into a monstrosity was reduced to the innocuous thing that it always has been. We offered up silent admiration for the man who had the courage to defy the philosophy of a nation, and we canonised him as the first man who publicly refused to accommodate what we held to be a fundamental wrong; Tony Scott's unafraid sense of justice is something which the Africans will talk about with respect for a long time. And before he left he accepted to make records with an African penny-whistle troupe.

The Bud Shank Quartet gave a very successful and satisfying concert at the Bantu Men's Social Centre, perhaps the only hall in Johannesburg where a mixed audience is truly integrated; the races of South Africa sat together and Western civilisation has not suffered from the experience.

The striking feature of these two visits was that the Africans felt—because Tony Scott and Bud Shank, with his quartet, spent several hours of most days mixing with black musicians, listening to their music and recording with them—that for once they were the essential South Africans; and after these experiments white South African jazz musicians began turning up at African jazz afternoons, what is called in the trade—jam sessions.

But all this was much later, in the 'forties and before the late 'fifties there was only the cinema, protest meetings, football matches and African jazz concerts, which were always dominated by the tsotsis. It was usual for the tsotsis to invade dances and concerts; at a Sunday afternoon jazz concert at the Odin Cinema in Sophiatown, which featured the Manhattan Brothers and their 'nut brown baby', Miriam Makeba, the tsotsis called the tunes and intimidated the artists.

'Not that one,' a tsotsi interrupted Miriam Makeba's song. 'Sing that other one.'

'Which one?' Miriam Makeba said, feebly.

'That one,' the tsotsi said, waving an impatient gesture with his hand. 'The other one. You know it.'

Miriam Makeba's voice rose with the lyrics of *Laku Tshona Ilanga*, there was a slight vibrato in her voice and the tremulousness was perceptible in her otherwise electric movements.

'Not that one. The other one.'

The tension in her body was by that moment clearly visible as her fingers metronomed the beat of the blues.

'Not that one.'

And by going through her repertoire she finally realised that during the singing of *Saduva* a maddeningly pulsating rhythmic conversation of sensual gyrations and sound and motion in counterpoint between Miriam Makeba, in dazzling scarlet jeans, the Manhattan Brothers, and the audience, swinging and stomping, and sweating with desire to the throbbing of every sinew of the volatile, voluptuous body of Miriam Makeba, she was not interrupted. She smiled an acknowledgement that *Saduva* was in fact 'that one'. They appreciated her gesture so genuinely that they requested 'that one' three more times before she was allowed to move on to the next song.

But I wanted more than the excitement of the senses; the doors into the art galleries, the theatres, the world of ballet, opera, classical music, were shut in my nose because I am black, and because of this fact I am, therefore, not considered capable of appreciating them; it was decided I am not sufficiently civilised to benefit emotionally and intellectually from the halls of culture; in any case, it was an alien culture, and I was encouraged instead to develop and cultivate an appreciation for my own culture of the shield and the assegai, of ancestral gods, drums, mud huts and half-naked women with breasts as hard as green mangoes; but these were the things for which I was declared to be a savage and not worthy of the 'benefits' of Western culture. And whilst I was encouraged to look back to the kraal, to revive the image of the noble savage, I was nevertheless expected to conduct myself in a civilised manner, to conform to the stereotype which answers to 'boy'. I was alienated and rejected by a culture which at the same time imposed upon me an observance of its values; but there was always present the provision that if I was law-abiding and accepted the denials of this discriminating civilisation, that if I conducted myself—even though I was a sub-human—like a civilised man, I might, God willing, be accepted and welcomed into the exclusive club in about 2,000 years. It took the white man that long to develop to its present degree of excellence his civilisation, unique in time and space.

And until such time as I shall have satisfied the requirements in regard to the time factor (I sometimes think that time is the imperative factor), it shall be considered an impertinence for me to arrogate to myself a pretension for Western musical forms, art and drama. I am not ready for them; an early plunge might leave me bewildered. But I am a freak, I do presume an appreciation for Western music, art, drama and philosophy; I can rationalise as well as they, and using their own system of assumptions, I presume myself civilised and then set about to prove it by writing a book with the title, *Blame Me On History*, which is an assumption that if I am a freak it should not be interpreted as a failure of their education for a Caliban, but a miscalculation of history. But this is heresy, a subversive plot of history against well established South African systems of beliefs.

Except that I do not care to be South African. The white men can take their South Africa and hand it back to the animals; perhaps they can find a way to live together under the will of a law which shall be acceptable to all: that the strong shall prey upon the weak. Man has failed. His principles have no integrity, his laws accommodate the inequality of man. The annihilation of the Aztecs in Mexico and the Incas in Peru by the Spaniards; the extermination of the Red Indians in North America and the Maoris in New Zealand by the English; the obliteration of the Hottentots by the Dutch, indicate that the white men did believe themselves so superior, and their civilisation so unique, and others so inferior that they had very little compunction in exterminating them, with the same disregard as one destroys vermin.

I do not care to be South African, nor do I particularly feel myself persuaded to become a Christian in accordance with the doctrine of a faith so heavily putrified by the ethics of Calvinism. The Dutch Reformed Church and its phalanges has offended me with the belief in predestination, which is nothing more than a justification of the condemnation of the majority of humanity to exploitation by the few on whom God has been pleased to plaster His grace. The precepts of race domination are found within the doctrines of the Dutch Reformed Churches, and their cause is championed by disciples like Rev. N. P. J. Steyn of Krugersdorp, who is reported to have received a double doctorate from London University for submitting a thesis which demonstrated that apartheid, as applied to the native races of South Africa, is a God-given command, that is scriptural, legal, just and fair.

This pronouncement is not to be confused with the expectoral rantings of a fanatic; for the Afrikaner race this is scriptural truth. The Prime Minister, Dr H. F. Verwoerd, in his inaugural speech, said: 'We firmly believe that all will be well with our country and our people because God rules. It must be stated at the outset that we—as believing rulers in a religious country—will seek our strength and guidance in the future, as in the past, from Him who controls the destinies of nations.'

A report on race relations drawn up by three professors of the Dutch Reformed Church, concluded with the 'therefore' that 'apartheid is incompatible with the idea that all human beings are equal'. The three professors: S. Du Toit, W. J. Snyman and Ben J. Marais, advanced as the foundation for establishing this incompatibility the contention that 'manifestation of God's purpose in the history of revelation does indicate that sometimes He allows the subjection of one people by another, if only as chastisement'. Of course there have been the cranks—even within the body of the Church —who have come forward with statements that they have been unable to find any justification for apartheid in the Bible; and the lone voice of Professor B. B. Keet, senior professor at the Dutch Reformed Church seminary in Stellenbosch, has spoken on the side of liberalism: 'Our fight is not between black and white, but between barbarism and civilisation, or, if you will, between heathendom and Christianity.'

I was surprised that the professor did not realise the essential error contained in his statement; I prefer to accept that he overlooked the development of his argument, because the reason he and the other intellectual storm-troopers of apartheid could not see the fight as anything but that between black and white is that at the moment it is the blood of the black man which is allowed to stream over the earth of the country because of the imbalance of power.

The battle is raging fiercely between—in this corner—civilisation, which is white; and—in this corner—barbarism, which is black, or if you will, between Christianity, which is white, and heathendom, which is black. Shake hands and come out hating.

But Professor Keet has also made more progressive observations, his mind has been recovered from the stagnation of Afrikaner intellectuality; he submitted the analysis that Christian charity is bedevilled by the fear of loss of political control, of economic competition, of debasement of Western civilisation, of racial inter-mixture, and that 'true civilisation is never accompanied, nor can it be served, by the witholding of human rights'.

Law-making is a function of the body politic, and the moment it becomes an extension of worship so that the letter of the law and religious ethics come into union, then my mind screams against both. The Bible and the God of Calvinism is being held up and interpreted to mean that the 'subjugation of one people by another' is justified in Christian ethics; if this be Western civilisation and Christianity I will have no part of it. I have renounced Christianity as a snare intended to rivet upon me those chains which have reduced me into a chattel placed in South Africa for the convenience of the white man; and until Christianity can begin to mean something which is more honest, its purveyors can go peddling it among the animals. I will not be honeyed with snippets about the life in the Hereafter, other racialists have sermoned that even there white angels sleep late whilst the tan cherubs bring the morning tea. I know this life, I demand to live it with dignity. What if my condition does not change in the Hereafter? Two existences in subjugation would be unbearable.

I was born into a Christian home of Christian parents, my

mother was a devotee who went to church every Sunday; I was baptised and confirmed into the Lutheran Church, Berlin Mission, learned the catechism and sang in the church choir. I remember that as a boy I was scrubbed with a brush, my ash-grey itching skin rubbed with vaseline and rushed regularly to Sunday school for religious instruction. At the end of the annual term I was awarded—for unbroken attendance—a picture of Jesus Christ; it was a picture showing the Ascension and I prized it highly because it was something I had earned.

I received a primary education in a Dutch Reformed Mission School in Meyer Street, Sophiatown, where every morning the lessons started with a prayer and religious instruction. At home, many years ago, there was a prayer for every meal and every night before going into bed—always the same prayers. I was raised by Ma-Bloke to be a dutiful Christian, and my rebellion was not her fault. When I became older I began to challenge the very philosophy of Christianity and embarrassed her with a tirade of questions, and gradually she realised the point I was making, that it was impossible to be black in South Africa and also be a good Christian. She was tenaciously doctrinaire; any and every action was pre-destined and willed by God: the poverty, the starvation, the oppression, the degradation, all these were willed by God. If a child died of malnutrition, it was the will of God; when a black farm labourer was flogged to death or if an African was shot down by a farmer who later pleaded in court that he thought it was a monkey ravaging his farm, Ma-Bloke said it was the will of God; and when the farmer was cautioned, by the magistrate, to be more careful in the future, and fined £25, it was the will of God. Man escaped the responsibilities for his own action, all the injustice, the inhumanity, was willed upon the bleeding body of Christ nailed to the cross. I refused to accept that Christ died so that the white man can plunder me and bleed my body.

The purpose of the religious instruction which I received was to educate me into an acceptance of the irrefutability of the scriptures of Christendom; they revealed to me that God in his infinite wisdom singled out the sinful issue of Ham for punishment even unto the thousandth and thousandth generation. This issue of Ham was invested—for the purposes of easy identification—with visual differences in skin colour and damned to eternal servitude. If God had not intended us to be different He would have made us all the same, and in His infinite wisdom He has invested with a high visibility them for whom no redemption is possible; even the dying of Christ on the cross shall influence no change upon their condition.

There is one incident which stands with indelible persistence in my memory; it was during the days of my primary education. It was the end of term and we were assembled in the church hall for the annual address to be delivered by a white elder of the Dutch Reformed Church. He stopped in the middle of the talk to inform us—the little black faithfuls—that we were singularly fortunate; there was a Christian sincerity in his voice and bearing. We were fortunate, he told us.

'My God,' he said, his fingers pointing to the ceiling, 'is far, far up there in heaven.'

I could not accept this faith which was demanding my obedience, was plundering my body and would not embrace; I was appalled by its tyranny and its honeyed words which taught me to seek for peace and comfort in bondage. The harbingers of this faith revealed to me that 'man was made in the image of God', then proceeded to dehumanise me; they taught me to repeat the Ten Commandments, with particular emphasis on, 'love thy neighbour as thyself', but in practice they showered denunciations on me, defined me as a savage and classed me among the beasts; there was one morality standard for white Christians and another for black Christians, and even the sermon they preach is a colour-bar one.

Someone ought to undertake to rewrite what—in South African terms—can justly be called, the ten fables of Moses; and may I suggest as a sample, perhaps the most appropriate one: Black man, thou shalt not steal from the white man. This is fun.

I am thy Nationalist Government, thy white superiors, thou shalt have none others.

Thou shalt not take the name of thy Nationalist Government in vain, nor blacken my name overseas.

Thou shalt not be misled by others (the Communists, the English and the Jewish liberals, the jingo press, the A.N.C. agitators) for I, thy Nationalist Government, thy lord, am a jealous god.

Honour thy Minister of Bantu Administration and Development that thy days may be long in the Bantustans.

Thou shalt not kill the white man.

Thou shalt not covet thy white master's women, nor commit an offence under 'The Immorality Act' by having unlawful, and sinful, carnal intercourse and other acts in relation thereto.

It is the disrepute into which Christianity has been brought which is responsible for my attitude, deplorable as it may seem, but yet perhaps the fact that the 'greatest faith in the world' should have to be divested of its spiritual nobility and to be thus shaded with such fearful overtones, is probably the most un-Christian act of all. Man's spirituality has come to a state of decay. It is perhaps for this reason that I carry my Jesus in my heart and turn my back from the Church; Fiki is a casual, non-dialectic Christian, but my unbaptised daughter, Chris, and I will not approach the temples of worship until the Church and the World Council of Churches shall stand up, unafraid, and speak out a condemnation—by word and deed—and a challenge, as once Jesus did when He went into the temple and flogged out the money-lenders; and the day the world body of churches shall command into the wilderness the churches of South Africa, shall refuse to deliberate with them, shall not sit at supper with them, that too shall be the day I shall stop to reject Christianity; for so long as the orthodox Church shall remain white, will continue to react white, for so long will black South Africa disrupt the perfect unity of the Church.

This break-away from white orthodoxy is an accomplished fact; by 1957 there were 500,000 Africans in what was described by the Anglican Bishop of Pretoria as 'separatist churches'. In other parts of Africa the Muslim faith is embracing followers at a rate which is causing considerable concern to the Christian movement. By acceptance and association, the Christian Church in South Africa is white—its authority and symbols are white; in religious paintings all the angels, the saints, the apostles and all the ecclesiastical hierarchy is white, but the devil is black, together with all the symbols of what is fearful, sinful and evil. The Church has become a symbol of everything that is white in a country where white is the symbol of political domination and racial superiority. There is a need for a Martin Luther.

The involvement of the Church with a system which is hated and must be destroyed can be assessed against the acts of violence committed against the Church during race riots, when Church buildings have been among the first edifices of oppression which are stoned and burnt down, and acts of violation have been committed against nuns. People have deliberately refused to face up to the truth surrounding these actions, the tendency to become melodramatic with shock, and the over-simplification of the issues has been all too frequent; people will not learn that shouting 'savage' has not helped the mind in the understanding of the underlying truth behind these acts.

There was little consolation in the statement of the Bishop of Pretoria that the 'separatist churches revive heathen customs', that 'they mix religion and nationalism', that 'they are a threat to Christianity'. There is this physical fact that more than half a million Africans have separated into independent churches.

This is the fact I discovered in the magazine enquiry for *Drum* when I was assigned to find out the facts behind the break-away churches; the intention of the story was to find out whether black Christians and white Christians were, in fact, brothers in Christ. It was a rhetorical question; every journalist in that editorial meeting knew the answer, so did I and so did every black man in South Africa; but *Drum* wanted a prestige story for its anniversary issue, and it was decided to attack the institution closed to the hearts of the man in the street, to confront the white Christians: How are your religious prejudices? How tolerant are you in practice?

The investigation was to spread over two instalments: the first, examining the extent of the break-away movement, and the second, the physical reasons behind the black rebellion from white control. The enquiry took me into the world of stormy religious sessions, of picturesque revivals, the colourful rituals, the free involvements, to biblical baptismals at the river, and brought me face to face with the demi-gods of religious big business and the excitement of informal Christianity. I spoke to the self-styled bishops, the prophets, the faith-healers, all the characters in the colourful world, and at times involved in the drama of the separatist movement. And because of the training I had received on *Drum* I approached the story with all the detachment and the cynicism of a hard-boiled journalist. I was superior, the whole movement was a circus; I was above it all and vaguely laughing at them, and this is how I felt when I confronted Mr Andrew Masekoameng, faith-healer of the Sophiatown Saint John's Apostolic Faith Mission, with the statement of the Bishop of Pretoria.

'If the Europeans want to work with us,' Mr Masekoameng said, 'then they must listen to us. Until they are prepared to listen to us, to practise the word which they preach, then they must walk out of our churches. They drove us out of their churches and now they call us heathens.'

And as I was taking notes my mind kept repeating that it was an articulate statement which would make good copy, I was pleased with myself, and unobtrusively a regard for the faith-healer insinuated into my consciousness, and more with respect than cynicism I read to him—from my note-book—the statement by the Rev. Benkt Sunkler, which he had made concerning the ritual of the sects, that 'it is an escape into history, into the glorious Zulu history, which was brought to an abrupt end by the whites—a colourful form of worship more compatible with African tradition'.

Mr Masekoameng invited me to judge and discover for myself the validity of the charge, and so I followed with Bob Gosani, the talented photographer, to a Sunday morning faith-healing ceremony at a stream in Orlando. The air was sharp and I was grateful that I was not the faithful apostolic who was to be led into the water, but the look of hope and profound faith on the face of the crippled Peter Morgan as he was being carried into the cold stream filled me with a sense of resentment. Why could I not believe in something, in anything, with the fervour which could bring me the same kind of inner peace?

The apostolics were clapping their hands to a rhythmic chant whilst Peter was being submerged into the cold stream. My mind was screaming. Stop it! Stop it! It is a sin to raise the hopes of anybody to the point where they expect miracles; the only way that man can be saved would be to drown him. At the end Peter Morgan was still a cripple, and dangerously exposed to pneumonia, and yet there seemed about him a happier state of mind; he was glowingly happier than I was and I envied him his simplicity and spiritual security.

As some sort of defence I saw into the methods of those religious overlords something for me to despise and thereby be drawn to the persuasion of the Rev. Sunkler. There was a Billy Graham kind of showmanship about them; we were permitted to take all the photographs we wanted, all of them were open and unashamed about the things they did. Faith-healer Tsoku, the Lion of Juda, was concerned more with the smelling out of evil spirits; Bishop Dhladhla conducted his faith-healing ceremonies with the sick in a bath of water round which was a circle of burning candles held by young girls in black skirts and white blouses; Prophet McCamel and Rev. Bhengu converted drunks and tsotsis who came to them to surrender their weapons and pledge themselves to the Church.

I attended several church meetings, faith-healing ceremonies and baptismals, and found myself in a world I never dreamt existed; the ritual was exciting and colourful, and there was a kind of showmanship and joyousness behind the pulpit which made this Christianity commercial; I was to find myself admitting that if Christianity was anything like this—a joyous noise unto the Lord—then I could allow myself to be re-converted. The sermons were animated and invariably attended by histrionics, the congregation sang happy songs to a rhythmic chant of hand clapping, and as the spirit moved them they went into epileptic fits, into howling shrieks which would have seemed more appropriate in a sanatorium for the bewildered; they stood in athletic trances or collapsed in the aisles possessed with fainting spells. The excitement generated from the pulpit probably intended the reaction in the aisles.

The investigation was reported in cynical prose in *Drum*, February, 1956, the tone of the story was decided by the editor, Sylvester Stein, who was cynical about the break-away sects; it was a cover story under the sub-heading: Ducking

For A Pretty Convert. The cover policy of *Drum* was that a pretty girl, preferably a pin-up, could sell any issue; I suppose sex will sell anything, even a story as serious as: No Room For Half a Million Christians; and it was unfortunate that the actual writing of the story might have implied the attitude that *Drum* was laughing at these Christians—the prophets, the bishops, the faith-healers and the converts—rather than making a studied criticism of colour discrimination in the white orthodox churches.

The second of the magazine stories on the question of colour-bar in the churches was to be an investigation into the state of the white churches; the article was to be titled: 'Brothers In Christ?'. It had been decided during those editorial conferences—at which all the major stories were planned—that this story was to be of far more importance in scope and depth. It was to be a Mister Drum assignment, the prestige story of the year to mark the annual celebration of the founding of *Drum* magazine. Other stories in the series had been, 'Mr Drum Goes to Bethal', in which the journalist, Henry Nxumalo, had volunteered as a labourer to one of those notorious farms of the Northern Transvaal to which Africans are either directly kidnapped and seldom heard from again or induced to contract themselves—under false pretences—to labour on the farms under slave conditions; the exposé of the working conditions, the contractual system, instigated a Government commission of enquiry. In the story investigating prison conditions—'Mr Drum Goes to Jail'—the same journalist, after several attempts for a whole week to have himself arrested, was sent into The Fort—known and feared throughout South Africa as Number Four—Johannesburg's concentration prison which for acts of cruelty and the thuggery of prison guards and African privileged prisoners is perhaps unsurpassed in twentieth-century civilisation. Henry Nxumalo, the first of the journalists to wear the title of Mister Drum, had set a standard in journalism and an exercise in courage which was not easy to equal.

Every junior reporter on *Drum* secretly cherished hopes of being selected as Mister Drum. In 1955 Henry Nxumalo was transferred to *Golden City Post* in his appointment as news editor, and Can Temba, next in seniority, was appointed associate editor of *Drum* magazine, and possibly because there was nobody else available for consideration I was selected for the top assignment of the year, to be Mister Drum of 1956.

In comparison, 'Mr Drum Goes to Church', was a less hazardous assignment, the possibility of physical danger to my person was minimal; but the honour of the election, the prestige, was incalculable, even against the fact that I was to be bodily thrown into the den of white Christian lions. It was ironic, though, that I, a self-confessed non-Christian, should be sent into the Church to test the validity of Christian brotherhood.

The challenge was far more important to me than the editor realised, it was to be for me the opportunity to confirm my convictions, in terms above those of the emotional; I had found the need to satisfy my intellect that the stand I had taken was moral, that the denunciations I was screaming against the Church had substance, not just the impatience of youthful enthusiasm. A man does not throw over the second greatest possession which has kept him secure on the visionary and the moral sphere as though it were a careless trifle.

The question of my relationship with God was something I had to resolve myself, a matter of personal conscience; so I locked my secret behind the flash of a smile. Man had failed me; Christianity had betrayed me, and I walked alone with my God in the loneliness to which man had committed me.

I accepted the challenge of the story and as it turned out this was to be the single event in my life which was to be the shadow whose influence spread long over me; the simple and seemingly inoffensive action of going into churches was to change my whole life, to bring fame in equal measure and proportion with the vindictiveness of the police department which was to force me to choose permanent exile from the country of my birth; but fundamentally it showed another view of people which has made it difficult for me to surrender myself into friendships.

In the divine sanctity of the houses of worship I saw Christian charity at work. I was shocked into a state of trauma by the unashamed godlessness of the white Christians, who emphasised—more clearly—that they were essentially white and incidentally Christian. I found a reception committee of two Christians at the main door into the Dutch Reformed Church in Troyeville, Johannesburg; they were handing out hymn-books and extending the hand of a Christian welcome to members of the congregation as they walked between them into the church. Jurgen Schadeberg, the white photographer who had his camera concealed under the jacket, had been welcomed into the church; the strategy was that if I could manage myself into the body of the church I should select to sit myself within the set focal range of the camera, so that Jurgen Schadeberg should not have to focus. There was little hope of walking past the welcoming committee, and this entrance was abandoned in favour of a side entrance through which I could inflict myself into the body of the church.

Inside the church I looked round for Jurgen and the sudden confrontation of those white faces confused me; I was unsettled and overcome by the enormity of the act, I became conscious that I was breaking the law. All the faces were similar, I had to pretend a casualness during that desperate search for the one familiar face in the presence of all that hostility; and when I did eventually find him I made a quick mental calculation and selected a pew within an estimated range of the focus the camera was set at, but actually it was the nearest pew. In the same row where I was sitting were two elderly women, both wearing hearing aids, and I was about three seats away from them; then suddenly I saw it happen, Christianity on the move, they jerked a shocked glance at me, looked at each other, then back at me, reacting in a manner to suggest that I was something which the devil had spat out; and gradually by inches they edged themselves away from me until their progress was barricaded by the solid wall. I could not summon up sufficient cynicism to sneer my reaction at them; I confess to an unbearable shock of seeing people— over sixty years old who had nothing left but their prejudice —respond so much like devils.

The minister—his spectacles pushed down the ridge of the nose—fixed his eyes most constantly on me, and when he said, 'brothers and sisters' I felt that somehow I was not meant to be included; I could not face up to the challenge of his stare, there was something hostile, reproachful and un-Christian about it, and that something in the cold stare, in the elastic movement of the lips, the freezing crispness of his voice, was shutting me out of the fraternity of his words. In the mass of the disapprobation they were unified by a thought, not directed against me as an individual, but against a symbol of what is hated and rejected; and all the crosses of Christendom could not persuade them from wishing me out of their midst, even by an act of death.

But the silent objection to my presence was soon to become more vocal, and physical; an elder of the church—in black suit and tie—whispered almost point-blank, to irritate my ear-drums.

'Come outside,' he said, 'I want to talk to you.'

I gestured that I could not possibly walk out during the service.

'Could it not wait?' I said, fixing my eyes on an enormous

Bible in Pedi, the Northern Transvaal dialect of the Sotho group language; and even though Pedi is my mother tongue I cannot read it; the ink was bleeding all over the page.

'Come outside.'

I appealed to him with eyes and gestures, with all the humility I could command; but essentially I was terrified, suppressing the panic inside my stomach which was limp under an ice-cold weight; I wanted to run from the embarrassment, but Mr Schadeberg was behind me with his finger clicking the shutter of his concealed camera and I could not afford the indignity of being photographed in a state of panic.

'Come outside,' he said, the politeness and the patience had dropped out of his voice; he must have realised that the situation was calling for a more stern handling; and gently, but firmly, I was physically lifted, from under the arm, off the pew and force-marched up the aisle, through the body of the church, past the congregation staring a silent approval of the expulsion, and out through the main entrance which I had so carefully avoided; and once outside the church the politeness and the Christian patience was switched on again, and once more Christian charity spoke with many tongues and the tongues of angels, and with the patronisation of the God of Calvinism.

The recovered Christian spoke to me—with politeness and patience—that I was not permitted to attend the service in that church, which was a place of worship for white Christians only.

'You go down this street,' he said, 'it's about a mile down this street—then turn right and continue on that road until you come to a church which is for you people.'

I listened politely to the directions, thanked him for his kindness and Christian goodness and walked round the corner to the car which was waiting for Jurgen Schadeberg and me.

This was the incident at one Dutch Reformed Church, but it was to set the pattern of Christian behaviour which I was to encounter in most of the churches I was to go into. In all I went to fifteen churches and in two of the churches the black intruder was to be bundled into a car and driven to the police station.

During the planning period for this story every detail was carefully worked out in the several editorial meetings; there was no detail which was too small to be considered. The basic strategy was mapped out. Everything was discussed and examined clinically down to the possible reaction of the congregation, and even the reaction of the minister behind the pulpit. The possibility that there might be acts of violence committed against the body of the reporter was raised for discussion, and anticipated. It was impressed upon the reporter that acts of provocation were at all times to be guarded against. The instructions were that I was to go into the churches and at all times behave myself in a normal and orderly manner, courteous at all times; to be careful of noting and reporting only the facts, without imposing comments on them. The details of the facts of the reception in the churches were to be reported with irrefutable accuracy.

The photographer was to be a man whose admittance into the churches could not be disputed, thus Jurgen Schadeberg, the picture editor, was assigned to the task; since all photographs were to be taken secretly the necessity of confining all the action within a set focal range was impressed on me; a car would be kept waiting within the vicinity of the church with a second photographer, Bob Gosani, to be on the alert should the action shift to the outside of the church. An unnatural emphasis was impressed, repeatedly, on the question of provocation either in manner or dress; I was to dress and conduct myself with unapproachable respectability, and in an appropriate dark suit and sober tie, carrying in my hand

194

a most conspicuous Bible—which belonged to Ma-Bloke—I began my church-going marathon on the first Sunday of the new year, 1956.

It was January and the summer sun was beginning to burn itself out, and the smell of burning autumn leaves, the snapping and the crackling underfoot was already with us. The green of the leaves of the branches had began to bleach into a burnt brown, and I could smell and dread the coming of another South African winter; the senses transmitted to the mind's eye the creeping reality of the drabness, the bleakness and the hibernation of the sun together with my dreams. Nothing happens in a South African winter, except for the gnawing cold, the icy breathing of the cold air through the cracks in the door, the window-frames and the ceiling.

The cold seemed to filter and to creep and crawl through the very structure of the walls, and I remember the interminable nights of shivering out of the blankets to stuff pieces of clothing and old newspapers under the doors, between the rattling windows; there were nights of dreaming myself against a woman's breasts, to press myself into the warmth of her body, but even that could not insulate me against the whispering bluster of the winter which was intruding into my room. The days brought very little comfort except that the sun would mock a promise of warmth, but the nights were always the same, cold and long.

I remember that every year was the same, the cold which seemed to arouse unpleasant remembrances of apartheid never seemed to relent; each year my room seemed to surrender to the cold just that little more, and each year I made determinations that next year will be better, I would live in a room equipped for the winter; but it was always the same, living in the terror of a recurrence of the attack of lumbago which each year forced me into bed to waste a few days from work, calling for my sister, Daisy, for another cup of tea.

But it was January and the comforts of a little respite warmed my mind, the dread reality was still a few months away. I left my room at eight o'clock on the morning of the first Sunday morning of the church story to meet the car with Sylvester Stein, Jurgen Schadeberg and Bob Gosani, to go over a few details before driving out to the Dutch Reformed Church in Bez Valley, Johannesburg. Jurgen went on into the church, to be followed by Sylvester on a mission of studying the layout of the church. He had found a side entrance into the church. I walked through the gate of the church opposite the main entrance and the reception committee, casually walking to the side of the church and into the door.

We drove round looking for another church and at Fairview we found a small Presbyterian church; there were the same reception committee, but it was an English church.

All of us in South Africa, black and white, accommodate the discrimination mentality of the Afrikaner, we accept this as an honest fact; the Africans admire it as a document of honesty, however wrong it may be; but the English-speaking South African has inherited all the hypocritical diplomacy of the British; the English South African is never either against or for anything, the African resents the insidiousness of his intolerance and his contemptible sense of superiority.

Because the Presbyterian church is English we decided on the direct approach; I walked up to the main entrance and confronted the reception party with the physical reality of my presence, to force a showdown right there at the front door; I knew that once in the church the old British diplomacy would paramount everything, we decided to offer them the exercise of private and individual discrimination, which is an English character trait. But they did not react, the men at the entrance offered to shake my hand and a book of hymns was offered to me; one of their number religiously placed his hand on my shoulder to lead me into the church, but leaving me to choose my own pew; I was interested to note that it was I who preferred to be the segregationist, I selected a row which was occupied by nobody else, and about three rows down from me were sitting two elderly women who did not even notice my presence.

I was sitting too far out of the focal range of Jurgen's camera, I changed seats to a further two rows behind the elderly women and discovered myself against a ray of light which patched through the window. I heard Jurgen's camera click a couple of times; the finished print showed three figures, mostly in silhouette, but the colours were clearly defined; the ray of light was to become a touch of suburban symbolism, the caption read: 'But There's a Ray of Hope'. The instructions were that if I were to be accepted and welcomed into any of the churches I was to remain in there just long enough for the necessary photographs, but I found myself unable to walk out of all that friendliness and goodwill; I sat through the entire service and upset the programme for the day. I disobeyed orders and wasted an hour in personal reconfirmation. I think Sylvester Stein understood. We drove to the house of Sylvester for lunch, and the being with Jenny, Sylvester's charming wife, and Jurgen's beautiful wife, Elsa, eased a little the tensions in me, and perhaps intensified the loneliness of my bachelor days; I wanted desperately, sitting in that family tranquillity, to be married and to be a part of the companionship I envied between the couples.

The Church story was a leisurely assignment which could only be done on Sundays; the days of the week were easy, and we waited, and the story waited, but the one thing which could not wait was the state of my nerves; the human element was the one factor which had not been taken into consideration, and this, the most explosive factor, had been left to chance. I felt the premonition of the impending explosion, but was constrained to brush it aside with the rationalisation that every action is nothing but a permission of the will; I resolved to will these thoughts away.

On Saturday morning in my newly-pressed suit we went to the Seventh-Day Adventist church which was not too difficult to steal myself into through a side entrance; and after a week's steeling of the nerves I discovered a courage, possibly inspired by the thought that the Seventh-Day Adventist was an English church. I threw my antenna to feel out the slightest hostility to my presence, but it was like trying to feel for something in a vacuum. There was no contact. Then I felt the warm breath on the back of my ear, the voice whispered: 'This is a white church, there's a Seventh-Day Adventist church for Natives in Sophiatown.'

'Yes I know,' I said, brushing his objections aside, 'but I want to worship here.'

I leaned forward out of the reach of his whispering voice which was breathing warm into my ear, and peered into my Bible. After a few more attempts which were ignored he rose from his seat and walked over to the main entrance to return with one of the elders who was a member of the welcoming committee; there were no polite insinuations in his voice. I was not wanted.

'I'm asking you to leave.'

I was determined that if I was not wanted it was their responsibility to have me thrown out, I was not prepared to co-operate with them for the benefit of my own expulsion; but their determination was very discreet, almost like helping a blind man across the street—you hold his hand firmly and steer him across the street. But Sylvester was dissatisfied, the expulsion was not emphatic enough; I have to force out of them an unequivocal statement, a definite: 'We do not admit Natives.'

The next day I was repulsed from a Dutch Reformed church, and segregated at the Methodist Church, Kruis Street, the congregational home of Rev. Webb, Johannesburg's liberal priest. In a little corner of the world where hate is stronger than faith, it is men like Rev. Webb who pray appeals that men—even as master and slave—should seek for a way to live together in peace; many clerics have selected to ignore that Christian brotherhood cannot exist until there is complete equality between all men; for only equals can be brothers and only brothers can be equal.

I was welcomed into the service in his church, was handed a prayer book by a member of the welcoming reception which in this church was working from inside the church; I was informed that the ground level of the church was full whilst being ushered to the gallery, but Sylvester, who had followed us into the church, later informed me there were several seats in the main body of the church; I stayed for a quarter of an hour and left with the feeling that although I had been admitted I had been segregated against.

In the editorial conference of the next week it was decided that one reporter could only attend two services, that joined by another reporter the story would receive a wider coverage in church attendance; Can Temba was invited to join me in the assignment, and he immediately proved luckier than I was, his personality invited a more violent reaction, in one church, than I had managed in mine; and I remember how we teased Can about it, that his irreligious manner invited hate at sight. There was something about him, un-Christian perhaps, which seemed to offend the white Christians in a manner that I could not.

His first church of call was a revisit to the Seventh-Day Adventist church; brash and bubbling with bravado, Can whistled his way to the main entrance and into the hands of a hostile, enormous Christian who with two others halooed for help and manhandled the black intruder into a waiting car; and as they were forcing him into it his head knocked against the top of the car causing a flow of blood. He was taken to the Marshall Square Police Station and charged with trespassing, and was allowed out on bail.

And during this violent reaction Jurgen was discovered taking photographs and within a few minutes he was running down the street, pursued by the disciples of the Seventh-Day Adventist church, behind him the modern versions of Peter, John, Matthew, Judas and others.

But within twenty-four hours Christian charity prevailed and the charge of trespassing was withdrawn.

The next morning, Sunday, Can and I set out to invade the Christian tranquillity in Langlaagte, an Afrikaner stronghold suburb which is a safe Nationalist Party constituency; it already had become obvious I had lost control of the assignment, all attention was being focused on Can Temba; Jurgen was assigned to him and Bob Gosani was teamed with me, the implication was obvious. And hoping to emulate Can Temba, I walked up boldly, perhaps with a little arrogance in manner, to the main entrance of the Dutch Reformed church, determined to make my intentions as positive as Can must have done; Bob Gosani fingered his camera nervously, and I pretended to ignore the elders at the door, impatiently pressing forward between them; but a hand was raised to block my way, and I was confronted by a sympathetic, but stern, look.

'This is a white Church,' he said. 'Are you a stranger?'

The politeness and the sympathy in his voice rubbed onto me, I was blackmailed by it; I could not provoke a crisis by forcing my way in, the instructions about blatant provocation had been explained too carefully. I had again been rejected without drama or the exercise of violence, and realised then that my contribution to the story lacked the sensationalism which made good copy. And as I was walking back with Bob to meet the others I could not help being overpowered by a depressing sense of failure and inadequacy; I did not, then and after, feel myself to be envious of Can, even though I was conscious of the fact that he had succeeded with the story more than I could have hoped to succeed. I felt the comforting need for rationalisations; I was not possessed of the necessary aggressiveness for this kind of story, perhaps it was not my day.

But it was Can Temba's day, and it was a big day for the story; on the way back to the place of rendezvous I was suddenly to become aware of police cars—the flying squad—driving around the area; not that it should have particularly disturbed me, normally it is a usual sight, except that within a few minutes I had noticed three different cars. This was unusual in a white area, it would have been acceptable in Sophiatown. To an African the police mean only one thing, the nearness of trouble. My instincts warned me to remove myself to a comfortable distance of the troubled area, but I was possessed by the uncontrollable curiosity of the journalist. I carried my Bible as conspicuously as to be dismissed for a Christian Native from church; but the editor's car was not at the place of rendezvous, and round the corner to the church which Can was to have gone to there was a police car parked in the yard and another was driving into the church grounds. The doors into the church were closed.

Something had decidedly gone wrong, I found myself suddenly compelled to find Sylvester and report to him, but it was he who found me; he informed me that Can and Jurgen were trapped inside the church. When confronted at the entrance into the church Can had requested permission to attend the service; the request was relayed to an elder of the church and a decision was taken that he could be seated at the back of the church; but one of the welcoming elders became suspicious of a mysterious car in which was a white man and a Native, Peter Magubane, with a camera, and they seemed to be watching the church. The doors into the church were closed and the police were summoned; but as Sylvester was filling in the details a police car drove up alongside ours, a plain-clothes policeman came forward to question us. Sylvester Stein identified himself as the editor of *Drum* magazine.

'And you?' he said, confronting me. 'Let me see your Pass.'

I told him my name and occupation.

'Pass.'

I was determined to be unpleasant by exercising a legal privilege that I was not obliged to show my Pass to an un-identified authority not in uniform; I wanted to humiliate him by demanding credentials of identity. This was something I had discovered a few days previously, and this was perhaps the single legal instance in which an African could humili-ate a white man: insisting on documented proof of authority from a policeman demanding to see an African's Pass; I was exercising a legitimate right, but Sylvester signalled to me to co-operate with the law.

The policeman made a note of my name, the identity number of that name, the poll tax receipt number and resi-dential address; and from that day a dossier was opened on William 'Bloke' Modisane of 101 Victoria Road, Sophiatown. Identity No. 947067. Tax Receipt No. 188/11/4388.

And during this documentation another police car passed by and inside was Can Temba, Jurgen Schadeberg and two members of the South African Security Police; one of them was Major Spengler, head of the Johannesburg Special Branch, and for three hours we waited not too far from the Special Branch headquarters in Von Weilligh Street, as Jurgen and Can were subjected to a clinical questioning.

The next morning the story of the black intrusion into white churches was headlined across the front pages of the dailies—English and Afrikaans—of Johannesburg, and all the excitement, the urgency, the revelation of religious apartheid was usurped from *Drum* magazine, the monthly. By the time *Drum* reported the story all the news value of it had been lost, and because the editor had insisted on a cold, sober, objective writing of the story—possibly to appease official reaction—in the end it was an impersonal account, where all the tensions I had felt during those religious nightmares were left out. For all the drama of the story itself, the assaults, the reaction of the Special Branch which behaved as if the story was a plot to dynamite the Christian faith of the country, the finished work was as vital as the sex life of rose buds.

It is not my fault that Christianity, as the President-General of the Pan-Africanist Congress, Mangaliso Sobukwe, said, was unfortunate—like communism—in its choice of disciples to South Africa. I have objected to the Christianisation of my daughter, I am unable to perceive why she should be a Christian in the South African context; and on this I stand unchanging, chloroformed against any other persuasion; I resisted and defied the deistic Christian parents of my wife and disregarded the influence of Ma-Bloke. I do not believe myself to be competent of the responsibility of committing my daughter into the fangs of a faith which is being pro-pounded as a sanctified weapon of oppression. I have reserved for her the right of choice to so commit herself; it was the exercise of perhaps the last remaining right which I could decide, and this in the full realisation that it was—if nothing else—to be my legacy to her. The liberal influences working around me insinuated suggestions that I should commit Chris and leave to her the margin of choice to embrace or reject the faith; but it was not the season for compromise, I could not face the dishonesty over so vital a commitment. I realised that this would project—in the schools of Christian South Africa —kaleidoscopic problems when she was to be enrolled.

This is a real and present danger, I had seen its viciousness in full operation. When Bantu education was imposed upon us by the letter of the law I attempted to evade it by the determination that children in my family shall not be exposed to the mockery of Bantu education, which my friend, Nimrod Mkele, has described as the education for a Caliban. The Roman Catholic Church in Sophiatown refused to comply with the terms of the Bantu Education Act, by which all private schools were to be delivered into the control of the Government, and instead exploited an advantage in the clause providing for the registration of non-State schools as private schools entitled to a separate curriculum. The Catholic Mission School in Morris Street applied for and was granted an exemption—which was later to be cancelled—from Bantu education. I admired the stand of the Catholic Church and was visibly moved by Father Trevor Huddleston who preferred to close down the Christ Church Mission School rather than surrender it up to Dr Verwoerd's Bantu education schools.

I took Daisy, Jeremy (Pancho) and Joseph (Butch) to the Catholic Mission School to request permission to have them registered for admission; I was informed by the Father that only Catholic children were being considered, but he held out hopes that there would be very little difficulty if I were to consent to the Catholicisation of the children. I submitted the decision to them: Daisy accepted immediately, the two boys were too young to assess the implications, nor do I think did Daisy. I thanked the Father and requested permission to discuss and receive Ma-Bloke's opinion; and thus it was that on count I discovered three active denominations in our family, and on request from Daisy—who had become an enthusecclesiast—made Friday a fish day.

This exploitation of the desperate needs of people in order to gain converts was acceptable to me, if only as an entrenchment of my cynicism. Suffer not the children to come unto me.

Chapter Thirteen

I PROHIBIT YOU! I prohibit you! I prohibit you! Wherever I turned—in my mind, in the waking hours, in my sleep—this was the confrontation glaring at me; it shouted at me out of the legislature, the Church, in the streets, I saw it in men's eyes, in the anger of their impatience, and like the sun against the sky it was fixed implacable in the soul of the white man. I came to be haunted by the premonition that the air I breathe may fall into the list of the prohibitions; the oxygen in the air was the last remaining amenity which I shared fully with the whites of South Africa, but since it is the policy of the country to separate all amenities, I believe there is hope that the air in the European areas will be pressurised, Europeans will breathe rarified air whilst the common, unpurified air will be set aside and guaranteed for the exclusive use of the African races. And as it is the policy of the Government to establish separate and unequal amenities for the black races, there is reason to suppose that a vital component of the air I breathe may be extracted to reinforce, and further purify, that of the whites. When this does happen I hope the Government will be persuaded to accept the rape of justice and fair-play, that the air reserved for me will be guaranteed in the constitution, and the right entrenched by a two-thirds majority of both houses of Parliament; it may not be the ultimate protection, but it will, at least, have been invested with the respectability of law and order.

Against the physical presence of these prohibitions I turn my face into the dust; dust be my destiny, lead on and I will follow. Like you the direction of my life is variable; together let us drift on, purposelessly, into a future without a future;

drift me to that place which Sophiatown has decomposed into, let me lie among the castaways of Sophiatown: the bricks which were once our homes, the sand which was the dreams and hopes crushed by the bulldozers. Breathe into me the energy of Sophiatown that I might spend my body—not unto its death—but to a demolition, that all that may remain of it will be the sand carried in the bowels of the dust so common that all the police can do is to spit in it. In me lock up the energy of excess that I may soon be burnt out, like the energy of promiscuous sex.

I know that for myself this gushing of energy, this intense drive for living to the brim all the energy of each full minute of every hour of every day, from taking out of each day the full capacity of my mouth, has developed my body into a gluttonous hunger; my stomach has become larger than my eyes, my hunger is indiscriminately distributed. I am enervated by this hunger to indulge myself, to submerge and annihilate myself in every pleasure, to feed luxuriously each appetite of the moment; to live only in the abandonment of each moment of every day, exhaustingly and completely; contemptuously disregardful of tomorrow, which, together with the Hereafter must await its turn in time. Who is it can tell me the fortunes of tomorrow? Perhaps Omar Khayyám?

> *Tomorrow?—Why, tomorrow I may be*
> *Myself with Yesterday's Seven Thousand Years.*

Somewhere in the locations there is a Three-Star knife or a bullet waiting for me, and any of the thousand tomorrows will bring my body to collide against that knife or bullet; every day I listen to the whining of the black maria, I see my blood flowing to mingle with the mud and the decomposition stagnant in the open gutters of Sophiatown. That is the tomorrow which is real in my life, and it is against the background of this knowledge that the moments of my life are provided for in the plan of my day-to-day existence.

Will there be a rising of the sun for me tomorrow? Shall there be a thrill by the smile of a woman? Shall my blood be rushed by the soft brush of her hair, the breath of her lips? I cannot invest in success, there is no guarantee that tomorrow I shall walk down the street, my nostrils following the perfume of a beautiful woman; the possibility of walking out of the air and falling into a grave are far more persuasive. I have reserved for myself a freedom from morality, surrendered myself to the lower freedoms: the freedom of all the vices; and since, according to Western civilisation's system of beliefs, savagery is black and promiscuity a heathen indulgence—and heathendom is black—I am persuaded into believing that this is the standard which is expected of me.

Western civilisation has failed to develop in me its steadying influence, but it has developed me to a state where I have cultivated what Nimrod Mkele has described as a bird-of-passage morality. It has become a moment of urgency in my life that before they lead me into a South African jail or my mutilated body is lowered into the cold earth, I must have savoured every pleasure, languished upon the taste of every experience of vice, and thus demonstrate an appreciation of the life I was permitted to live. I searched for new vices, did research into little-explored experiences; sought out and devoured anything vaguely pornographic, and then turned round looking for rationalisations, a philosophy to justify the depravity of my life.

I found the Marquis De Sade satisfying, but I could not accept that pleasure and the perversion of pleasure in torture were necessarily complementary; torture can only feed on sadism, pleasure is an enjoyment which is shared—and although it may be sadistic in pursuit, its ultimate is a shared enjoyment; of course, one may become enslaved to pleasure, to seek only the pleasure even in place of enjoyment. It was Omar Khayyám who provided the articulation for the thing I had become; I committed to memory the entire text of *The Rubá-'yát*, almost to convince myself that there was positivism in the life of licentiousness, particularly in an existence of negatives, in which even my physical being was a negative of the white man; it argued then that the act of a licentious existence must, in fact, be a positive reaction. Whenever my life outraged my conscience I recited:

> *Ah, make the most of what We yet may spend,*
> *Before We too into the Dust Descend;*
> *Dust into Dust, and under Dust, to lie*
> *Sans Wine, sans Woman, sans song—sans end.*

I am afraid of the confinement of the coffin, the endlessness terrifies me; in fact I felt that I needed to erect around me monuments which might survive the insignificance of my life. I believe in achievement, I would as soon live in a meritocracy. But I have been denied recognition, denied the opportunity to develop whatever talents I thought I might have; but throughout this calculated system to rivet chains upon me they neglected slight freedoms—the freedom from morality and freedom from the vices—which I exploit for the little pleasures of my regulated life.

Invested with this short-term morality I delivered myself up to a life of extravagance; fortunately crime and violence are too closely allied, and I am neurotic about violence, thus sex and vice became the pursuits of my life; I read furiously on the subject; I was stimulated by the satyrs of Henry Miller; I was masturbated by the morbid sexuality of the Marquis De Sade, and because of the attitudes to sex of the culture into which I was born, my enthusiasm was restrained by far less taboos. And thus gradually—in place of the prohibition notices—I saw only sex symbols; I was undressing every woman I happened to be looking at, I could hear them sighing the sounds of sex pleasure and there in the streets I would experience the satisfaction and the stimulation. Every woman I met was valued in sex symbols, they were nothing more than naked bodies I caressed with sweaty lust; none of the women was an individual personality, beauty was only an incentive which stimulated the lust; I resisted intellectual rationalisations like compatibility of interests, the very suggestion of falling in love was rejected and guarded against.

And always there were those women who sought to trap me into professing love, and this at the most awkward moments; I resisted this as a blackmail tactic of women who will go to bed only when a man admits to loving them, but I was soon to realise that principle can go too far. I learned to say, I love you, with an emptiness which would have amused the Marquis De Sade; always I managed to make it sound like, I want to go to bed with you. I regretted the fact that women invariably insinuated love into the sheer ordinariness of sex; why should sex be complicated by side issues when it can be enjoyed in its own right.

And yet for all the sophistication in my attitudes towards sex I was aware of entrenched reservations, and because of this consciousness I was able to joke that my experiences were limited, and in a sense, snobbish.

'The only vices I haven't explored,' I said, 'are drugs and boys—I found dagga tedious.'

When I moved into my own room I arranged and furnished it for the purposes of seduction, the atmosphere was designed to persuade the Miss to unbutton her blouse; the couch was low, spacious and contemporary, so were the two armchairs, there was a radiogram and schmaltz records; and with experience and time I perfected the art of seduction, even reading books on the subject; the system was perfected with such

209

arrogance I could decide at a glance the approach most suitable to effect a quick and successful seduction. It became a most important challenge to set records, to actually work within a time limit, setting the clock and proceeding to operate on the reluctant Miss. I became inconsolably depressed and frustrated by the presence of an immovable blouse, it was an affront to my ego, and as a last resort I would fall back on the 'I love you' hypocrisy. If this did not succeed then there was something decidedly wrong with the woman.

There was something paranoic in the will to succeed; every success was an achievement, and I was being driven by a Tikoloshe into an intense drive to prove myself; anything which frustrated me in the realisation of this was resented, I was rude and disgusting to women I could not seduce. There was a time when I was attracted to older women, and at twenty I had an affair going with a woman nineteen years older; it was an achievement to be accepted into her favour, she thought I was intelligent and was impressed by the books I was always carrying about with just that intent. I used to study in her room late into the night whilst she fussed about in a transparent negligée, and I remember how the scene always reminded me of a line by Moss Hart: 'But, my dear, I could see Buckingham Palace.'

But through all the adventures I found nothing which was substantial, the journeys through the night provided very little real satisfaction; the conquests were like the effect of drugs or a state of drunkenness, and when they passed they left in their wake an emptiness even lonelier than that which had set me on the pursuit; only the hunger remained, nothing else was lasting.

It was not essentially a question of depravity, I was obsessed with the need to express something in me, even if it might have been a dedication to the programme of seducing every single woman in the world; then perhaps some day I might earn the respect and admiration of at least one man—one man in the whole world to stand up to me in acknowledgement: 'Bloke, that was some achievement.'

Yet, ironically, I felt through all this a desire to love and be loved, but calculatedly—in a resistance of this consciousness —I avoided emotional involvements, allowed none of the affairs to touch me, reiterating that sex should be enjoyed away from strangulating sentiments; but I could not suppress the inadvertent intrusion of a capability to love. I lived those hangover moments of loneliness in fantasies of a clean love, but when I looked for it among the women I knew, the disappointment of finding something else was even more exhausting than the affairs themselves; when I wanted, purely, to love and be loved, I found only an overlay of sex. I met a young woman who had recently won a beauty competition, she was the most beautiful woman I had ever seen; the quality of her beauty represented to me the purity of virginity, there was something chaste in her beauty; almost 'untouched by hands'.

I reasoned that if I could surround myself with that quality of beauty the ugliness of my life would be purged, this beauty could cleanse the stain of vice from my body, could pastel the colour-bar. Looking back on it today I concede—rather shamefacedly—that the thing I loved was not the woman, Mary, but the possibility of a Jacaranda tree to lean against, a branch on which to hang my illusions up to dry. It was a reasonable assumption, there was an angelic quality about her, a purity which implied the image of the sobriquet perfect woman; I was awed by her to dimensions of such absurdity that the mere articulation of love for her seemed a desecration of a virginity. For this idiocy I lost her and the equally stupid notion that she could have saved me; the reality was that she was human, even though what I felt for her was not.

Perhaps it was just as well; in the rhythm of sex I found a

diversion almost equal in quality to that of the penny-whistle music, its pleasure fed upon itself and one remembered only the exhaustion and the hunger to feed again on the pleasure; and for a moment, at that point of saturation, there was the feeling of a peaceful inability to feel the tensions; it was that moment of release when the congestion of fear vomits a loud scream registering the presence of fear. Through sex I proved myself to myself. I am a man. In the scream of that assertion I surrendered myself to the numbness of the pleasure, but there was only the exhaustion in the end, not even forgetfulness and satisfaction. When the trance of sex had passed and the pleasure exhausted itself out of my system there remained only the anger and the violence to repeat and indulge myself into a more lasting satisfaction—to build up a reservoir of pleasure to draw on until the coming of the next craving —but there was never a point of satiation.

I felt automated by this craving, could not free myself of it because I could not begin to understand it in my own mind. Perhaps a psychoanalyst could have isolated it and confronted me with the truth of its meaning, and perhaps explain also the sex mores of the Africans of South Africa, who are reported to hold an alarmingly high record of illegitimacy, which is seen by the white South African as nothing more or less than social degeneracy; another one of those examples in which urbanisation is held responsible for the break-up of tribal institutions and a general lowering of morals. Essentially, of course, there is as much concern about it as that of a respectable man looking at a prostitute: 'What a pretty face she has.' It repels, and yet fascinates, like it is said about a rotten mackerel by moonlight which 'shines and stinks'. They are fascinated by this degeneracy because it is black, and since the fear of black sexual invasion is fundamental in the making of the white man's prejudice, miscegenation is invariably the fountain-head of this hysteria. The black man is seen in almost all Western societies as a phallic symbol, and in South Africa this sexual hypochondria is articulated by pornographic statutes like 'The Immorality Act' and 'The Mixed Marriages Act' which have legislated what used to be tolerated public practice into 'unlawful, carnal intercourse or other acts related thereto'.

And because prohibition places a high premium on restricted goods, degeneracy in South Africa is not all black; all of us are struggling with a sex complex, sex apartheid is fundamental in our social and political thinking, and even when there is no legislation to sanctify it—as among the non-white races—it functions under various guises, with the South African Indians as major offenders. This again can be traced to their caste system, and since Africans are considered lower than the untouchables, Indian women are inculcated with customary and national propriety against Africans; but Indian males show a difference, they will go philandering among African women whilst they keep their own women inviolable, and no degree of sophistication or educational standard will persuade the Indian male from this; this single factor is a major constituent of the conflict between the Indians and the Africans.

As working journalists on *Drum* publications, Indians and Africans worked in perfect harmony, our Indian companions often requested us to introduce them to African women, but the courtesy was never reversed. Gopal Naransamy was proud of his assurances that he was not prejudiced, often invited us to his house for extravagant curries, he was careful to request from us a restraint in manner and speech, because his wife was 'orthodox', and when Casey Motsisi behaved badly it was viewed as a conspiracy against Indo-African solidarity. Africans are expected to be the eternal students at the school for good manners, and if an African behaved badly it reflected upon the entire black race. Once Gopal Naransamy and I were assigned to report on a society Indian wedding, and at the wedding reception I became aware of a most attractive school-teacher.

'Hey, Gopal,' I said, in a determination to titillate his prejudice, 'how about it? You know her—come on, fix me up.'

'Why not,' Gopal said, 'she's that kind of girl—she'll go out with anybody. I don't bother with her. She's a prostitute.'

'Forget it,' I said, smiling knowingly.

Gopal Naransamy proved himself far more intelligent than I had normally credited him; he was beholden to us for far too many favours, a bland refusal would have been unintelligent, but I submit he was not completely aware of the more profound implication which was contained in his reply. Any Indian woman who would consent to go out with an African must therefore be 'that kind of woman', at best, a prostitute. Among white circles the label is even more brutal, 'that kind of girl' is described as 'white trash'. Of course, Gopal's intention was designed, primarily, at discouraging me; that woman could not be a prostitute, not for all the Indians in the world.

As an African male I was a sex outcast; Europeans, Indians and Coloureds locked up their daughters when I was present, all Natives are potential rapists or perhaps more precisely described by a friend: 'Natives have a rape-utation.' The Nationalist Party has won an election with the slogan: 'Would you like your daughter to marry a Native?' This was after Seretse Khama's much-abused marriage to an English girl—an action which was to lose him the paramount chieftaincy of Bechuanaland—when Nationalist Party canvassing teams did door-to-door campaigns with photographs of a black and a white woman, confronting the voters with the dread possibility.

The race purists delight in reiterating—with a morbid accuracy to detail—the statistics of sex crimes committed by Africans; every individual African is either a satyr or a nymphomaniac—African males are more potently virile, women have greater expression and mobility; it is important for their sense of security to believe this, it emphasises the bastardy and the inferiority of the Africans.

'The Immorality Act' prohibits all sex between black and white, labelling all such acts as sinful, immoral and unlawful, but because lust is unlawful and rebellious the South African law courts function at double shifts to cope with offences committed under the Act. It has never ceased to interest me nor to become a source of ribald comment from Africans that a law intended to curb the lusting of Africans for white women should count its greatest offenders among the whites. Some of the country's most respected citizens have come to court on charges of committing an offence under the Act by having indecent carnal intercourse with black women; highly placed citizens like a prime minister's private secretary and a few dominees of the Dutch Reformed Church have confessed a realisation of the enormity of the implication of the deed, the dominees bowed with grief and humiliation at their 'enormous contravention'.

It is perhaps not surprising that Western civilisation, Christianity, everything, has failed to make an impression on me; I submit, however, that the fault is all mine, there would be something fundamentally wrong with me if they had. Only a congenital moron could learn anything from a culture which has produced a Minister of Justice, then Mr Charles Robberts Swart, whose sense of responsibility was concerned because the existing law could not adequately deal with a case where a white man was discovered kissing a Coloured girl; the nation's time and money was spent in the legal process of moving an amendment clause by which the physical act of kissing can be constituted as evidence establishing a conspiracy to commit an offence under the Act. The Kiss was to be submitted as a court exhibit, a factor for the consideration of a Magistrate to decide was whether the Kiss was one of those tonsil-touching scorchers capable of arousing indecent desires. If my failure to understand this legislative necessity proves that I am uncivilised, I accept; even the child-like games we played in the locations were nothing as childish as this.

Those liberal white friends who repeatedly informed me that the law is the law could not see the humour contained in the judgements of some of the cases tried under 'The Immorality Act'; in the earlier scenes of this legislative farce white men were discharged on the submission of the plea that they were the unwilling partners; they were either acquitted or had their sentences suspended, whilst the African women—who had pleaded guilty in a separate trial—were imprisoned for the maximum terms required by the law. The cause followers who campaigned to have this view reconsidered could not understand my careless attitude; I was amused by the morality of the campaign which sought to gain a minor correction in a mechanism which was fundamentally wrong. Of course, I do not pretend a knowledge of the complexities of law and morality.

My limited knowledge has imposed an understanding that the function of the law is to prevent men from a life of crime, but, except for the Pass laws, 'The Immorality Act' has made criminals of more people than any other law in the statutes of the civilised world; and from this record I am expected to develop a respect for the law.

Even conceding to the South African arrogance that Africans are children whose progress must be guided, I have found very little of value in their education, except a consciousness that I have been injured and twisted. Children learn by imitating their parents, by repeating words, picking up mannerisms from their parents; education is a process of repeating what others have learned, a long process of imitating.

The boast of the colonialists has always been that theirs is the divine function to prepare and educate Africans for positions of responsibility; but all through Africa the Natives have been placed outside the process of the democratic rule of law. If Africans are to imitate the rule of law as they have seen it exercised against them, then perhaps one can understand the convulsions in that continent; I have learned that in South Africa the law is white, its legislative and executive authority is white, and if I am to have learned from my educators, what reason is there for me to suppose that when the legislative and the executive authority of the law becomes black, the law should not become black? I have also learned that the law may be manipulated—by the process of the law, not to conform to principle—not only to protect the interests of the few, but to maintain and perpetuate them in positions of arbitrary authority. There are no other interpretations to read into this.

Rationalisations have their place and function. It is easy to blame the failure of my life on the colour-bar, in the same sense that it is easy for the white South African to be grateful to the colour-bar for his privileged positions. I could perhaps present eloquent argument that in a normal society I could have made this or that of my life. Perhaps all of us in South Africa have reason to blame the hypocrisy, the race attitudes, the dangerous state of race relations, on the colour-bar; there are even those who see it as a sequence of history, we have been committed by history to this condition. Blame the subjugation of one race by another on the commitment of history; blame the bigotry on history; blame black nationalism on history. I have heard argument that the white races have had their turn of being on top, and that history has come round for the coloured races to be on top. It is a logic of history, they say. Until then we South Africans, black and white, will put our heads together, and in a spirit of pure South Africanism —speaking in concert the song on our national emblem: Ex

Unitate Vires—blame all our problems, and ourselves, on history.

And as a true South African I am tempted to blame the emptiness of my life on history, and pretend a reason for the loneliness, the need for love and companionship; but these are diversions. I want acceptance in the country of my birth, and in some corner of the darkened room I whisper the real desire: I want to be accepted into white society. I want to listen to Rachmaninov, to Beethoven, Bartók and Stravinski; I want to talk about drama, philosophy and social psychology; I want to look at the paintings and feel my soul touched by Lautrec, Klee and Miró; I want to find a nobler design, a larger truth of living in literature. These things are important for me, they are the enjoyment of a pleasure I want to share. Somewhere there must be a woman who could look deep into beauty and hard at ugliness, who could feel a hurt and an injustice suffered by others as though it were her own.

I have felt too much, alone, and bled too deeply, alone, the being alone is unbearable. I am the eternal alien between two worlds; the Africans call me a 'Situation', by Western standards I am uneducated. If I had my life again, although I would select to be black, I would want a university education, to read philosophy, social psychology and history; in my loneliness I tried to learn too much and live too many lives, I tried to concentrate 2,000 years into thirty. Perhaps Dr Verwoerd is right: Natives should not be educated beyond certain forms of labour. The inadequate education I received is responsible for my unrequited hunger; if I had been the simple kaffir I would have found happiness in my simplicity and appreciated the good things about my marriage and loved Fiki with the simple respect and the dignity with which my father and his father before him had survived.

I was left to develop along my own lines, and discovered that with sex I could bridge the 2,000 years, to become decadent before becoming civilised; I found sanctuary in oblivion and with application I managed to complete the circle. The periods of drunkenness were longer than the moments of sobriety; the thinking and the preparation for the next conquest provided a purpose for living, expressed the violence of the desire to belong to something; those bland moments of blind drunkenness were without remembrances, and although they were basically unsatisfactory, I desired them because there was nothing else to replace them. When I worked at persuading the woman I employed all my sensibilities and the tensions were pushed back.

But it was all carnal, there was no spirituality in the relationships, even the enjoyment was mechanical, just animal enthusiasm; there was no tenderness in the act or passion for the woman. I wished I had loved one of them, any one; and when I married Fiki it was with the intention of freeing myself from the frightening depravity, in a desire to hide behind the façade of respectability. But I cannot blame the hurt I have caused her to suffer on history; I had learned, but too thoroughly, to disregard the attentions of others; when I should have understood, I was callous and vindictive; I have never learned to accommodate her, because if there was anybody I deserved to have loved it was Fiki; I wish to God I had learned to love her before it was too late, I was essentially concerned with the problems of living with my colour, and at the time I behaved as though I were the only black person in South Africa; I persecuted Fiki for her colour as viciously as the white men did.

Before I met Fiki I had already been working myself into an attitude ready to fall in love with somebody; I had visions of a woman I could talk to through the night without having sex on my mind; I thought that perhaps if this woman could be a virgin I might want to preserve her against the dirt of my hands, and in my mind she became a kind of Shangri-La, a something which, although desirable, was situated outside my grasp. When I did consider myself to be in love I could not then understand that it was with the public image of South Africa that I had fallen in love; the painful admission is that this was a realisation so private and guarded I could not recognise its existence or if I did I succeeded in submerging it completely into the subconscious. Today I am disgusted in acknowledging that in spite of the resistance, South Africa has succeeded in having educated me into a total acceptance of the values of its dichotomous society. I am able to admit that my marriage decomposed because Fiki is black; the women in the sex pilgrimage left me in a coma of screaming loneliness because they were black. They need not have failed me or done anything, the fact that they were black was sufficient supposition that they were not good enough; only the state of being white could satisfy me, and in a tedious succession I thought myself to be—of course, always for the first time— lyrically in love with every white woman I met. I was poet- ically in love with Ruth, then with Frankie, and with Mira, Erika, but it was consistently with Ruth that I was in love, and perhaps came to understand that between us was the dominat- ing presence of colour. There was the inevitable moment of recognition when the white woman becomes white and the black man is actually black.

The recognition that the moment a white woman is involved with a black man she immediately assumes all the problems of the blacks—the discrimination, the insults and the humiliations —became a restraint on our relationship; I could not commit Ruth into this world, so we lived in a silent world aware of the tensions of loving against the odds of South Africa. I was suffocating with it, I wanted to tell it to her, to unburden my- self to a friend, but like the anger and the humiliation, I pushed it down into my system; there was pleasure in the knowledge that I could love, that such a woman is real and breathes, even though she was in another galaxy. We are divided by millions of light years of colour and hate, I was afraid that if I told her of this prohibited love, the prejudice against the colour of my skin would rub onto her, there is no place in the whole world where we could hide this stain. The ugliness of the hollow thing I had become prevented me from talking to her about it.

I reasoned myself into believing that I was a happy man because I held a controlling interest over my emotional estate; I held the hollowness in control, concealed behind a ready smile and a personality my friends were kind enough to find charming. I could not bear to be alone. I love parties, where I dance feverishly, inflicting myself on people and insinuating into conversations. I was afraid of my thoughts, avoided discussions of intellectual involvements, afraid that I might betray the fears I guarded so carefully. I desired only to be extrovertly happy, quick on the smile with an adroit tongue.

But in my room in Sophiatown—away from the prying crowd and the promiscuous relationships—I lived through a thousand moments of recognition. How could I be so cavalier? So glib? How could I smile and wave flags? What was there to smile about? Was it that because I loved her I felt myself, therefore, to be a part of this enormous human race? So enormous and so inhuman. When the lights went off in the little room I could not see the smile or the waving of the flag; in my mind was the agony of a thousand questions. Where is that smile and the charming little man?

Where?

And there in the darkness the lid jumped open and out wiggled the loneliness, the fears and the doubts, the silence screamed in my head, the being alone was the suffocating in a crowd. The stale smelling air, the longing to draw closer the woman divided from me by the many years and the hostile world.

Where is she? Where?

Where are the flags?

Behind the façade, the deceptions?

She is sitting opposite me at table in Uncle Joe's restaurant; looking into my eyes, daring me to love her; but always I am afraid, there is only the silence.

Why the screaming silence?

Where is the comfort?

On the ceiling of the room, through the darkness, she is smiling down at me; so near and fading into nothingness.

Where is she? Where?

We are driving down the street, she smiles beautifully; there are no words between us, only the awful silence. I am afraid of words, she is afraid of the commitment of the spoken word; we guard against the careless inflexion of the voice, against the tyranny of words; always there is the cautiousness.

What is there to say? What?

What words can be found to mean the things beyond the spoken word? Nothing must be allowed to escape caution. What can I find in the sound of words which the eyes could not speak more eloquently?

Nothing.

But nothing is silence, and silence speaks with the eloquence of consent. I swing this thing round to small talk and congest the desire in the blood knowing I will sweat it out in the darkness of my room.

What else is there to do?

In the darkness I need her, the longing burns me into the streets looking for a woman; to return with a feeling of being unclean, then I want to hide from her the filth of my nakedness; but when I am with her I am cleansed, and there is the smile and the left-over happiness. Then I forget, and I dream, and think that perhaps I may yet reconstruct my life and be free of the bitterness of South Africa.

I have no illusions now of realising such a love in a future framed by South Africa, I am black, she is white; South Africa can be depended upon to provide the circumstantial conditions which will corrode and fester this love. We are separated by this silence because both of us have been trained for our racial roles; there were times when I was not sure whether she would not scream rape if I were to talk to her, and always there was the ordeal of walking in Eloff Street together.

They glared at us with murder in their eyes, they stopped to look at us with dismay and shock, then reproach and resentment and finally disapprobation and hatred; the arrogance of a black man walking abreast with a white woman staggered them, the reaction was qualified. They look at her and become bilious with nausea, struggling to control it like an attempt to contain vomit; I could feel their contempt for her which was sliming between teeth and lips.

And out of the corner of the eye I saw panic gathering in her body, her mouth twitched nervously and the colour in her cheeks changed; confusion was flashing her eyes about, and gradually she become dominated by fear; her step faltered, I become nervous and concerned, and look at her with a forced smile to reassure her the comfort and the protection of my presence, feeble as it might have seemed against the accumulation of their hatred. Thus surrounded by a world of hate I began to feel myself helpless and inadequate, even the protection was impotent; in desperation I wanted to hide my blackness, to obliterate this thing which disorientated her, making her actions crotchety.

Her pace quickens and our company is publicly divorced as she moves ahead of me, forcing me to satellite behind in the South African social habits of mistress and servant; the silence comes between us again, to separate us for a more desperate need. She has been let off easily.

The reaction becomes focussed on me with something more positive in its promise of violence. I am being considered for chastisement. I could see it in their eyes, and more solemnly explicit in the violence of the man who bounces his shoulder against mine. It is the deliberate physical provocation. I am staggered by the impact and turn round to find myself staring at a vicious dare. Waiting. Impatient. The world seemed to be waiting. Everything was waiting. The anger of race purity was waiting to devour me. I was waiting too, like the sacrificial goat. All the anger, the bitterness, the violence which I had been storing in my stomach began to rumble, convulsing with the fire and the burning lava of gastric volcano; it is threatening to erupt into a single burst of violent ejaculation.

The anger is waiting. I am ready.

Any time you are ready! The words scream against the suburbs of my brain.

Let's resolve it. Now.

I'm ready. It's your strike.

I look at her, in her eyes there is hurt and anger; I am challenged to protect her pride, and to defend my masculinity. She is waiting. Her judgement is waiting.

I look at the white confrontation, this thing, this South African dynamo cranked by race hate. It is waiting. Violent. Deadly.

Don't be a fool, this is exactly what they want. What is to be gained by this useless way of dying? Die on the stand of a principle more noble in reason than a selfish whim to defend a personal pride. Die in the fight for a sane South Africa, and in this fight there is no place for personal vendettas—there is only South Africa. Death is the badge of the coward, life is for life; be brave to live for the chance to die for something more cardinal. There's always a time to die.

'I'm sorry, baasie,' I said, turning my back from that sterile anger.

And later, during a moment of sophistication, she appreciated the sanity of the decision, but I could not suppress the feeling that behind the cultivated understanding and the sympathy was the accusation of cowardice; women tend to situate great emphasis on the protection of strength, I know that cowardice consumes love and could be a barrier of shame between a man and a woman. And because of the decision I have come to know her despisal.

The coward is the first person to classify, identify and recognise this condition. I know all the manifestations of cowardice; I do not mean the physical act of retreating from a fight, that is the final reaction of a mental state in confusion. There is the cowardice which could perhaps more adequately be labelled: made in South Africa. There is cowardice of living in dignity with one's colour, and this employs a complex variety of behaviour patterns, like escape or flight from the colour-bar; those with low visibility escape into the classification of Coloureds—if they are light-skinned Africans—or into the privileged world of the whites, if they are fair enough to pass for white. And there are the Jews who change their names—not to easier-to-spell Jewish names—but to pukka English ones; modern surgery has facilitated in vanishing from the scene the essentially Jewish nose.

There is the cowardice of the respectable African who, because of a concern for the progress the educated ones have made, is versatile in the reiterations of anti-black generalisations, and will endorse that Africans are peculiar; when Africans massacre each other during those all-too-frequent faction fights, these brain-scrubbed Africans will eagerly join the white world in being suitably horrified.

'How can they be so savage?' the integrated voice of black and white respectability will mutter.

Savagery is particularly savage when it is black, but is viewed with 'concern and regret' when it is white. When Ghana's Kwame Nkrumah imprisons or deports people without trial he is screamed down—even by the white progressive racialists of South Africa—as a savage dictator; emphasis is stressed on 'without trial', which makes the point of criticism imply heavily on the contention that President Nkrumah should have invested these acts with the respectability of the processes of law. But when the same thing is done by South Africa's Charles Robberts Swart—in his office as Minister of Justice—it is viewed with 'concern and regret'.

Since I have developed a psychosis against the word 'savage' I will view 'with concern and regret' the Africans who have adopted the white attitudes of South Africa, even accepting their motives and justifications for it. The choice is between pride and bread and butter. There was this house servant who probably believed her security depended on a disclaiming of an affinity with Africans; she was talking to her 'madam' with whom I was friendly:

'You know, madam,' she said, 'it's true what they say. Natives is Natives.'

There is also the cowardice which is responsible for the smile policy and the legendary inarticulacy of the Africans; but behind this is the man who is afraid to lose his job or is avoiding arrest. I have been the victim of several instances of cowardice, accommodating the taunts of a white employer; I have cringed before the white boss who has the might of the law behind him and the power over the bread and butter of my family.

White Man Boss: Why did you do it? Even you must have known it was wrong.

Black Man Slave: (silence).

White Man Boss (condescending): If you were not sure, why didn't you ask?

Black Man Slave: (silence). (Off) Because you never listen. You're impatient—you always say I'm too stupid to understand, anyway.

White Man Boss: Surely there must have been a reason.

226

You must have thought something. (Pressing) Go on, tell me—What did you think you were doing?

Black Man Slave (carefully): I—I thought . . .

White Man Boss: Ah! So you thought—that's nice. Tell me, what did you think?

Black Man Slave: (silence).

White Man Boss (seizing advantage): What's the matter? Lost your voice? Come on, tell me what you thought.

Black Man Slave: (silence).

White Man Boss (impatient): Speak up, boy. Damn you Natives—all the same. Stupid.

The anger, the turmoil and the swearing are unnecessary. I thought of my job, the idea of losing it; the nightmare of the Pass Office, the long queues, the emasculating medical examination; fresh permits for seeking employment, the permission to work; I thought of my family, the food, the rent, the school fees for the children. These are the evaluations I had to make at that moment of crisis. This is my kind of cowardice. My self-respect is derived from a knowledge of fidelity to my responsibility. If I had been civilised, with a highly-developed sense of honour, I would have spat on the boss, told him to go to hell and probably kicked his teeth in.

During charitable moments this cowardice is called discretion, but whatever it is, this attitude is almost solely responsible for the white arrogance which is aware of the motives behind the legendary good-naturedness of the African. Because of the African's economic dependence the white man places a high reliance on the fact that the African is rational. But the white man fears the tsotsis who are perhaps among the only Africans who have personal dignity; they answer white arrogance with black arrogance, they take their just desserts from a discriminating economy by robbery and pillage. The educated African is confined by academic rationalisations, the tsotsi is a practical realist; he is sensitive and responds to the denials and the prejudice with the only kind of logic Western man understands and respects. Tsotsis are seldom the victims of white chastisement, when white hooligans gang up on a tsotsi, he pulls a Three-Star knife, then fear, the guardian of safety, will prevail upon them to scatter.

But the respectable, educated Africans will negotiate a polite settlement of grievances even to the point where the purveyors of Western civilisation spit on them their despisement or kick them in the stomach. Because I am a coward I have tolerated white hooligans to insult and emasculate me publicly, all because I was afraid of being kicked to death in police cells; but I have always hated myself for it and in the end preferred death to the analysis of cowardice; I would shriek and swear and pound my bare hands against the walls of my room until they were numb with pain, which would become the ceremonial moment of atonement.

And what has been the meaning for it? Because I was not man enough to protect the love of a woman embarrassed by the colour of my love? A woman who fidgets and capitulates when confronted by the scorn of the colour of her own colour. Perhaps I was ungrateful, I should have been satisfied with the private moments of a love which was torrid in locked rooms, shut in from friends and confidants and the eyes of reproach. If I am to be kicked to death for my love, then it must be a love worth dying for; it must be a love bigger than the mark of infamy and disgrace, a love which will sing hallelujahs loud unto the sky.

I was risking imprisonment and probably the gallows by loving white women, there was always the consciousness that some day one of them will shout 'rape' and beyond that scream was the hangman's noose; but I was fortunate, usually they sobbed elegantly and spoke about being unworthy of my love—because I was such a wonderful person—confessing a consciousness of human weakness; the strength to have loved me would have made her a better person, I was told. It was the most eloquent rejection ever pressed on me.

This scene contributed to my sense of rejection; I retreated into my old cocoon to lick the blood off the scars and return to the quick smile and the flags; then with time came the acceptance that the only reliable existence was that of the bedroom athlete. I wanted to erase the memory of her face from my mind, to switch off the music of the sound of her voice, to blow my nose and clear it of her perfume, to dull my senses of the soft-silken feel of her hair, the virgin softness of her voice. Music is the organisation of noises, not any particular voice should be confused as the whole sound of music, and once more into the many I went in search of forgetfulness in sex.

Avoid the commitment of love. By breaking this rule I had destroyed perfectly satisfactory flirtations; but I did learn in the process that my life was not unique, its attractions has fastened on others—like me, desperately conscious of the death of man's spirituality—who had come to realise that emotional insecurity and unrest becomes promiscuous for company, that flirtations and liberal sex are a way to drawing closer to people.

Because of the search for a larger existence I was to become an alien situated between the scorn and the hatred of both the white and the black world; the white world wanted to fasten a noose around my neck for soiling that purity which is white, the blacks were distrustful, eager to spit on me for thinking and loving white, which is the symbol of their oppression. The whites would not see me as a man, and the blacks could not see her as a woman. I had reached that moment in history where I could not bother.

Chapter Fourteen

THIS IS the situation I must tolerate because all around me people have been educated into an acceptance of the fundamentalism of colour difference; there are those who believe the perpetuation of the differences is not the seat royal of the tensions of our country, that with a more equitable distribution of the good things of life the different groups—as separate units—can exist under a more temperate climate. I have tolerated South Africa and her attitudes to the moment where I do not care for fineries, now there is only the brutality of truth. Only South Africa the country is worth preserving, her attitudes must be destroyed even unto a destruction of physical South Africa; the attitudes are bigger than we are and perhaps we might have to destroy ourselves if we are to get at them. Because they are so fundamental I have had to arrange myself under their will.

I accommodated the attitudes of South Africa because it was convenient to do so, because it saves trouble; I did not wish to expose myself to the violence of insult any more than I already was by the unavoidable circumstance of being black. I have adjusted myself to police hooliganism, white trusteeship, the Pass laws, I have to accommodate them a little while longer; and whilst I am doing this I imply the stamp of acquiescence, which I do probably because I am afraid of freedom, I would not know what to do with it; I do not possess the price to pay for it.

My sensibilities have been dulled by the violence of oppression, my energy has been dissipated by the struggles, the plots, the repressed violence simmering within my body, the insatiate demand for the blood of the oppressors; I had reasoned myself that only in blood will I see an end to my oppression or be myself destroyed. This was the harsh reality. It has been impressed on me that only in the blood of Caesar could the conspirators prevent the abuse of power which might sway Caesar more than his reason; but it was Brutus who realised the margin between power and the physical man, warning that since the 'quarrel will bear no colour to the thing he is', let us concern ourselves with the destruction of a symbol, which we hate, but not the man.

Like Brutus I am haunted by the immediacy, the direct presence of blood between oppression and the freedom which I must snatch; I stand against the power complex of the white man, I hate and intend to destroy white domination, determined to explode the myth of white superiority. I do not particularly hate the white man, but white domination and white superiority is white; white is the symbol of what I have to destroy. Do I hate whites? The question is irrelevant and arrogant. When confronted with this question—which is always used as a red herring—Robert Mangaliso Sobukwe, the President of the Pan-Africanist Congress, replied that 'it would be dishonest of me to say I hate the whip and not the hand which wields it'.

The whip lashes only at the will of the hand which is willed by the mind. Do I take the whip away or do I amputate the hand to remove the power to hurt others. This is the confrontation of Brutus, the serpent which must be killed in the shell.

> We all stand against the spirit of Caesar;
> And in the spirit of men there is no blood:
> Oh! then that we could come by Caesar's spirit,
> And not dismember Caesar. But alas!
> Caesar must bleed for it.

It is an inhumanity therefore which we have earned by the

labour of our intolerance: we refused to love each other, decided, rather, to die than search with pure reason for love, knowledge and human wisdom. We must now die in the convulsions of seeking for love, through force and blood, because man has a propensity for responding to blood. We must die, brutally and horribly, that those of us who shall survive our intolerance shall by the cruelty of our death be so struck to the quick that they shall fear the intolerance which divides people into race groups which would rather perish— in their racial groups—than love one another. We shall annihilate one another in the hope that the world will come to understand that man is not threatened by the bomb, but by himself. Man is the danger, and by his actions he shall destroy himself.

The search for knowledge from pure reason has brought a new generation of nationalist Africans, the young intellectuals who are as arrogant as truth; they have removed African agitation from the emotional to the intellectual through the doctrine that the ultimate principle of reality is reason. To liberate himself the African must destroy white domination and smash the myth of white superiority, and against their determination is the white dedication that South Africa shall never be ruled by Kaffirs, Hottentots and Coolies. These young intellectuals assert that Afrika is for Africans, that South Africa must assume a democratic morality and be ruled by the real democratic majority. These nationalists identified themselves as the Africanists, and by their stand immediately aroused the sympathetic indignation of Africans, like myself, who had been disgusted by the dishonesty of South African thinking; and by attacking the sacred cows of those whites who desired to be publicly identified as the friends of the Africans, the Africanists found themselves labelled as racialist, a term which white liberals manage to make sound like a crude curse.

I was surprised by the arrogance with which the Africanists ignored this charge; this criticism against them, the Africanist submitted, is a desperate design by misinterpretationists who read their policy like some people read newspapers, looking only at the headlines. Afrika is for Africans. We are against multi-racialism. Africans must go it alone. These points read in isolation, are an invitation to misinterpretation.

'What's there to be said when people choose to misinterpret us,' Matthew Nkoana said.

This was around 1957 when, because of the frustration at the immaturity of African politics, I had separated myself from political involvements. I was to find myself stimulated by the Africanists in the same detached manner that I was by the Hollywood films, and there the attraction stopped. I was not going to charge ahead and take out a membership card. I had learned my lesson. The Africanists never failed to excite my mind and to disturb the friends of the Africans, especially by the assertion that the Africans have reached that time in history when African liberation can no longer be entrusted to left-wing or right-wing or left of right-wing groups of the privileged and powered white minorities.

Mangaliso Sobukwe, with his usual bluntness, proffered the integrationists the realism of his thinking, by submitting —without apologising for the political expedience—that African people can be organised only under the banner of African nationalism in an all-African organisation where they will, by themselves, formulate policies and programmes, and decide on the methods of struggle without interference.

This was sharp criticism against the Congress Alliance, and was the direct point on which the Africanists had become restless within the body politic of the African National Congress; Mangaliso Sobukwe was critical of the dilly-dallying and the racial ganging-up against the Africans by the powered minority groups inside the Alliance. There has been too much talk by these reformists but nothing honest and forthright and positive has been done about halting the system of apartheid. The significance of this was later to be analysed Jordan K. Ngubane—a respected integrationist who rose within the reformed Liberal Party to become vice-president —that 'with the African National Congress paralysed by the conflicting loyalties which are the logical by-product of multi-racialism and racial ganging-up, and therefore unable to assert positively the dignity of the African person, the Pan-Africanists are in a position to assert it freely.'

The statements of Sobukwe were immediately interpreted as a rejection of white friendship or white help or white leadership; and it was curious that the casually committed African intellectuals were among the first to criticise the man and his statement; they wished to be produced as black witnesses that racialism is criticised even among the Africans. Black and white liberals criticised the Pan-Africanists for prohibiting membership to individual whites—even against the fact that as individuals whites cannot become members of the African National Congress either—the issue was reduced to personalities, people were saying: 'Why can't I be a member? The Pan-Africanists are anti-white.'

And yet the same whites who wanted to become members were the ones most hysterical in their criticism of the Pan-Africanist policy of gaining liberation by violence if necessary; it was interesting to note that the main body of criticism fastened on the policy of violence. I have been audience to white friends who, though they profess a willingness to understand the historical standpoint of the Pan-Africanists, will not accept it because they are personally denied membership.

'You have voted,' I said, to one of these reformers, 'for a white political party which denies membership and the vote to Africans. When did your sense of morality become so keen?'

The concern of the whites was understandable, albeit selfish, because the mere suggestion of violence was a threat to white interests and their physical body; whatever else the white South African may be, he understands that the fight is between black and white. The efforts of the South African Communist to divert this to an issue of class and capital has been exposed as an effort to divide effects; the Communists of South Africa stand under a charge by the Pan-Africanists as being unconcerned—as a matter of urgency—with the liberation of Africans, that they would rather accommodate the furtherance of apartheid than organise Africans as Africans for an armed revolution. The Pan-Africanists demand that the Africans be allowed to freely choose communism, and not have it dangled as a bait in their struggle for liberation. The position of the Communists is also understandable, when it is accepted that they are principally interested in furthering the aims of communism, and the African struggle can only be seen in that context; the conflict of aims is here exposed, the African is desperately concerned with liberation from white domination.

But the Communist Party was officially banned by the 'Suppression of Communism Act' of 1950, and infiltrated its African members into the African National Congress; the white members were to be seen in the ranks of the Congress of Democrats, which is a white organisation. These whites realise the dilemma of being white, they are in danger of being swept aside together with the Afrikaners in the event of an African uprising not directed by the Communists. I find it difficult not to admire their efforts in delaying this force, no man will work towards the destruction of his own sense of security; and it would be uncharitable not to commend them as brilliant strategists in their efforts to contain an armed African revolt, they have become the chief doctrinarians of multi-racialism, which as a policy of securing a place for the white man in South Africa, and guaranteeing their interests and privileges, has persuaded even professional anti-communists like Patrick Duncan, Ronald Segal, Helen Joseph, Bishop Ambrose Reeves and others, to be produced on the Communist's side of the fence against the Afrikaners. The advent of the Pan-Africanists has had the unique distinction of having forced a unity of purpose between the Communists and the 'democratic' whites.

The Africanists stirred violent condemnation of the policy of multi-racialism as being a dangerous weapon of perpetuating racial exclusiveness and racialism, and it was only a matter of time before the two separated, with the Africanists emerging as the Pan-Africanist Congress; the attack on multi-racialism excited reaction against the Pan-Africanists, and I began to suspect that they were seen as a greater danger than the Nationalist Government. The charge of racialism against the Pan-Africanists became a criticism which gained sympathy in and out of South Africa, but most significant—for me, at any rate—was the fact that the Pan-Africanists did not deem it necessary to answer to such an emotionally-charged indictment, and it was at this point that my interest in their course became more than academic. I was disturbed by so drastic a charge, one was accustomed to having it associated with the Afrikaners.

I inveigled Pan-Africanists like Matthew Nkoana and Joe Molefi into talking about Pan-Africanism in South Africa, listened to multi-racialism described as 'democratic apartheid' with much arrogance and impatience at a mind which did not instantly understand the premise of their argument. The reputation for being a lady's man and an uncommitted playboy exposed me to their patronisation, they condescended, and with slow deliberation they were at pains to persuade me to their trend of thinking, but filling in only the main points. If they had not been so earnest I would have inflicted a Casey Motsisi joke on them: Never mind the gist, just give me the details.

'But why doesn't the P.A.C. explain the muddle?' I said. 'Make people understand your point.'

'What for?' Matthew Nkoana said. 'We are not selling ice-cream.'

It is a fair supposition that in a world inhabited by racialists the liberal thing to do is to cultivate an intellectual dogmatic psychosis against racialism, to make it the pivot of reaction and a point of reference; at this point one would surround himself with the togetherness clichés, and any reaction against the clichés becomes a rejection of liberalism. It is easy to become lyrical about multi-racialism, it is a simple concept to understand, requiring, as it does, very little mental exertion, and this was the point at which I found myself in the discussion with Matthew Nkoana. When this concept was desecrated by the Pan-Africanists I immediately became incensed, but after listening to Matthew I was disgusted by my simpleness. One only understood multi-racialism against the background of the African National Congress policy; the thesis is that South Africa is a community of multiple races, the different race groups must deliberate together and constitute a foundation of a multi-racial society. The Freedom Charter, which is the documented doctrine of multi-racialism, was adopted at a Congress of the People in Kliptown, Johannesburg, on 26th June, 1955, and under the sub-heading: 'All National Groups Must Have Equal Rights', are listed two statements which, on analysis, struck me as dangerous.

All national groups shall be protected by law against insults to their race and national pride.
All people shall have equal right to use their own language, and to develop their own folk culture and custom.

I became disturbed by the basic principle and implications of these statements. What was it the Freedom Charterists were implying? Surely they must realise the dangers involved? Even making the concession that South Africa is made up of a multitude of races which have been educated by a deliberate separatist policy into reacting—not as a nation—but a community of racial units, one cannot suppose that race attitudes can be banished by a system which seeks continuance of racial separation in the pretence that peace is possible if the different race groups work out a formula of existing together, in perfect tranquillity, as separate national groups. It was a criminal affront that any man should be organised to pledge himself to the foundation of a society which history has proved dangerous, not only in South Africa, but everywhere in the world where man has erected barriers which prevent a free exchange of ideas, culture and human relationships.

Multi-racialism came to be a nightmare. South Africa has seven main national groups, the English have as much a right to their language, folk culture and custom, as the Afrikaners, the Jews, the Chinese, the Moslems, the Hindu, the Africans; but the problem does not even begin to emerge in all its horror. The Zulu are as different from the Basuto as from the Venda, the Shangaan, the Xhosa, the Pedi, the Bechuana, as also from the Malays and the Coloureds. If all these national groups are going to be guaranteed—by the letter of the law—an equal right to their language, folk custom and culture, then South Africa shall have more ghettos, igloos, Pakistans, Hindustans, Bantustans, Dorps and Counties than even the segregationist Afrikaners are planning. If this is what I am being asked to fight for then the multi-racialists and their projected South Africa can go to hell. My children shall not be confronted, in another hundred years, with the same fight which is before me; our children must inherit a non-racial South Africa. There is nothing to gain by preserving racial divisions, I have no privilege, authority and prestige, for me there are only the chains to lose; whites tend to speak academically about racial domination. For me it has been my whole life. I want to obliterate all possibility of this evil ever showing its head in South Africa.

The South African whites must either be embarrassingly stupid or Machiavellian; there are nine million Africans against their three million, how do they propose—in a democratic arrangement—to balance this numerical superiority? It would, perhaps, be unfair to suppose that this might not be a problem for them. But let us suppose a situation in which the multi-racial society is arranged on pure democratic lines— proportional representation on population figures—in which the rights and interests of the minorities are entrenched in the constitution and protected by the safeguard of a two-thirds majority of both houses against violation, what guarantee have they got that the Africans may not employ the terms of the law, following the letter of the constitution, in lobbying the required majority and then legislating their rights away? The Afrikaners have done it to disenfranchise the Africans and the Coloureds, why should the Africans not do it? I would place a greater reliance on a State which guarantees and protects the rights of an individual and not those of a race group.

This is the confusion and the dishonesty which the Pan-Africanists attacked in their rejection of multi-racialism, arguing that the ulcer of the problems of South Africa is the policy of race exclusiveness. In his inaugural address, President Mangaliso Sobukwe said that he accepted the existence of observable physical differences between various groups of people; these differences, he asserted, result from different factors, principally those of geographical isolation. He restated the Pan-Africanist's objection to multi-racialism, that in his opinion it springs from a principle of safeguarding white interests.

'It is a mockery and a complete negation of democracy,' he

239

said, 'implying proportional representation irrespective of population figures. There is also an implication here that there are such inseparable differences between the various national groups that it's best to keep them permanently distinct.'

It was exciting to work out the difference; the Pan-Africanists were demanding a non-racial society whilst the Congress Alliance was pleading a multi-racial society and shouting down the Pan-Africanists as racialists. One has to be a South African, I suppose, to realise the margin of difference. Mangaliso Sobukwe ignored the charge and avoided the indignity of making counter charges. 'The history of South Africa has fostered group prejudices and antagonisms, if we have to maintain the same race exclusiveness, parading under the name of multi-racialism, we shall be transporting to the new Africa these very antagonisms and conflicts.'

By beginning to understand and accept the Pan-Africanist view on non-racialism I was to find myself as the public defender and apologist to the whites who questioned me about that body of Pan-Africanist policy which disturbed them particularly; but they never seemed to be listening or seeking to understand, the main intention seemed to be a desire to find illogicalities which they immediately documented in their list of armour to criticise and ridicule. In the capacity as an unauthorised public relations man I probably did more harm to the cause of the Pan-Africanists than did their detractors; and because of my association with whites the Pan-Africanists would probably have refused me membership, then perhaps I could have accused them of being anti-black. The fact that I was a conscientious apologist for the Pan-Africanists seldom failed to infuriate my white friends, who did, at times, resort to the technique of ridicule; because I lacked the brash arrogance of the Pan-Africanists, I allowed myself to be baited with old South African wormwood like: 'If, as you say, you're going to kill whites, what would you do if you came face to face with me? Will you slit my throat?'

It took a long time to sidle out of this baiting, and when I did discover an answer my white friends derived a masochistic fascination about the possibility; word was passed around and in the end it was to become a term of endearment.

'When the revolution starts,' Myrtle said, 'will you slit my throat? And Monty's?'

'Because I love you, Myrtle,' I said, always with the appropriate dramatics, 'I would like to be the one to do it. That way it'll be quick and merciful.'

It is a sad commentary on the human character that an area of amusement could have been found in so earnest a sentiment; I found no one who understood with absolute sincerity that by being white, and in South Africa, they were a part of what must be destroyed. I could not joke about it, I have lived through too many riots in which the sten guns were crackling all around me; the rat-a-tat of the sten guns is dinning in my ears, vibrating the eardrums with vehement reiteration; I am being shot into a cul-de-sac, the noise is maddening. It must be shut off or I will go mad. But they will not stop pushing and shooting, now I hear only the rat-a-tat; it will not shut down. I throw a stone into the muzzle, to indigest the sten gun, but still they cough at me. I stand up, determined to stop the spitting or die, and my friends think it is a subject of amusement. The black cemeteries are full of the graves of unrequited heroes, perhaps they too thought it was amusing.

These friends failed to realise how fundamentally they violated my sense of morality, there were very few to whom I was constrained to explain this stark reality; I believe it was Clara Urghurt I spoke to.

'After it's done,' I said, 'I would be unable to live with all this blood on my mind. I shall kill myself.'

It was an insult to reason that there were to be found those who sought to reduce the attitudes of our society to the banality of personalities. What about me? Will you slit my throat? When the dominant fact is that there is going to be a slitting of throats, I would have thought it would be irrelevant —especially to the throat—whether the knife is held by me or somebody else. The individual has been rendered unimportant, the attitudes of our society transcend the individual. The white man has laboured earnestly, sincerely and consciously to deface the blacks, with the result that the black man has ceased to be an individual, but a representative of a despised race; they hate me, not as an individual, but as a collective symbol; the African has been reduced to a symbol which has to answer to labels like, Jim, John and boy, and when the whites feel any affection for him it is characterised by forms of endearment, such as, My boy, which is intended to impress liberalism and fond possession. The operative word is 'my' which is used as an adjective of detached intimacy, something in the area of 'this is my Siamese Cat', perhaps an unfair figure, decidedly prejudicial to Siamese cats, which, relatively speaking, enjoy a greater measure of attention and care.

White South Africa was morally disturbed, and with demonstrative indignation they protested with banners and solemnity when Russian scientists orbitted Laika, the space dog, and when a signal was released that the dog would be poisoned because it could not safely be brought back into our planet; the Society for the Prevention of Cruelty to Animals in South Africa and most of the world bodies conducted prayer meetings bubbling with Christian ritual; yet African children die in their hundreds, every day, because there is not enough to eat, and African prisoners and the labourers on forced labour farms are tortured, flogged and kicked to death by white farmers and police hooligans. This does not so much as raise a mascara'd eyebrow.

The de-personalisation of the African has been so thorough that I have no name, none of them care to know whether I have one, and since there was very little point in having a name—in any case, I have no name, the only one I had was buried on the coffin of my father—I adopted the label Bloke; it was a symbolic epitome of the collective thing I was made to be. The African is a collective which cannot be classified and distinguished apart, or hated apart, as an individual; this is perfectly justified, there are nine million of us, it is humanly impossible to hate nine million people individually, it is, however, less exacting to hate them collectively.

It is this collectivist mentality which has mutated me into a destructive monster which cannot, politically, see people as individuals, they have trained me not to. Because I am black I must conform to the needs of nine million blacks, it is not accepted that my individual needs may be different from that of other Africans; if Meadowlands is appropriate to the requirements of Africans, then it must accommodate the individual requirements of every single African. By the consistency of this reasoning, if Italians like spaghetti, then every individual Italian must therefore eat spaghetti. There is the opinion that the English have an insulated sense of superiority, are contemptuous of other nations; the Americans are said to be loud and uncultured. The polemic therefore would be bigoted and prejudicial.

And because man learns by imitation the system of depersonalisation has transported over to the Africans; they have been trained and conditioned to see the whites as 'baas' and 'missis', and in their collectivist reaction every white is the signal of authority, a symbol to be hated and feared. There are no individuals among the whites, and by their actions the Africans do not regard them as people.

'Don't worry,' an African will console a friend who has been injured or humiliated by a European. 'It's all right, they are not people.'

A human injustice is regarded with grave significance

by Africans, the injured party will brood for hours, with incredulity and dismay, that such an act could have been committed by a human being. 'I would understand if this was done by an animal.'

During a riot in East London eight Africans were killed in a clash with the police, three of these were struck down by stray bullets whilst sitting in their homes which were built of wood and iron bars; the incensed Africans went on a vengeance prowl in the streets, seeking to avenge themselves on the whites. The first car they encountered—with two whites in it —was stoned, but they failed to bring it to a stop; the second car—driven by a nun from the Saint Claver's Mission— following almost immediately was stopped. The nun was outraged, killed and placed in the car which was set alight, and it has been suggested by white friends—probably in the hope of insinuating that there is a left-over savagery in all blacks—that the nun was desecrated and cannibalised in a ritual and parts of her body removed to reinforce medicines. They made it sound like an Edgar Allan Poe tale.

The desecration of the nun's body horrified white South Africa which was shouting the familiar platitudes: these Natives are savages, not fit to take their place in the white man's world; Western civilisation, culture, religion, everything, has failed to make an impression on them. Why the nun? She was their friend, devoted to their welfare. Why kill her like that? I listened to the individualists talking, it made me sick.

Why the nun? This was the precise point, and it held up two lessons of warning. White South Africans are not famous for the ability to think. The nun had been working in the only African clinic in East Bank location, she visited the sick in their homes, was a familiar sight in the location; every African in that location must have known her on sight, her figure was far more personalised—by dress—than perhaps any other white, but all this did not divert the vengeance from striking out at her. The Africans saw only a symbol of a hated race, the nun's dress became, itself, the mask of that symbol. This symbol which they saw must have conjured up another symbol of fear which man is seldom satisfied by mere killing of it; the thing must be annihilated, the memory of it obliterated from the face of the earth. It is how a man kills a snake, he continues striking at it long after it has ceased to be a danger.

None of us wanted to look this tragedy in the face, like Oedipus we blinded ourselves behind easy rationalisations, we determined not to look at this issue of our intolerance. The nun was killed because she was white, not any particular white, just white. The nun was desecrated, not because she was a white nun, she became a representative symbol of something they hated so much the only way it could be destroyed was to obliterate it physically and organically.

Such is the passion of the hatred which the gold and the diamonds of South Africa have purchased.

And whilst my mind was being paralysed by the moral conflict that I might have to destroy life that I may preserve it, they laughed, the whites of South Africa, they were humorous. I knew that man could no longer be saved by saviours, we have used up too many of them. Man's only salvation is himself, he has to save himself. Now. The saviours in religious history brought salvation to man through love and humanity and faith, but modern man's spirituality has decomposed, he responds only to blood. The conflict was ever present. What is the value of humanity? Can I attain immortality by destroying humanity? What will be its worth to me, as a morality, a philosophy? Can I monument anything lasting, full of love, from the ashes of destruction? I hoped the white man would kill me with as much thought.

The young intellectuals of the Pan-Africanists have wrestled with this moral conflict, for two years they debated it, but they managed to confine their dialectics to the doctrine of truth from pure reason. It must be by their blood, they resolved. The advocates of patience, who sanctify the virtues of passive resistance and consecrate the depth of Christian martyrdom have all failed; so have those pathetic anachronisms, the gradualists, who are waiting for Moses, and the historical time when their condition will be erased. I was told the delightful story of the American Negro who said: 'Man, it takes time. Yessir. Sure does. Man, fifty years ago us niggers wasn't even allow'd near dat bus. Now we's sit at the back. Man, that's some doing, times-a-movin'. Twenty years—maybe thirty, an' us'll be a-drivin' them, man. Sure takes time.'

The Pan-Africanists were submitting, with cold precision, that Africans have been shot by the police in a thousand instances; no amount of goodwill and the dishonest rejection of violent means for the securement of liberation will protect and safeguard the Africans against police hooliganism, which had already been publicly sanctified by Mr Swart: 'It is significant,' he said, 'that in the recent disturbances (following the Eastern Cape riots of 1952) not one policeman had been murdered or hurt. It must never happen.' Thereupon he instructed that there were always to be sufficient men and weapons, the police must shoot first, they would have the authority of the Government behind them. The Pan-Africanists warned that even if Africans were to march in protest, with Bibles in their hands or to fall on their knees, the police would open fire on them; methods of struggle which had failed must be abandoned.

We must fight. We demand total commitment to our programmes of liberation, of action; the appeal is urgent, our people are dying. There is no time for moralities. I responded to the call. To hell with morals, my mind was screaming, morals have not—and will not—free us from apartheid. This is our fight, we are the most brutally crushed of the victims of apartheid, we face alone the Saracen trucks, the dum-dum

246

bullets, the jet planes, the reserve army, the skiet commando, the farmers with the sjambok, the police truncheons. The urgency to destroy the system of apartheid is a crucial reality to the Africans. The people are dying, I have said to my white friends, this thing must be done quickly. With the Pan-Africanist I say, this is my fight, I must do it alone; I have passed the point of debate, the issue is quite clear. I will kill. But it is too great a moral responsibility for one to confront a white friend with the possibility of having to shoot at their parents, brothers and sisters. How long would it take such a man—dedicated as he might be to the policy of the Pan-Africanists—to wrestle with the conflict, to take a decision, then to press the trigger? The element of risk is too great. South Africa is armed with the means to destroy an armed revolution within one week, our situation is dangerous enough without risking additional hazards.

There are those whites who pretend a willingness to fight on the side of the Africans, even against their own sense of security; and on this score I found myself having to argue against Lewis Nkosi, who is erecting around himself an intellectual reputation of uncommitted innocence and liberalism. Lewis has argued, in the presence—and to the delight—of white South Africans, that the Pan-Africanists are racialists because they deny membership to whites.

'How can you be sure, Bloke?' he has said. 'I think some whites will shoot at whites.'

At one of these interminable discussions Myrtle and Monty have verbally committed themselves to a willingness—when confronted with the decision—to do so, and this Lewis threw at me with his usual candour. Mr Nkosi is welcome to the risk. Possibly I lack his faith in human beings, but I sometimes think it important to examine what people do about the things they say, rather than what they say about what they more often than not do not do. There is nothing in the records to

247

prove a justification to those hopes men like Mr Nkosi and other multi-racialists have been pleased to solace themselves with.

The African National Congress is congested with sexual energy because of the racial ganging-up; when the Congress Alliance was formed, the policy-making machinery became a body known as the Co-ordinating Committee, on which the African National Congress—which claims a membership of 100,000 card-holding Africans—has the same vote as the Congress of Democrats. It seems a peculiar kind of democratic alliance in which a man who holds 60 per cent of the stock has the same vote as the man who holds 2 per cent; perhaps this is what the whites in the Congress of Democrats mean by a democratic multi-racial South Africa. But what in effect is being manipulated is that the Congress of Democrats has a controlling influence over the South African Indian Congress, the South African Coloured People's Organisation and the Trade Union Congress, forming a formidable block vote of three against the African National Congress's one.

Thus it was that the A.N.C. exposed itself to the charge that it is being controlled by the Communists, that it had ceased to become the directional body of African liberation; in this Co-ordinating Committee proportional representation is irrespective of population figures or card-carrying membership figures. The joint membership figures of the three organisations constituted not very much more than 15 per cent. The Co-ordinating Committee created the unusual circumstance where the campaigns decided by this body involved and exposed the Africans, alone, to police hooliganism in the locations—as in those stay-at-home campaigns in which none of the ordinary members of the Congress of Democrats, the Indian Congress and the Coloured People's Organisation, were ever present either before, during or after the shootings. During the Defiance Campaign of 1952 we seldom tired of the joke they told about the Indian politician who said: 'We'll continue the campaign to the last African.'

Although I felt a mental accord with Pan-Africanists I retained my political alienation, I was exhausted by South African politics; everywhere I turned there was politics and there were flies and there were the attitudes of our country. There was politics even in the seemingly innocuous social gatherings like coming-out parties, when African children are taken out of the house for the first time since birth. There were always speeches. A friend of the family—usually a schoolteacher or some frustrated man who should have been a public speaker—would assault us with one of those pretentious speeches which Africans delight in making and listening to. And after the usual fripperies—toasting the general health of the host and the guests, and the friends present, and telling of how very happy he was for being given the opportunity of saying a few words; it was a pleasure, a privilege, and, indeed, an honour, for which he thanked the esteemed host and the ladies and gentlemen, at which point there would be a general applause, and from the speaker a theatrical pause —the speech invariably assumed political overtones.

'I wish to pause at this juncture,' the speaker said, literally taking the pause to sip, theatrically, from a glass of mineral water. 'I'm sure you'll all join me in taking this opportunity to thank these parents for having given us another soldier for the fight. Ladies and gentlemen, a toast to Mr and Mrs African.'

The coming of this fight was discussed in all kinds of circles with a casualness which was frightening; I began to appreciate a fundamental difference, these people felt an emotional identity with the fight coming on, whilst I felt an intellectual involvement. It was my hope that things will not be allowed to develop to the point of fight, but I discovered Africans, like myself, who were seemingly pretending a disinterest in political involvement, yet talking with casualness about the fighting. It had become a state of mind. There was a terrifying possibility that the fighting might overrun political direction and be carried on by a momentum of hatred. In my mind I saw the violence and the blood and the death, and I had seen enough of all three, my mind could not take any more killing without unbalancing. I wanted a little peace, some amount of freedom and a little time to reconstruct my battered soul under an easier political climate where I could humanise myself. Ezekiel Mphahlele had been writing me sane letters which implied that he was on the road to a human recovery, the letters contained a happiness which we had failed to realise even in our most riotous moments during those promiscuous white parties.

Chapter Fifteen

THERE IS a Kafkan sterility in and about South Africa. Every endeavour, every action is like an orgasm in a bed of which the sheets are soiled, but there is no release of the sexual tensions; there is always the anticipation and the pursuit, the excitement of climax and then, nothing. All our efforts could not save Sophiatown from dying, nor all our violence wash away the blood on our hands. There were little excitements, always the promise of bigger things, but never satisfaction; like being seduced by a professional virgin, who is always hinting at promises, allowing a man to work himself into a towering desire, herself being carried along through all the stages in the sex play; then refusing, in tears, at the climax of passion, and, feeling the man going through the agony of congestion, she will apologise for her virginity.

The excitement of my having been one of the reporters who were involved in the Church Story never failed to fascinate and shower upon me the fame which was to make for me many white friends; I was to discover myself seeking out white friends almost as a hobby, imposing exhausting demands on myself by collecting a variety of interests in an effort to reach a wider circle of friends, and to feed these interests, I read, as Dylan Thomas says, 'all the time with my eyes hanging out'.

On several occasions I found myself caught in situations where I knew nothing about the subjects which were being discussed, and it meant inheriting yet more interests for which I would do more reading; but it was difficult to be cultured when all the cultural institutions were closed to me. When a new play opened in Johannesburg all conversation would close around it, and they spoke of the performance of William Sylvester in *Street Car Named Desire*, and the Old Vic season at the His Majesty's. This was an area in which there was nothing I could do, except perhaps read the plays and all the reviews; I was also confronted with this problem when the better films were issued, with a screening certificate which censored white children between the ages of four to sixteen, and this automatically included me. *Carmen Jones* was one such film; but my habit was to buy screen magazines and read the reviews, the story of the films and the life and loves of the film stars in the cast. In certain circles it was important to know how many times Lana Turner has been married and divorced.

In this manner I managed to keep in with the new trends and at times I found myself arguing against people who had seen the films; in a way it was some kind of an achievement to become an expert on the American and the English cinema. Then there were circles which talked nothing but boxing, others who knew the mood and the colour of the shirt Duke Ellington was wearing when he recorded, say, *Mood Indigo*. It was terribly exhausting.

African friends presented another kind of problem; I was amazed by the inexhaustible knowledge of the 'Boys' who knew the make, style and name of all the tailoring houses in New York and London; then the jazz fans, the football enthusiasts, the detective-story addicts, the film experts who could reproduce the dialogue of almost every cowboy and gangster film they had seen. I was living in two different worlds which I tried to bridge, and at times with amusing results, like trying to bully jazz fans into listening to classical music; the more charitable ones would sit quietly—with only an occasional nervous impatience for the coming on of the jazz session—through all the movements of a piece by Mozart, which Dwarf described as the squeals of a woman being strangled.

'What is that?' Dwarf would say.

'Mozart.'

'Who?'

'Mozart.'

'No wonder he has a name like that.'

But the effect was even more astounding to the whites, at least Dwarf meant it as a joke. Philip Stein and I had been arguing about a tune he was whistling, which I recognised as snatches from Mozart's Piano Concerto, K. 466; Philip thought it was something else and I was insistent and finally we decided to go over to Recordia, the record shop, and listen to the concerto. Philip introduced me to Roy Carter, the salesman, who who was devastated by the fact that an African could know anything about European classical music; it was vastly amusing, and Philip too was amused, and I pretended a casualness.

'He's intelligent,' Roy Carter whispered to Philip.

It was precisely because he thought I was intelligent that we became friends, and it was for this reason I accepted the invitation to dinner at his house; this friendship never ceased to amaze and stimulate his interest, and that evening he was to find himself exposed to another shock. We discovered that we both liked Dylan Thomas and poor Roy was constrained to shake his head in disbelief, he was excited to discover that *Do not go gentle into that good night* was also my favourite Dylan Thomas poem. I was deliberately baiting him into a realisation of my wide range of interests; he had recordings of dramatic readings from Shakespeare by Sir Laurence Olivier and Sir John Gielgud and I knew most of the excerpts which I spoke, either together with or over the voice of the reader; as Roy discovered a 'cultured' African I learned a bitter lesson: our attitudes rise from a lack of rapport between the peoples of our country. From the moment Roy Carter discovered we had a wide variety of interests in common, the differences between us vanished and I discovered a very warm individual human being who suddenly ceased to be white.

My little room in Sophiatown was a fly-over which connected the two worlds, and in it I erected all the symbols of the world which rejected me: on the walls were hanging reproductions of Lautrec, Van Gogh, Chagall, Klee and Miró, there were books and folders of the Impressionists unobtrusively lying about; the cabinet was stocked with cocktail glasses, wine, brandy and beer glasses discreetly paraded, and those of my African friends who came to dinner were meant to be impressed by the ritual of making American martinis served in chilled cocktail glasses before meals, wine with meals and after-meals drinks in fresh glasses. All this was done for the pleasure of hearing them say, Bloke you're a white man; why not, if I could not be white physically and legally, I could pretend a white existence.

Because of the experience with Roy Carter I went on a calculated safari to find white friends under the pretence that personal contact with whites on a human level was far more important and realistic in the breaking down of racial barriers, looking upon my friends as converts to racial harmony; if South Africa could not be subverted politically, then perhaps culturally and socially the whites could be seduced into realising that integration was a sane policy, particularly since it was an alternative to violence. I became a black apologist, preaching the doctrine of brotherhood, desperately trying to avert the danger I saw coming on, looming over all of us. Unless something was done to reduce the political imbalance the Pan-Africanists might build into a striking force, and because their case was so persuasive, the temper of the Africans willing to dare anything, I was afraid.

It was like a mania, this search for white friendships which multiplied almost every week; there was Malcolm Hart and his wife, Jeanne, there was John Goldblatt, whom we converted into an honorary African, and there were the beautiful girls who always looked as if they had strayed from a Dior fashion house; but in the end the friendships became like the sex in my life, my wandering eyes spread promiscuously over every white person I met in the succession of parties. There was an emptiness about them, they always returned to the opulence of the white suburbs as I crawled to the bleakness of Sophiatown, and instead of being enriched by these friendships I found myself drying up like 'a raisin in the sun'.

When I met Fiki I was looking for a change, to find meaning in all that chaos, and as it turned out, she was the first woman in my life who wanted something more than an existence which was like a long party. And during one of those weekends we were wont to spend together, she confronted me: 'Bloke, marry me.'

Why the hell not, I decided, and we conspired together, Fiki and I, to subvert African customs surrounding marriage; first we decided to do it and then present the fact to our parents, but she thought it might be courteous to do it with their knowledge without conforming to the ritual; she took me to talk to Ma and Daddy Plaatje and in cold blood coaxed me to ask for permission to marry her. Mr and Mrs Plaatje seemed unconcerned about the travesty of custom and tradition, they were overjoyed and from the ease of their manner I found the courage to recover from the enormous decision I had taken.

'Daddy,' Fiki said, 'we are not going to have this nonsense about lobola.'

'Of course not,' Mr Plaatje said. 'But what about your mother, does she know?'

'No, sir,' I said, 'actually I suggested to Fiki that we surprise both our parents, but we decided against it. Fiki and I are going to Ma-Bloke after this.'

Ma-Bloke was furious, could not conceive of the effrontery of my actions which had been disregardful of her authority and of established custom; she insisted on having it done properly and with respect to the customs of our ancestors.

'You have no right,' Ma-Bloke said. 'What will the people say? Are we heathens?'

'Mama, I don't care what people say.'

'You'll shame me with people's laughing,' Ma-Bloke said. 'Don't put people's eyes on me. What kind of people are they—Fiki's people—to even have listened to you? Hau. I will talk to your uncles, and we shall go and talk to Fiki's people; we'll do this properly. You didn't spoil things?'

'No, mama.'

'We'll talk nicely with them,' Ma-Bloke said. 'We'll ask for a fair lobola.'

'Ma-Bloke, please listen,' I said. 'There's no lobola, Fiki and I. . . .'

'No lobola,' Ma-Bloke said, completely destroyed. 'What kind of heathenness is this? Of which place is it? You'll make people to be laughing at me.'

'Mama, Fiki and I don't believe in . . . Ma-Bloke, Fiki is not a cow; I won't buy her, we don't think it's right. Besides, I haven't got the money.'

'People work first if they want to marry each other,' Ma-Bloke said. 'To marry is not a small thing. You know what you are doing?'

Ma-Bloke recruited two of her sisters and their husbands and the Modisane delegation went to Germiston to present the case of my marriage to Fiki; whilst they deliberated Fiki and I were amused by the formality, we were told to go outside whilst our future was being negotiated. We sat in the front stoop necking and somewhat unconcerned by the dramatics which were being insinuated into the simple act of our wanting to get married; when it was over and the families sat down to lunch Fiki nudged up to me whispering the minutes of the indaba: the Modisanes had insisted on paying lobola, and Mr Plaatje, after being bulldozed into setting a price on his daughter, had—as a gesture of courtesy —asked for £25 lobola, the modesty of which had staggered my negotiators so profoundly they were constrained to have the figure repeated.

'I don't understand these people,' Ma-Bloke said, when we got back to Sophiatown. 'Anyway, you are lucky.'

'All right, mama,' I said. 'Now that you've insisted on lobola, who's going to pay the money?'

'You must work hard.'

'The custom, mama, is that the money must be paid by my uncles and my father,' I said. 'I'm sorry, mama.'

The next problem was to persuade my traditionalist mother that although I am the first-born there was not going to be a white wedding; she immediately interpreted this as a deliberate design to humiliate and injure her pride. All the first-borns of her sisters were married in a style appropriate to the social standard of the families, with prime slaughter and pretentious celebrations.

'You'll make me to be struck with shame.'

'Ma-Bloke, I know it's a big day for you, but we haven't got the money,' I said. 'I'm still paying the accounts of last Christmas shopping—Christmas is round the corner again, I'll have to start all over again. Please, mama, let's swallow our pride just this once. We'll have a great big party and all our friends and relatives will come. Okay? Come on, Ma-Bloke.'

She smiled. And although I knew it was not an easy decision we both realised it was practical. She enormously enjoyed the social prestige of a party—in her house—which was attended by Europeans, and this gave her the something she could throw at her relatives; and she has not survived the rare distinction of having had a white man acting as best man at her son's wedding. I have on certain occasions discovered her relating the account to her friends with joy and tears. It made

R

me happy that she had found something to compensate her disappointment.

The white Native Commissioner who performed the marriage rites was perhaps more astounded than the African clerks who were peering at us through partly opened office doors, and when the Native Commissioner asked for the ring I stretched out to Roy Carter; after the ceremony Jeanne and Malcolm Hart, Roy and John Goldblatt, kissed the bride, and Jeanne kissed the groom; this was too much for the Afrikaner Commissioner, who glared at us, and for a brief moment he looked as though he was envious of our company. Ma-Bloke, Aunt Letty and Mrs Plaatje sniffled, and Fiki and I were married, full of joy and expectations.

That night of 28th August, which was our wedding night and my birthday, we all squeezed into two cars, Ma-Bloke and two relatives, Jeanne, Malcolm, John Goldblatt and Roy, drove off to Germiston to a party given in our honour by Fiki's parents. And in the car, stuffed into handbags, pockets and under the overcoats, we smuggled bottles of brandy. Because Europeans are not allowed into African locations after nine—even with permits—we were bold enough to drive to the Police Station to request special permission for my white friends to attend my wedding party; the white sergeant was about to dismiss our petition without further debatement when I winked at Jeanne who immediately drew closer to confront the sergeant with her blue eyes.

'Well, you see,' the sergeant said, 'it's against the regulations. It's not safe. Perhaps I think I better come with you for two hours, then I'll escort you safely out of the location.'

The first hour of the party was painful, the sergeant and his African aide were sitting there like a clause in the Liquor Act; Jeanne and I decided the party would flop if things were not to liven up; Mr Plaatje, who was ordinarily honoured by the social presence of the law in his house, was vastly frustrated, obviously going through the discomfiture of a legal conflict; Mr Plaatje is employed as an interpreter in a Magistrate Court and as the son of the famous African author, Sol. T. Plaatje, the humiliation of being produced in Court on an offence under the Liquor Act would have been devastating. There was a clear further need for Jeanne to charm the sergeant, and a few flutters of the eyes later, a bottle of brandy was produced on the table; but it is illegal for a white person to serve drinks to Africans, Jeanne persuaded the sergeant to do the honours. And there, in South Africa—at a Native party in a Native location with Europeans illegally present after nine o'clock—the spectacle of a police sergeant, in full uniform and wearing his gun, serving European liquor to Natives was vintage.

For the first time in my life—presumably for any African —I was instrumental in causing a white policeman to commit an offence under the Liquor Act; I was fascinated by this power, and every time I held my glass out at him I chalked up another count against him. It took the sergeant a few glasses of brandy and some coaxing from Jeanne to release him from his Afrikaner chains, and we were to see a human being wriggle out of the uniform and the gun. Around ten o'clock there was an ease and a charm about him, the gun belt had been loosened and the gun placed on the table, and the sergeant was talking, laughing, drinking, singing and dancing as animatedly as Fiki and I. We had set aside our prejudices, the thought never occurred to any of the Africans present, nor to the sergeant, that it might not be safe for a white policeman to disarm himself in our presence. After midnight, when the drinks were finished, we decided to bring to an end an altogether memorable day. The sergeant escorted us out of the location, wished Fiki and I the best of luck and waved us all a very good night; it was a memorable occasion to a marriage which gave off some of the sparkest moments of my life.

During December of the same year I was to be invited to the house of Dr Ellen Hellmann to meet Norman Cousins, the editor of *Saturday Review of Literature*, a meeting which was to change my entire life. Norman Cousins wanted to see the effect of the system of apartheid on the Africans; I guided him through a sight-seeing tour of the mind of the people who lived in the squalor of the locations, took him around the people I knew, showed him how they lived, worked and how they overflowed out of the crowded trains which transported them from work, the long wait in the bus queues for buses; but I did not intend to show him how we died, he was to learn that for himself. We spent some time in my room in Sophiatown discussing the dynamics of life in South Africa; Fiki was expecting Chris and away to spend the holiday season with her parents, and in our discussions I expressed a fear for the future of our child, about exposing her to the attitudes of our society. Norman Cousins listened to a longing I felt for a fuller existence, and we talked about the violence which I explained as a sterile gesture against the tedium of life in Sophiatown. I was afraid that this violence was circling around me.

'Why don't you come to the United States?' Norman Cousins said.

Norman Cousins could not have been much older than I was, but he was successful at his profession and was financially independent; I was thirty-three years old, without a bank or an entry in the telephone directory, how could I say to another man that I was a failure, a used-up, left-over man without enough money to buy him drink. It was, of course, easier to blame South Africa, to explain that the economic policy is designed, in intent, to produce this state of insecurity in the Africans; how does one man say to another, I want to remove from my wife the frustration, the sense of insecurity she must feel in the company of my white friends whose wives were dressed and maintained at a standard which made my wife feel inferior; the sense of shame for having to offer hospitality in a single room, continually asking friends to move about, to sit back and allow room for greater mobility when serving courses of the meal. How does a man say, I pretended not to notice the moments I thought she would explode into tears; that normally she suffered those indignities in silence, the compensatory methods I adopted, buying dress items for her which I could not afford and entertaining on a level far above my earning capacity. I signed away my labour and low wages in various hire-purchase agreements to erect symbols in our home, trinkets of opulence for show to our friends, but, in effect, monuments to our own insecurity and in some small way my desperate attempt to compensate my wife. We had a child on the way, I was disturbed by thoughts of emotional security for her, of the simple things that make for happiness: a home to sleep in comfort, the food to nourish the body, the right to friends of one's own choice, to dream, to love, to mate, all in perfect peace. I could not tell these things to Norman.

I told him of the intent to go to Britain, to work my way to Canada, and even on and finally to the United States, a country, I persuaded my mind, that could offer Fiki, Chris and I the opportunity of building up a security both spiritual and material. Money was important in our lives, it was the foundation of the only security we knew, and we never had enough stability to think it unimportant. I could not inform Norman that I lacked the funds to travel directly to the United States or to Britain or to fifty miles from Sophiatown, and as I talked to him I thought he believed that I was too proud to ask him directly for help. Perhaps he was right, this was the virtue I learned from Hollywood films, particularly from *The Fountainhead*, that everything which I claim to be mine is all that these hands have earned; there was a degradation in depending my life on the charity of another man, begging is an emasculation, and although South Africa mocked at this, together with my manhood, I held this side of me free from stain. There was this pride, the integrity and the independence.

There were many things, between Norman and I, which were unstated, standing between us like a barrier, and when he left I retreated into my black igloo, in the interminable repetition of living the tedium of South Africa.

New Year's day was on the other side of the week-end, I had persuaded white friends in the office to procure European-type liquor for me, and with three bottles Henry Nxumalo and I utilised the office car to drive us to Sophiatown; it was Saturday night and we were going to have ourselves a real South African nice-time. Fiki was away and I had organised two girls to come and have a nice-time with me, and with Henry present it would balance out adequately, I was not in the mood for a two to one orgy. We were drinking for some private intent to annihilate ourselves and stop the progress of time, two solitary black masks intent on exploding the old year with the violence of noise; Africans destroy the old year violently, and sometimes in this process we kill each other, that the old year should not spread its influence into the new year. But we could not become drunk, the girls were late, we needed them to complete the perfect period of the annihilation, where the convulsions of the mind, the tensions of the body and the ugliness of the old year were to be obliterated in a long wail of a violent noise which would exhaust us.

A restless impatience came over Henry, the nice-time was not as yet stereophonic, the drinking and the noise from the record player, the inability to become drunk, only strengthened his impatience; he wanted to go to Western Township to keep an important appointment; I argued against the intention, pointing out the dangers of being abroad on New Year's eve, assuring him that if it was a girl there would soon be two to join us. It was only after seven. Henry was determined, promising to be violently stubborn. I hoped and prayed for the girls to knock—at that precise moment—on the door, I offered him more to drink, but every drink and every gesture to restrain him, the feeble noise, only increased the determination to go; and when I could not persuade and divert his attention any longer I went out to find a taxi for him, and Henry walked out of my room, out of my life and out of the air.

The girls arrived after eleven, shouting my name from the street, laughing and talking excitingly loud as they crushed into the room, throwing their arms around me and kissing their wishes on my face: merry, merry. They were from another nice-time, the fumes of gin were floating round every word which they breathed at me, and their bodies tingling with the smell of love.

I turned the record player on very loud, we began to drink and frolic, dancing to the orgiastic rhythms of the kwela, our bodies vibrating with sex rhythms; after we had finished the first bottle of gin one of the girls said clothes were cumbersome, and we peeled them off from our bodies becoming three masks with naked bodies commemorating the festival of sex. We danced the motions of love-making without touching our bodies together, the sweat gleaming on our bodies as we were drinking and dancing and teasing the body with a desire which we frustrated in a kind of carefree test of endurance. Our bodies were stimulated, titillating with desire, and they giggled and I laughed as the bodies touched by a will of their own, slapping aside the hands which reached out from a momentum of the body. The muscles of the nerves stretched to cracking, but we endured and mocked at the strain.

For more than an hour we stimulated and frustrated the body, until, each in turns, we collapsed to the floor, the bodies as under a magnetic field, locked together as the tensions exhausted themselves out of our bodies.

'Who first?' one said.

'I don't mind,' I said. 'Hey, why don't we toss a coin?'

'I got a penny,' the other said, reaching for her half-coat. 'Head or tail?'

'Tail—no, head.'

'Tail, you shouldn't have changed.'

'Anyway, I don't feel like it just now. Let's drink and dance.'

We commenced again to excite the body with the dance which was like a love-making of people separated by a glass divide, and we worked up another sweat, but the desire became more unbearable to contain; the girl who had lost the toss tripped me and fell on top of me, and both of us made love as a kind of contest during which we drove our bodies and the will to a climax whose tension was dementing the senses. The bodies carried the storm to another beginning of driving and working to another climax which was a false alarm, and the disappointment sharpened the will.

'Okay,' the other said, her foot pressing my bottom down, 'my turn. Right, Blokie, let's see how strong you are.'

And I battled against the exhaustion of the body, spurred by a destructive impulse of the will to explore the endurance of the body to the point of collapse; I was curious of the results when the body is exhausted to a numbness, would it become demolished? There must be a point at which the will surrenders its influence to the exhaustion of a body which has become too numb to respond to signals, but I had a reputation to maintain, the will to justify and vindicate my manhood; and the effect was like the fear of regurgitation, my body was afraid to vomit the energy and surrender to the taunting of the will, until in the end, after more drinking and more eroticisms of the dancing, we finished all the liquor and a kind of sadness came over us. Twilight was beginning to break all around us and the girls said it had been a nice time and left.

I became lonely afterwards, my body was saturated with sex and I was dissatisfied, there was the compulsion to scream a prayer to Fiki for forgiveness; the things for which I was looking were not all to be found in sex. I was sick with it, the smell of it was glued inside my nostrils and spreading over the flat of the tongue; the smell of liquor disgusted me and I wished to God I could vomit it out of my system. My body was wilting, the entire room smelt of the seventh commandment, and I collapsed, in shame, on to the bed in a desperate effort to sleep the ugliness out of my body.

I was woken from this heaviness by the pounding on the door, the smell of stale sex and brandy and gin was overpowering; I opened a window and staggered on to the door to admit Mrs Ben Gwigwi Mrwebi, who, with a dignity and solemnity, informed me that Henry Nxumalo was discovered early that morning, about fifty yards from Coronation Hospital, with twenty-two stab wounds, in a voice which was halting and jerking and jumping.

'He's passed away, Bloke,' she said. 'His body is waiting for the Black Maria.'

I looked across to the cabinet, there were the glasses and the bottle of brandy, the Mellowood brandy which we were drinking, the glasses which the girls had been using, also the empty bottles, and the top of the cabinet began to look like a glass cemetery. My mind vomited into my stomach. Mrs Mrwebi implied a willingness to take me to the spot where the body of Henry was lying, waiting, and festering in the sun, but I was overcome by a numbness; I could not think or feel or stand on my legs, I wanted to be alone with the pain, to force down the biliousness and the being afraid. I saw the mutilated body of my father, the blood and the broken flesh, and this woman was asking me to look again at this sight which nineteen years had failed to purge from my mind. I was afraid to look upon the body of Henry Nxumalo, could not face the twenty-two knife wounds, and in my mind I fought against the interpretation which might be insinuated on this refusal to go and look at the body of a man who was my friend. What possible repudiation could I make against such a charge? I did not care. I was afraid. I was among the last people to see him alive, and it was precisely because of this fact that I could not be persuaded; Henry was close to me, I did not want another gored and mutilated memory of a man I knew and loved and respected. I thanked Mrs Mrwebi and with many larded divergences I managed not to go with her, and I doubt if she ever understood or forgave me.

Thus when I received the letter from Mrs Sanford it was like a dying man's echo for help which was on the way but could not find the spot where I lay in waiting, and it echoed back to me, I echoed on to it; there was the possibility of running away from the sight of death, and all around me there was the tolling of the bell for my body which I saw festering in the sun, to attract friends and strangers to stare at the blood and waving aside the flies of the location pestering about the blood which had curled on the skin. I immediately made application for passport facilities and placed our names on immigration forms to the United States, and Hank Margolies, the assistant editor of *Golden City Post*, wrote a flattering letter of character and another to the United States Consul to facilitate the issue of the passport and of visas. I approached my old school master, Mr Harry Madibane, and proceeded to request another from Dr A. B. Xuma, a prominent and respected—even by the Government—member of the African community.

'I can't just issue you with a letter of character,' Dr Xuma said. 'A letter of character is earned, I don't feel qualified to give you one.'

It was a disappointing reaction, but I was not bitter, the doctor lived by a set of ethics that even the imperfections of our country could not throw into disproportion; I submitted

266

to the Native Commissioner the letters and other requirements, then was informed I was required to deposit £200—
a hundred each for Fiki and I—a guarantee required by the
Government from all Africans wishing to travel abroad; the
explanation is that the sum is to be held against the possibility
of Africans being stranded abroad for funds to return home. It
has been interpreted, though, as a studied discouragement
for Africans wishing to travel abroad, and it was resented
because it was a colour-bar arrangement; possibly the Government is negligent of the interests of white South Africans once
they leave the country.

Fiki and I decided to travel from South Africa on 4th
January, 1958, allowing the Government about eight months
to accommodate the go-slow machinery of the Civil Service
to give us a decision. The United States Immigration Office
required forms from my sponsors showing the state of their
finances and a written guarantee that I would not become a
burden on the State. Entering the United States presented
more problems than an entry into heaven; problems seemed
to loom all around me, I swallowed hard and pawned my
pride, my integrity, my sense of independence, and approached
friends for the £200 guarantee which I raised in three separate
units. The waiting list for immigration to the United States
was over-subscribed by three years, and the information officer
in the United States Information Service, Dave Du Bois, who
was also a very good friend, advised that I should put my name
down on the immigration list and also apply for a special
work visa which is issued for specialised employment in the
United States. Everything seemed to become more and more
complicated. My name, and that of my family, went on the
waiting list in September, 1957.

By the end of October we had not as yet been advised about
the application for passport facilities which had been filed
in May, but I was optimistic and proceeded to make travelling

arrangements; the Consul's office informed me that very little could be done about our visas without a passport, and I started phoning Pretoria persistently, being told to phone next week, then the next week and even so into the next. In the seventh week I was informed on the phone that my application for passport facilities had been rejected. No reasons were offered, there was no point in pressing for them: the Minister of the Interior is not obliged to give any reasons. By laboursome petition and enquiry I was given the advice to appeal to a Rev. Thema, who was the only African on the Dutch Reformed Church synod, and had some influence in the executive departments in Pretoria. I journeyed to Pretoria twice before we discovered that Rev. Thema knew a rich uncle, Mr J. K. Mrupe, who was my mother's brother, and after this discovery Rev. Thema expressed a willingness to investigate my case. A week later he had discovered that the Security Police had submitted an unfavourable report to my application, and had arranged an interview for me in the Special Branch headquarters in Pretoria; and in my best suit I was taken, on 23rd December, to the place of interview. It was a most impressive system, almost as exciting as in the Hollywood espionage films. We were led through various offices and corridors, finally to this door with a spy window which opened to reveal a face which seemed to recognise Rev. Thema.

I found myself in an enormous room with the one wall covered by a giant large-scale map of South Africa, with coloured pins and arrows around various points on it; there was a long impressive desk and behind it sat Major Colonel Prinsloo, second in command of the South African Special Branch, a little man with a tight skin which seemed to stretch like elastic around the cheek bones and the forehead. He was extremely polite.

'Please be sitted, Mr Modisane,' Major Colonel Prinsloo said, motioning me with his hand to a seat. 'Rev. Thema.'

'Thank you, sir,' I said, accepting the hospitality of his politeness.

Major Colonel Prinsloo fingered a dossier placed strategically to the left of him, and with pointed casualness he hooked his finger through the ribbon band and drew it over until it was opposite him, he pulled one end of the ribbon, gently sliding the knot to unfold. I thought of Alfred Hitchcock.

'Why do you think you were refused a passport, Mr Modisane?' Major Colonel Prinsloo said.

'I'm not sure, sir,' I said, looking an appeal to Rev. Thema who sat there like a silent arbiter.

'Have you no idea?'

'Not exactly, sir,' I said. 'I think perhaps it is because I was involved in the Church Story'.

Major Colonel Prinsloo looked at Rev. Thema.

'Now, Mr Modisane,' he said, opening the dossier. 'Why did you go and cause a disturbance in our churches? You know the laws of the country, there are churches for my people and there are churches for your people; we don't go to your churches to cause a disturbance, why did you do so in our churches?'

It was impossible not to have been struck by the sincerity of the man who insinuated upon me a sense of guilt for having gone into white churches, I had violated this mutual courtesy without any provocation, and for a moment he had succeeded in making me feel ungracious and disregardful of the sensibilities of the white Christians. I had committed an enormous contravention.

'I'm a working journalist, sir,' I said, in a feeble voice. 'I have to do the stories assigned to me.'

Major Colonel Prinsloo's police mind fastened on the words 'have to do', and his manner suddenly changed to that of the father figure, his reasoning becoming an intended assault on my sense of morality.

'Even if what you are asked to do may be wrong?'

'There was nothing radically wrong in going to church,' I said. 'We are all Christian together.'

'If your editor told you to go out and kill, murder a man,' he said, 'would you do it because it is your job?'

'That is a moral issue,' I said, 'there's no parallel. I don't think going to church was an issue on that level.'

There was a slight pause at which I thought there was a silent acknowledgement from Rev. Thema of my point, and I believe Major Colonel Prinsloo realised the indelicacy of pursuing this line in the presence of Rev. Thema.

'I understand it was your job, you had to do it,' Major Colonel Prinsloo said. 'I realise that your job depended on it.'

'Yes, sir,' I said, then sharply realising I had committed myself to the development of his argument, that I would be patronised to an obvious conclusion.

'You did it because you didn't want to lose your job, and those people took advantage of this,' he said. 'You must be careful of these Jews, Mr Modisane, they'll get you into trouble. Your people and my people understand each other, we live in peace together, we respect each other's wishes. I know you didn't deliberately go out to cause a disturbance in our churches—Yes, you're right, it's the police department which gave an unfavourable recommendation to your application. You have a job in America, a chance to study—let me see, yes, the University of Southern California, this is a good opportunity for you, to study and then come back to help your people. I don't want to stand in your way, I personally would like to help you, but I don't make the final decision, that's the responsibility of the secretary of the Department of the Interior, he will have to decide. I could help by changing the recommendation, but I can help only if you are honest with us. You tell us a few things, I change the police report, but I cannot guarantee you a passport, that's for the Department of the Interior.'

I had anticipated this development and was curious to hear the rest of it; except for the fact that it was done with such courtesy I could have sworn I was being blackmailed.

'I don't want you to think you'll be betraying your friends,' Major Colonel Prinsloo said. 'You'll be telling us nothing which we don't already know, we want to think you are being honest with us. I'll call in a stenographer and she'll take down what you say, the statement will then be given to you for your signature. We want to know all the names of the people involved in the story, we want to know what each did; why the story was done, whose idea it was; the motives behind the story; what was hoped to be gained by it; why it was that you went to Afrikaans churches only.'

I fought against the impulse to spit in his face, I was disgusted by the suggestion that this man was implying a simplicity on me, it was an affront to my intelligence; I searched my mind for the precise terms which would adequately impress upon him the loathing I felt, and although it was probably true they knew the names of the others in that assignment, it was nevertheless rude to present a man with such an ultimatum. There are far more practical means of gaining such information, they could torture it out of me. Because of the training, developed over the years, of suppressing everything into the stomach, I fell into a silence, afraid of the release of anger which was throbbing like cross rhythms; I willed myself into a calm, I was afraid to speak.

'I can see you don't know what to say,' Major Colonel Prinsloo said. 'You don't have to reply now, go home and think about it; I will phone Major Spengler in Johannesburg that you're coming to see him—after the holidays will be a good time, let's say the 27th of December. If you want to telephone him before he'll have a stenographer in the office.

Go and see Major Spengler, he'll arrange everything for you."

I returned to the office to report to my editor, Cecil Eprile, who was immediately disturbed by this development; he went into the office of the proprietor, Jim Bailey, to report on the matter of my confrontation. Cecil Eprile reacted and commiserated in the manner of a friend, and felt a new consciousness of respect for me as a person, congratulated me on the sense of loyalty to the paper. He and Jim Bailey thought that perhaps it might be better if I did not go to see Major Spengler, fearing that I may be tricked into making a statement, and although I might be mistaken, I seemed to note that both Cecil and Jim Bailey did not place a high reliance on my sense of judgement; the temptation of having to choose between America and South Africa could be resolved without too much effort, the prospect of a milder political climate was exciting.

'He might have hidden microphones in the office,' Cecil Eprile said, 'you might say something which might be held against you.'

'I don't think so, Cecil,' I said. 'I think I want to go.'

Major Spengler was equally courteous, but his approach was far more reasoned and realistic, he presented me with a case which was difficult to argue against, and the disturbing element is that the truth of his statement was later to be vindicated; but I suppose it was difficult for Major Spengler and Cecil Eprile and Jim Bailey to understand that the confrontation violated my individual sense of integrity, there was not the slightest doubt in my mind that the matter merited any consideration. I was curious.

'Mr Modisane, it makes no difference to us whether you give us this information,' Major Spengler said. 'It's your future that is at stake. This American trip is a good chance for you. It's your life, and you must look after yourself—or nobody will. I know you think you owe your paper a loyalty, but do you think if you were in real trouble they'll lift a finger to help you? People help themselves. We've got our files on the people we need to have, if we must help you, then you must help us; I don't promise you a passport, you must understand that.'

'Yes, I know that sir,' I said.

'This is your future, you must help yourself,' he said. 'Look, phone me tomorrow if you want to do it. If you don't I'll know your decision. When do you want to leave?'

'I've booked passage for January fourth.'

Back at the office Cecil Eprile, after consultation with Jim Bailey, asked me for a written report on the two interviews which he thought ought to be published in the newspaper with the possibility of having the issue raised in Parliament as a question to the Minister of the Interior; but nothing was done about publishing the scandal and although I was not particularly concerned with questions asked in the Commons, I did think the story was worth publishing.

I wrote a rather long and impassioned letter to Norman Cousins explaining that I would not be coming to America as planned, describing the circumstances of the two interviews which I described as an effort by the police to get me to 'sell my soul' for a passport document; Norman wrote requesting urgent permission to publish the letter.

Dear Bill:

Your letter is a powerful and moving document. It was written by a big man, a very big man, and I am prouder than ever before to know you. Your handling of the passport challenge reflects as much credit on you as it does dishonour to those who have hobbled you.

I don't know the situation in Johannesburg, yet I hold fast to the hope that there may be some way to crack through the barrier of human smallness. Is there any reason to believe that a request or appeal from influential circles in the United States might be useful? Is there any American firm in particular that your Government finds especially deserving of attention? What about a request from our own Government circles?

Your letter carried such an impact that I am emboldened to ask whether I can publish it. We must weigh of course the possible resentment it may stir up in Johannesburg against the sense of outrage it will produce both here and in South Africa. It may well be that our best chance is to put a sliver in the public conscience. Please let me know soonest how this strikes you.

> *sincerely,*
> *(signed) Norman.*
>
> *January 17, 1958.*

The letter which Norman published was picked up by *Contact*, the Cape Town journal, then by *The Star*, the Johannesburg evening paper, which had seen it in *Contact*. *The Star* published the story under the headline:

A PASSPORT TO U.S. . . . . IF RAND NATIVE REPORTER TOLD ALL

I suppose it was flattering that somewhere in the story I was referred to as 'Mr Modisane, who is essentially a Native journalist'.

'Why did you give the story to *Contact*, and now, *The Star*?' Cecil Eprile said, with the newspaper in his hand. 'Why didn't you give it to your paper?'

I did not cherish the possibility of becoming annoyed with Cecil, I ignored the question, but I had become disenchanted with *Drum* publications. I thought to phone Major Spengler to inform him that he was right. I began to lose interest in my job, did not care to do anything else except the column on music and the frustrating social page which I loathed. But I suppose the objection arose from the fact that I had reached the point at the wall, and although it is true Can Temba became associate editor, Henry Nxumalo and Arthur Maimane were elevated to posts of news editors, these were nevertheless prestige appointments, the Africans in them were paid far less than the white sub-editors.

I had surrendered all hopes of 'the great prospects' which every African reporter joining the staff was promised against the low, prejudicial wages determined for Native reporters, a scale lower than that of the white typists. I had approached Jim Bailey on the subject of a raise in salary on the event of my marriage to Fiki, hinting that my salary was inadequate to my standard of living, that with a wife and possibly a family my situation would become acute. I was told—between irrelevances and jokes which were not funny—that getting married did not constitute a basis for a rise in salary. And thus Fiki and I, Ma-Bloke and the four children hobbled along on the low wages and 'the good prospects'. Gradually the sterility of our life, the lost hope of going to America, the prestige job which brought home more 'prospects'—which we could not eat at table—than the money for a civilised existence, began to nibble at our relationship, and Fiki, understandably, preferred her mother's house in Natalspruit which had four rooms.

I sneered at the defeat, challenged the right of any man —be it Dr Verwoerd or Major Spengler—to dictate the fortunes of my life. My mind began to grow criminal tentacles, on beam to pick up the frequencies of advantage, sensitive to the exploitation of a situation. As music critic I was approached—with the usual courtesies and smiles which were too broad—about a mention in my column, 'which was very good', of a musical train to Basutoland, it was the greatest musical invasion on the Protectorate, a sort of musical tour of goodwill. As I listened to Peter Rezant my mind leeched to the advantage for using the trip as camouflage for another intent to work my means. People who show all thirty-two of their dentures for a one-inch column in a newspaper would have all their teeth extracted on a verbal promise of four inches, and taking this unfair advantage of Peter Rezant I suggested that, perhaps if I were allowed on the musical train the tour would benefit from a more extensive coverage, with photographs of the actual performances. Free transportation was immediately promised, in exchange for the privilege and honour of having, as a special guest, the columnist of the most widely read music column in the most widely read newspaper in South Africa. I wished I could have made a recording of that high praise to present to Cecil Eprile as a Christmas gift.

I was accorded the attention and grace of a celebrity, and as Peter Rezant's Merry Blackbirds were entertaining in Maseru I spoke to Mr Kotsokoane, a former science master at my old school, employed by the Basutoland Government in their agricultural schemes to combat the urgent instance of soil erosion, about the possibility of being issued a British passport; whether there were circles of influence which he could buttonhole; perhaps, since Modisane is a common name, we could find this surname in the British Protectorate of Basutoland, and with a princely largess and the fact that we are brothers under the apartheid boot of Dr Verwoerd, he might be persuaded to recognise me as the long-lost grandson of a prodigal son, which would make me a British subject entitled to a British passport. Mr Kotsokoane was discouraging, he had been away from South Africa for too long and was probably shocked by the criminal recesses of my mind; it was not possible, the right way to do it was the legal way: establish residence in Basutoland for one year.

I did not have the year to spend in Basutoland, particularly since the prospects of making a living were limited. In Johannesburg I requested a week's leave of absence from work which I used for travel to Serowe, the capital of Bechuana-land, also a British protectorate, to present a plea to Seretse Khama.

'I'm sorry, I can't help you,' Seretse Khama said. 'If your father was born in Bechuanaland it could have been possible. In any case, I don't think I would have wanted to help you; what are you going to do in England and America, your place is in South Africa to continue the fight. I can't help you to run away from your responsibility—I can't.'

I returned to Johannesburg with the awful acceptance of the realisation that Major Spengler was right, it is intolerable to allow my attitudes towards his race and the resentment against the police to become a suit of armour over the man, so that even the truth is suffocated in the encasement; the truth is, in the final analysis, it will be by the effort of my actions that men will rise to the standard of my cause. Major Spengler had presented against my manhood a challenge which seemed to insinuate, in a total context, the implication that I was incapable of looking after myself; it seemed to reflect the South African attitude that Africans are children who must be guided through every stage of their lives; the normal reaction was to prove myself, to resolve that it must be by my independent effort; the dare that until it shall be proved otherwise I shall be but what I am—less than a man; this immediately generated a swashbuckling compulsion to succeed and confront the result before his face: Major Spengler, I have helped myself.

I began to make enquiries about the British Passport Act, to read the definition of what is a British subject and a British citizen, and was intrigued to discover that a man born in the British Isles, colonies and possessions is by law a British subject and the children of British subjects and British protected peoples have the birthright of being British subjects. It was an interesting thought which was worth exploiting, and I wrote to the British Passport Officer in Cape Town, pointing out

277

that my father was born in the South Africa which was then a British Colony administered directly from Whitehall.

15th January, 1958

Dear Sir,

In reply to your letter dated 7th January, 1958, I have to inform you that under the terms of the British Nationality Act, 1948, you are not entitled to a United Kingdom passport or United Kingdom passport facilities as neither you nor your father were born in the United Kingdom or a Colony as comprised on the 1st January, 1949. The status of South Africa at the time of your birth and your father's birth is immaterial in this context.

However, since both you and your wife were born in the Union of South Africa, you are presumably South African citizens by birth and, as such, are British subjects in United Kingdom law.

I can advise you that under the Act of 1948, mentioned above, it is possible for you, as a British subject, after residence in the United Kingdom or Colonies, for a period of one year, to apply for registration as a United Kingdom citizen, which if granted would make you eligible to hold a United Kingdom passport. However, your attention is drawn to Section 15 of the South African Citizenship Act, 1949, which states 'A South African citizen who whilst outside the Union . . . acquires the citizenship or nationality of a country other than the Union thereupon ceases to be a South African citizen.'

You would be ill advised to attempt to enter the United Kingdom without a passport, since upon arrival there, it is likely that you would be refused leave to land by the Immigration Officer at the port of entry.

Yours faithfully,
(signed) A. E. Huttly,
United Kingdom Passport Officer

I was surprised by the inefficiency of the sources which supplied the United Kingdom Passport Officer with his information: South African citizenship, by the letter of the law, is open to white South Africans only, and the fact Fiki and I were 'presumably South African citizens by birth' was immaterial against the reality that the law did not recognise us as such, therefore we could not lose what we did not possess. I had made independent enquiries about entering the United Kingdom without a passport and discovered that as a Commonwealth citizen, with documented proof of this status, I could not be refused 'leave to land' in the United Kingdom, unless, of course, I should be singled out for some other reason.

I accepted the principle and the responsibility of committing a criminal offence by leaving my country without a passport; I had made notes on the trip to Serowe, possibly I could travel through Bechuanaland on the escape route, but there were still many problems to be worked out and the most important was that of financing such a trip. It was impossible to save up for the journey from the 'monthly mockery' which *Drum* was paying me.

A few weeks later a man came to see me in the office. Lionel Rogosin, the American film producer and director who had made *On the Bowery* and *Out*, had been advised by Dave Du Bois to bring his problems to me; I had become a kind of unofficial filing index, people came to me for photographer's models, tickets to African shows, suggestions on the launching of a new product on the African market, and, generally, I was an all-purpose man, an index of information.

'My name is Rogosin,' he said, 'Lionel Rogosin, a mutual friend asked me to look you up.'

He explained to me the project which had brought him to South Africa, the desire to put on cinematographic record the system of apartheid, wanted to meet Africans to listen to them and look into their lives; I listened courteously, there had been too many people who came to film, dishonest people who exploit Africans as cheap acting labour force, and since African entertainers were not strictly considered as professionals or protected by an effective union, up and down the country there had been people who have cast Africans in leading roles for £33 for an eighty-minute feature film. Lionel Rogosin explained that since he was an independent producer he could not afford to pay Hollywood salaries, and there was an honesty about his face. This, together with the fact that he was having trouble with the Government over visas for his crew, two cameramen and a sound engineer, was perhaps all that was required for me to change my attitude towards him. Anybody who was in trouble with the South African Government inspired in me a sense of identity.

Lionel became an exhaustive enquirer, penetrating into the squalor of the locations to feel the heart-beat of the Africans; I took him into the shebeens which were reeking with sweat and the smell of stale beer to listen to the people talking, sometimes with bitterness but always with humour, about the injustice, the misery, the poverty which was a part of their lives, and I remember that one evening we dragged him through a ceremony of pouring beer over his head to make him an honorary Zulu, taught him to do the Zulu war dance. One evening, during a drunken session, he was standing in the middle of the room with a fighting stick in his hand saying he had to rush home to protect his family against the Zulus. 'The Zulu warriors are coming.'

By the time he was ready to start filming we had accepted him as an African, conditioned him to see black, to feel black and to react black, but to be black he had had to become a piece of the problems around that colour.

It never occurred to me that morning when Lionel walked up to me that I was to become enmeshed in a gigantic fraud, in a colossal challenge which was to cause me to resign my job and earn a life-long friendship. The South African Government was suspicious, they wanted Lionel to submit details and the script of the film he wanted to make. After Ed. Murrow's film, *African Conflict*, American film-makers were suspect.

Thus began the exciting merry-go-round. At one time Lionel was making a travelogue for an international airline company. The Government wanted to see documented proof, the actual contract. Lionel found himself having to live that lie through to the end and produced a contract, a vague noncommittal commission from the airline. The Government threw the contract out as too vague. The next decision was to film an African musical. Lionel took the suggestion to Pretoria with the near-plausible story that he wanted to present the music of South Africa to the world, to show that Africans were basically a happy people. To support this story we had gone round the location shooting scenes of penny-whistle troupes, gum-boot dancers, singing troupes, shooting hundreds of feet of film to be shown to the Department of the Interior.

The police were following us all through the location, seemingly casual but noting all our movements, and during a very crowded street scene I suggested to Lionel that he might ask the police—for the promise of being in the film—to help in regulating the crowds, which they did more efficiently that I had done. After more than a month's fooling around and travelling to Pretoria, the visas were finally granted, but by this time Lionel Rogosin had fed the white papers with the story that he had become fascinated with Denys Reitz's book, *The Commando*, which he wanted to film in South Africa with local actors. *The Commando* is a weighted account of the Boer war, and the newspaper record was enthusiastic over this and the Government attitude turned into a more sympathetic assessment of Mr Rogosin's applications.

From Zurich came Walter Wettler, the sound engineer,

and Ernst Artaria, the cameraman, and from Israel came Emil Knebel, another cameraman.

The police seemed to have deserted us, and Lionel and I began the long search for actors—not professionals, but faces —we looked at thousands of faces, coming out of the cinemas, in the bus queues, in the streets, everywhere, until I began to develop a feel for faces; because of the advertising space we bought in a newspaper we spent an entire afternoon looking at faces and managed to cast all the smaller parts, but were still confronted with finding the right face to cast in the lead. One morning Lionel rushed up to me with the excited news that he had found the face he was looking for, and as it turned out the man suited all the requirements for the part, he was himself a country man who had been forced to migrate his labour to Johannesburg because the land could no longer support the needs of his family. Zacharia was merely being asked to live again his life before the camera, the life of a simple rural African: inarticulate, halting in speech, very little education. But he was a man—as it emerges in the film —with a quiet dignity and tremendous integrity, and since the dialogue was not scripted, Zacharia spoke, improvising, his own dialogue; the words were his own, and so was the grammar.

The terrifying scene at the end when he returns from jail to find his wife, Vinah, murdered by Marumo, the mountain man, was even more agonising to watch in front of the camera; the script called for him to break down mentally, and in a rage of hysteria, to smash up whatever his temper directed him to. The crack-up of the character, and the man, were so closely linked that we were horrified to be in the presence of the destruction of a man. It was a nightmare which we could not control or stop or turn our faces from, and when Lionel did assume the presence of mind to shout 'cut' we were sick; the scene had come—for us—too close to the real thing, and for Zacharia it was the real thing, it was in his face.

The script which Lionel, Lewis Nkosi and I had pieced together was shot almost entirely in Sophiatown where we drove round with blankets over the cameras whenever we sighted the police; this secrecy extended even to the actors as a protection to them against police reprisals when the film is finally shown. When all the safe sections of the film were photographed Lionel became daring, he wanted to go into the mines to shoot the sequences of the training of the new recruits, the Africans who go down into the mines, into another world, of tunnels, with flashlights on their foreheads, drilling for gold. The black of the skin of the miners seemed to flow into the black of the tunnel, the flashlights on the helmets seemed to move without bodies, one after the other, and photographed in long shot they gave an impression of a long snake winding in the dark. The Africans scratching into the bowels of the earth for the gold which is the symbol of South Africa's white prosperity, and the fundamental of the greed that oppresses them.

To photograph the mine scenes Lionel wormed himself into the confidence of a mine official with the glowing account of making a film on gold mining in South Africa which would show the high technical standard of mining, the remarkable achievement in transforming, by specialised training methods, rural Natives into proficient miners.

The most stimulating scene was the alienation of the rural African, the confusion of being in the midst of black intellectuals—whom Nimrod Mkele describes as displaced intellectuals in search of a morality—listening without understanding but being stimulated; for the scene we assembled Can Temba, Lewis Nkosi, Morris Hugh Letsoalo and I, Lionel Rogosin provided the liquor and we had managed to persuade Martha Maduma to play the shebeen queen, but Miriam Makeba was not as impressed, the fee offered for the part was ridiculously low, and it was embarrassing that I, the music critic who had taken up the issue of exploitation of African artists, should have to be produced persuading an artist to accept a fee which I knew was not fair. But I believed in Lionel's film, that something will come out of it, so I offered Miriam Makeba some of those prospects which *Drum* always offered us.

'It might be a break for you,' I said. 'You might be noticed by the right people in America; you never can tell about these things, if for nothing else, do it for me. Please.'

She returned about twelve-thirty in the morning from doing a show somewhere in Vereeniging, and with a look-out posted outside one of the classrooms of Christ the King mission school which Father Huddleston had closed rather than hand the school over to the department of Bantu Education, we filmed the scene.

When the film was completed and the rushes sent to New York Lionel threw an enormous illegal party where black and white drank together, danced together and got drunk together; I saw Lionel Rogosin smile genuinely, not just with the teeth, but with the eyes, the face and the whole body. He had survived the ordeal of being black in a white skin, and the hoax, the lies, the deceptions were all justified in his final bold statement of the African's case.

Chapter Sixteen

I HAD become unaware of the progress of time, sitting in my little room which had become a piece of the darkness that had settled about and above the flat roof-tops of Sophiatown, and the darkness had settled around and infused me into it so that I could not see the scars and feel the wounds of my life which Sophiatown and South Africa had gored into my body. And there in the dark I could see the Three-Star knives of Sophiatown, their pointed blades zeroed on my body, and I was alone, my body exposed to the naked ugliness of my life, afraid of the things which had montaged the destruction of my soul against that of Sophiatown; I could not tell us apart, both of us had spent ourselves, but they had not swept the refuse into the incinerator. Remembrances of that life made me feel dirty, I longed for Chris and Fiki to come and wash the corpse of my body before it is finally lowered into the grave, so that I could appear before my God clean and sanitary.

The door was flung open, the light switch clicked and a galaxy of light fell about, below and above the darkness which had camouflaged the decaying body sitting over the wake of the dead soul.

'Hau,' Daisy said, 'I was saying there is nobody—I come to take the tea things. Why is auboetie sitting in the dark? Was auboetie asleep?'

'No, sweetie,' I said, then a desperation came over me for a human contact. 'What did you want to ask me when you brought the tea?'

'Does auboetie want some more tea?' she said. 'But auboetie has not touched this one—it's cold. Shall I make another one?'

'Yes, please,' I said, 'but you must tell me what you wanted.'

She carried away the tea-tray and I realised that I might have frustrated her; she would talk to me when she thought I was in a responsive mood. When she returned there was a nervousness about her. She was jogging from foot to foot, selecting the words in the dialogue which was to cost me money; I had seen this method in operation before, I had employed it myself, except that there were slight variations depending on the temperament of the children and the adult to be assaulted.

'Auboetie, next week is school competition,' Daisy said. 'Is the tea strong enough? Is it too strong? Does auboetie like me to pour? It will get cold, auboetie.'

'No, sweetie, the tea is fine,' I said, pouring a cup for myself. 'Would you like a cup? I've got very nice pastries.'

'Yes, auboetie, but I will drink it in the kitchen.'

'You can drink it here with me if you like.'

'Thank you, auboetie, but I was washing dishes.'

It was my fault for not having been strong in encouraging the children to break through the formality of big brother, auboetie, and little sister relationship; it was the same resentful system which had separated my father from us, and it was distorted by the strict observance Ma-Bloke had imposed on this formality—she was often critical of me because I wanted the children to call me Bloke. How can the children be respectful if there is no difference between themselves and their elders? It was difficult to argue very strongly against this since it might be interpreted, by the children, as a challenge against her authority as our mother, who by her years has the right to command obedience. A secret covenant was made with Daisy, Pancho, Butch, that in the privacy of our company they could call me Bloke, and this way a free rapport was established except that when they wanted something from me the formality would come up to separate us into our roles in the family.

'Why don't you call me Bloke?' I said. 'You know you can. Where is your school choir going to sing?'

'At the Bantu Men's, auboetie.'

'What do you sing?' I said. 'First part or second part?'

'First part,' she said. 'Auboetie, I haven't got shoes, and Ma-Bloke says she hasn't got money.'

'But I bought you two pairs last Christmas.'

'Yes, auboetie, but they are not nice.'

'Sweetie, you chose them yourself.'

'They are black and the other is brown,' she said. 'I want white shoes.'

'I see,' I said, 'but surely Ma-Bloke won't just refuse to buy you shoes.'

'Ma-Bloke wants to buy me shoes at Nanabhai,' Daisy said, contemptuous of wearing shoes which have been bought in Sophiatown. 'They are not nice, I saw very nice one at ABC.'

'At ABC,' I said. 'Now I know why Ma-Bloke refused. But they don't usually sell school shoes, I suppose you want to be a lady. You know Ma-Bloke doesn't want you to wear grown-up shoes, I'm not sure if I want to. Schoolgirls should wear school shoes.'

'I want shoes like sis-Fiki,' she said, her voice having softened. 'Au, look, auboetie's tea is cold, I'll make another one.'

She knew she had won and could afford to take her time about it, the offer to make fresh tea was a peace or victory celebration, we both recognised it as such; when she returned I blackmailed her into sitting down to tea with me. I had laid out the pastries, her small plate with knife opposite mine on the coffee table, one of the armchairs had been moved into place for her; we both knew it was a bribe, and a mischievous smile came on her round face as she accepted the invitation of my hand waving her into the seat. We had both won.

'If you'll sit down I'll serve you,' I said, more grateful for her company than the money for the shoes she could have bought. 'Do you know how much Fiki's shoes cost?'

A sadness came over her face which seemed to darken and become unattractive, to age a little, as when she cried her mouth—the lips are thin and the edges join into the roundness of her cheeks—and nose flow into the oval contour of the face; she bit the upper lip and nodded her head.

Lionel Rogosin and I talked about the film, the reaction it would arouse in Johannesburg, and eventually we came round to my journey to the United Kingdom where I would establish a year's residence and apply for registration as a British national and then for a United Kingdom passport, by which time my immigration visa to the United States would have matured and I would travel to the United States. We discussed the payment for my work in the making of the film.

'I prefer not to be paid, Lionel,' I said, 'but rather that you pay for an air ticket to New York for me.'

'There's no point in having money tied up in a ticket for over a year,' Lionel said. 'I'll pay for a ticket to London, then when you're ready to come to New York I'll send you a London–New York ticket. I'll give you £100 in cash to help you with the journey.'

The offer was far more generous than I could have hoped for, we agreed that I would travel until I found a country where I would be allowed to board a plane without a passport. I had met Miles Jebb, an Englishman who must be the gentlest human being I know, there was a preciousness about him which made me envy the gentle society which made such a softness in people; Miles Jebb was working for an airline and had promised to investigate the possibility of being transported without travel documents. We had a final drink and a meal at his place and Lionel, Elly and their child which was born in South Africa left with the promise of a meeting in New York and a search for a bar with American dry martinis like the ones we had in Sophiatown.

Because I was without a job I operated as a business the function of supplying advertising agencies with photographer's models, until almost every advertising space in the African newspapers and magazines featured models supplied from my unregistered agency, and every attractive girl in show business and out of it was on my booking list. But I was unemployed and Bert Riley, who had continued to endorse my Pass every month, pointed out to me that it could lead to trouble if it was carried on too long, and we agreed that he should discharge me; I spoke to Henri Schoup who offered me a token employment with United Press International, and the Pass was endorsed. I helped in assembling background material for feature articles.

The money which Lionel had left me was soon spent and I was back in my usual state of being without funds; I kept pushing back the going away, it seemed I could not break with South Africa. During August Sheila and Athol Fugard came to see me with a bottle of brandy and the request to fill a replacement in his new play, *No-Good Friday*; it was explained that there was no money in it, the actors pay their own expenses with only the promise that if it should make money the actors would share in the pool. The part was that of a gangster, Shark, a violent little man with an external charm and eruptions of violence which were locked inside the man.

I had acting pretensions, probably as a result of seeing too many Hollywood films, but the interest in acting was basically academic, having read studiously, analysing and doing exercises in front of the mirror, the technique of acting which Stanislavski describes in his books; the interest was mainly scientific with stimulations from watching the work of Marlon Brando, even though most of his films were too old for me, being the mental level of an under-fourteen white child. *The Men* was the only one which received a screening certificate which allowed juveniles to see it. I was fascinated by Rod Steiger, and because his films were available to us I was able to observe, analyse and utilise his method; there was a similarity between his character in *The Harder They Fall* and that of Shark, both characters had an inner violence which was under a silk veil of gentleness; the violence was implicit and intellectual, an aspect which I found more terrifying than physical violence.

I had read about the methods of torture employed in breaking down prisoners during the Second World War and later in the Korean war, without the administration of a single physical blow; the torture of the mind was to me a terrifying concept, because the mind is more responsive to pain. It was with this in mind that I approached the part of Shark, to work from inside the man, and the result was a nasty insidious terror, almost always implied, which at times had its effect on the other actors on stage.

We played before such small audiences it was discouraging, and it seemed that all the effort, the money, the sheer physical hard work Athol Fugard—without any backing, even from the Union of Southern African Artists which only invested in certainties at the box-office—had put into it would have been in vain. The play was given two nights in a small hall in Johannesburg—the first before an all-white audience—and attracted the interest of a white impresario who booked the play for four nights in the white Brian Brooke Theatre; but this booking almost destroyed the play itself because Athol Fugard, the playwright and white man who plays the priest—a kind of Father Huddleston figure—was not allowed on the same stage with black actors, and Athol Fugard had accepted the principle without consulting with the actors.

The actors confronted Athol with this betrayal, protesting

that there was an agreement not to pander to the bigotry of white South Africa; the actors refused to perform without him in the cast, but he argued that it was a big break for the play, and we became sentimental and relented because it seemed to be his whole life, the disappointment on his face was too heavy for us to ignore and Lewis Nkosi was recruited to play a white priest who had to be discoloured because of the attitudes of our country.

For three months the play had been an adequate diversion, and I was approached about considering the possibility of being cast in the ambitious all-African musical, *King Kong*, which the Union of Southern African Artists was assembling as a show-piece of black-white unity of purpose; the gala première was set down for 2nd February, 1959, and it looked almost certain that the show would enjoy a marathon run. I could not commit myself to an indefinite stay in South Africa; the readiness was there, only the decision was waiting, I filled in time by working at odd jobs like the one in the film library of the United States Information Service splicing films, duplicating information sheets on the Roneo machine, assisting during screenings and sitting in when new films, particularly the President Eisenhower press conferences, were being watched by Dave Du Bois, then catalogued and filed in the library. Dave Du Bois amazed me with the information and the rapport he created with the feuding sections of African politics, creating among them the image of the new Americans which the Africans could trust; and it was Peter Raboroko who, in honest admiration, said: 'When South Africa is ours we shall petition the American Government to appoint you ambassador to South Africa.'

When Philip Stein went on holiday he requested me to assist his father-in-law, Mr Manchip, to manage the shop in his absence. Everything seemed to be waiting upon the decision to go. I had sandwich lunches with Mira, Myrtle and Francie, spending the week-ends with Margaret and Morris Milner, Joan and Henri Schoup, the Bermans, Dolly Hassim and Gesse. Dr Ellen Hellmann was the constant spiritual light to which I turned for the peace and quiet of her friendship, a sit in the garden and listening to records with her daughter, Ruth, whenever I was afraid to look at the pleas in my mother's eyes.

In her desperation she confronted me with the uncles in the family but they accepted the futility of her restraining attempts; every kind of argument and explanation failed to impress upon Ma-Bloke that South Africa was pressing down on my mind. I made an attempt to manage her affairs, decorate the house in Alexandra Township which was a property she had been paying off for the last fifteen years; I saw her begin to die of the thought that I was deserting her without a protector, and I prayed for the words to persuade her to understand that I was sick with shame for the selfishness which was driving me to betray the love of a mother who needed me more than the sanity I claimed to be losing.

'Who are you leaving me with?' she said, her eyes having abandoned the hope of tears. 'What is to become of us? What will happen to you in a strange country with people you don't know? Who will look after you?'

'Mama, I'm not going there to die,' I said. 'Soon our country will be right, all will be well and I will come back. You will see, Ma-Bloke. It won't be very long.'

I had seen her eyes wet with grief and several times I kept delaying the journey, yet I knew that the longer I stayed the greater were increased the chances of being stabbed to death or being arrested on charges under the Immorality Act. I had ceased to care or be afraid of the hooliganism of the police in the prison cells. I invited Mira to Sophiatown staying very long together alone in the room, in the full knowledge that if the police were to visit us the fact that all we did was talk and listen to records would have been immaterial; that we were together was sufficient supposition that we were conspiring to commit an offence under the Act. Even though we sometimes slept together in the same bed there was no question of sex entering into our relationship. There was very little need for sex. I think that she, too, had somewhat ceased to care, for some reason or blind negligence she never seemed to conceive of the possibility of danger, it was never brought up in discussion. I had invited her to spend Christmas Day of 1958 with me. We talked, played and laughed the time away, until we discovered it was one o'clock in the morning with no possibility of finding a taxi. I asked her to stay the night, and in the morning she was perfectly normal with the people in the yard, even in spite of the obvious implications people would insinuate into the fact that she slept in my room. This single fact made me feel a very strong affection for her. We seemed to be deliberately creating the impression that we slept together in a sex relationship without in fact consummating the deed, and we did it almost in vengeance against South Africa and its attitudes. There was a time when I was insane with wanting her, but she managed to maintain the balance.

In January of 1959 I began saying my goodbyes, I had exhausted all the excuses for delaying the journey; then began the careful study of train schedules. Three times a week there were two trains going to Bulawayo, and although the Cape Town train left twenty hours ahead of the Johannesburg train it arrived at Mafeking forty-three minutes behind the Johannesburg train, and this difference was maintained all the way to Bulawayo. This information was especially interesting and useful, since the Rhodesian immigration officers begin the checking of travel documents at Mafeking, which is about twelve hours to Palapye and another twelve to Francistown, which is under two hours to Bulawayo. Travellers with tickets

293

to Bechuanaland were not asked for permits to enter the Rhodesias.

The Rhodesian authorities are only interested in persons travelling to Rhodesia, and the South African Government is not keen to create immigration barriers against the migrant labour, thus Africans from and to Bechuanaland travel freely without any checks; there was no reason to suppose that my intentions to travel to Bechuanaland should be questioned or even noticed, I was as black as an African from Bechuanaland.

During the trial run to Bechuanaland when I went to see Seretse Khama, I noted that the Rhodesian authorities go through a check of all the passengers before the train reaches Palapye and reasoned that there would be no necessity for another check between Palapye and Francistown since this area was contained in the territory of Bechuanaland; if there was to be another check it would probably begin from Francistown, but the time factor was working in my advantage, because since Europeans received the courtesy of being attended to before Natives, by the time they get to the Native coaches the train would have been to Bulawayo and back.

This precaution was a protection against the misfortune of a second check, which is unlikely since the Rhodesian Government also places a high reliance on migrant labour from Bechuanaland which it does not wish to frustrate by placing immigration barriers. But since there is always that margin of probability that an immigration officer may for some reason be travelling from one end of the train to the other, there was no guarantee that it would not be the one who had examined my ticket, in which case I would be recognised and confronted with a demand for travel documents. I resolved to travel by the Johannesburg train up to Francistown, then get off the train and wait forty-three minutes for the Cape Town train which would have been checked twenty-four hours ago, and even if there would be another check I would be travelling on a ticket from Francistown to Bulawayo. It was therefore necessary that I travel with two separate tickets bought at separate railway stations.

The train schedules also showed that there was a train from Bulawayo to Salisbury every evening at eight-thirty, and as the Cape Town train reaches Bulawayo at five forty-five there would be only a little over two hours of waiting for the next train. The times would be especially appropriate since the immigration office for Natives would be in the same building with the department which deals with Native affairs, and this department would be closed and the Custom's officials would advise me to report in the morning, by which time I would be in Salisbury. But the time-tables also showed that Salisbury was the last stop for 'civilised' transport to the north, except for the rail to the Copperbelt which started at Bulawayo. There was no reason why I should not travel the first 1,000 miles of the journey in reasonable comfort.

The première of *King Kong* was a gala affair at the University Great Hall, to which I took Fiki—as a parting gesture— because I always took her to first nights; after the show I took her to a party at the Berman house, and found myself saddened by the promiscuousness of the South African society, men were making advances at each other's wives; white men were glued to African women in a dance which was like fornicating on the dance floor, white women were sandwiched between walls and African men. It was a disgusting reflection of the emptiness of the gestures of our lives, and it was perhaps because of this consciousness—the fact that our lives are empty and the boredom drives us in a pursuit of this emptiness—that I was a part of it. A white friend was obscenely pressing Fiki against him on the dance floor. I could feel my mind vomiting; but both she and I were being promiscuous too, I turned the other way to breathe an appropriate-to-the-occasion desire on a white woman stranger. We soaked each other with our breath and words whose remembrance would destroy us.

I took Ma-Bloke to the second night, and as she had complained of not having anything to wear appropriate for such a great event, we had gone into town to select what she described as a suitable dress for an elderly woman; it was perhaps among her happiest experiences when I introduced her to all those fashionable white women in mink. The next time was to take Mira, and because she is white I had to have a special talk with Percy Tucker who managed a theatre booking service in Eloff Street; it was impossible to sit us together, but we worked out a solution, Mira would be seated at the last white row immediately behind where the black rows would begin. All through the performance she would lean forward to whisper into my ear or offer me chocolate, and during the interval we would walk out together to the foyer for refreshments. The time drifted on and I returned seven more times to see the show and be excited by the volatile appeal of Miriam Makeba.

I made the decision to travel in March over the Easter holidays, relying on the Christian nature of the white Rhodesians who should be celebrating in church and festivities; the immigration office would be closed from Thursday to Tuesday, enough time for me to reach Salisbury and perhaps even beyond before there would be a search instigated in the event of an alarm being raised. I arranged with Fiki to come to Sophiatown to supervise the transportation of our furniture —the relics of our life together—to her parents' home in Natalspruit.

'Do you want to keep this?' I said, showing our marriage licence.

'No.'

I threw it into the waste of papers, we bargained over the records, books and perhaps reaffirmed the unspoken promise that we might rediscover a need for each other, in which case I would save money for their passage. We kissed and she left in the lorry with the pieces which were a piece of our lives, I sat in the room which now had only a bed, packed the suitcase and safely stowed the money which I had raised by borrowing from friends: there was the dinner with Neil Herman and the envelope he pressed into my hand as we said our goodbyes; the night meeting with Robert Loder for a loan, and the help of a friend whose help must remain anonymous.

A very drunken and loud Dennis Kiley staggered in with a bottle of brandy, and we drank and talked until two in the morning when he drove his car over all the lanes of the street; the packing was finally completed, then I waited for the morning. I remembered other nights and other bottles of brandy, the nights when John Rudd came for a chat and a drink, then suddenly everything seemed very far behind me. I had called for the taxi of the man who used to pick up Mira at Clarendon Circle. Ma-Bloke was sitting forlorn on a stool on the stoop, defeated and unable to cry; I cannot say goodbye, there is something too permanent about goodbyes. It is difficult to say goodbye to Ma-Bloke.

'I'll be seeing you, mama,' I said, kissing her on the mouth for the first time in my conscious life. 'Look after yourself for me. Because I love you, mama.'

I was afraid to look into her eyes, afraid I would change my mind; the possibility that I would never see her again was terrifying, for so long as South Africa shall remain white, for so long shall I be an exile from the country of my birth. We exchanged farewells, the children and I, and Daisy cried because she is a girl; Pancho and Butch were brave about it, Suzan was silent as she got into the taxi with me. At the station was Martha Madumo's sister, Buti, Fiki and Chris. As I held my daughter in my hands, there were no words to explain to her why I was leaving and to explain that it was not because

I did not love her. The pain of being separated from her, to be away during the days of her growing when she would need me most, were thoughts which were whispered to her in sounds which were not words. There was the faithful friend, Lewis Nkosi, the boy I had privately and unofficially adopted as a brother.

There was an unbearable silence on that platform, so I decided that I needed to buy cigarettes. Lewis came with me to the kiosk and he waited outside as I stood whilst those two Afrikaner women went on talking together deliberately ignoring my presence.

'If you don't mind,' I said, 'I want cigarettes.'

'Can't you wait?' one of them barked, she was one of those pharmaceutical blondes who are pink and round all over; her beer-barrel body seemed to be swimming and shifting inside an apron, the colour of which flowed into her face and hair. She had an unattractiveness which made me impatient.

'No, I can't wait.'

'Then get out,' she bellowed. 'And don't come back here— Get out, cheeky Native.'

'With the greatest pleasure, madam.'

I joined Lewis and returned to the platform; we talked until the final bell and I got on the train with Chris, smothering her with kisses of betrayal, then I handed her to Fiki and we kissed with discomfort; there was one for Suzan and for Buti, and shook hands with Lewis. And the waving of the hands were retreating into background until there was nothing but the structure of Park Station through the smoke; I looked hard at every sight, and as the train smoked past the stations there were a thousand remembrances of a world whistling away; when we passed Newclare I looked, with loathing and longing, at the shacks and the slums of the Western Areas, tried to see through the sweeping panorama the last view of Sophiatown, but all that I could see were the slums, the bleak disarrangement of houses.

Postscript

YOU ARE BREAKING the law, my mind kept repeating. The law is the law. I fingered my pocket for the Reference Book, conscious that there was no permission stamped into it; this is illegal, it is illegal to escape from apartheid without the necessary permission. The law is the law. But what is the law? I held the Reference Book, and thought, this is the law, I remembered the arguments which my liberal white friends delighted in impressing upon me: the law is the law, it must be obeyed. The train was rushing past the small stations, at times too quickly to read the names of the stations, which seemed to be flowing into the mouth of the train, being chewed up like a stick of sugar cane; the stations were being chewed up in spite of themselves as I had been by the law which ruled over me without my consent. The standard of this law is white, its legislative authority is white, its executive authority is white, and as a black man I had to adjust myself to it though I accepted it as unjust. The discriminations are written into the law, to protest against the discriminations is to be produced against the authority of the law. I see the South African law as the basis and the instrument of my oppression. I am black, the law is white.

But the law is the law, they said. Well, this is the law.

The 'Natives (Abolition of Passes and Co-ordination of Documents) Act' No. 67 of 1952 abolished the Pass Laws, so instead of carrying a Pass I carry a Reference Book No. 947067; it has ninety-six pages, is bound in buckram and comes in two colours, the brown and the green. It is divided into five sections, the index is as follows.

A: Labour Bureau, Efflux and Influx Control and Registration.

There are three permissions stamped into this section.

1. *Permitted to seek work in the proclaimed area of Johannesburg until 23/6/1955 and remain therein for duration of contract of service entered into during this period.*

In terms of the 'Natives (Urban Areas Consolidation) Act' of 1945, a white person who employs an African who has not been granted permission to seek work or take up employment in that town, commits a criminal offence and is liable, on first conviction, to a fine not exceeding £10 or, in default, to imprisonment not exceeding two months, or to both such fine and imprisonment.

It is a criminal offence for an African to fail to have this permission stamped into the Reference Book; the permission is issued and valid for seven calendar days and is renewed twice, but if approved employment is not secured by the end of the third week, the efflux authority is empowered to endorse me out of the proclaimed area—of, say, Johannesburg—to an area which is depressed of Native labour.

This is the law.

2. *Permitted to remain in the proclaimed area of Johannesburg while employed by UNITED PRESS as staff assistant until present contract of service is terminated.*

The termination of the contract of service automatically terminates my right to seek employment, to take up employment and to remain in the proclaimed area of Johannesburg; fresh application must be made each time I become unemployed, failure to do so is a criminal offence. This stipulation is provided in Section 14 of the 'Natives (Urban Areas Consolidation) Act'; an African who has been convicted of the criminal offence of being in a proclaimed area unlawfully may be removed, on the sole discretion of a Magistrate, or a Native Commissioner, to his home or his last place of residence. But right of residence becomes unlawful the moment the African becomes unemployed, and fails to secure employment during the approved period. It is of little consequence that I know no other home than the proclaimed area of Johannesburg, the fact that I was born in Sophiatown, which falls within the boundaries of the proclaimed area of Johannesburg, is unimportant.

This is the law.

3. *Resident of Sophiatown in terms of Section 10(1)(a) or 10(1)(b) of Act No. 25 of 1945 as amended.*
   B: Employer's name and address

This page is divided into six sections: Name of employer, Address of employer, Date of engagement, Monthly signature of employer, Month, Date of discharge and signature.

An African has no right, by law, to be unemployed, the documentation in the Reference Book is proof the African is employed; the monthly endorsement by the employer is required by law, and if for some reason the employer should forget to endorse the Reference Book, the African is guilty of an offence and liable, on conviction, to a fine not exceeding £2 or, in default of payment, to imprisonment for a period not exceeding one month. It is the responsibility of the African to see to it—whilst in employment—that the Reference Book is signed regularly.

The 'Natives (Abolition of Passes and Co-ordination of Documents) Act' provides, in Sections 13 and 15, that any policeman may at any time call upon an African who has attained the age of sixteen years to produce his Reference Book; if the Reference Book has been issued to him but he fails to produce it on demand, because it is not on his person at the time, he commits a criminal offence and is liable, on conviction, to a fine not exceeding £10 or to imprisonment for a period not exceeding one month. Failure to produce the Reference

Book on demand is a criminal offence, the fact that the Reference Book is in the room about ten yards away is unimportant.

This is the law.

The penal system of drafting African prisoners to work off the term of imprisonment as labour on private farms in private farm jails—often in slave conditions—is a state so dreaded that Africans beg and borrow to pay the fines. Mr De Wet Nel, the Minister of Bantu Administration and Development announced in 1958 that a total of 55,474 cases were heard in the Johannesburg Native Commissioner's Court alone (one of the many such courts in the area of Johannesburg) under the Pass laws last year; the sum collected in fines amounted to £51,908.

C: Union Tax

In this section is stamped the Poll Tax receipt for the current year; this head tax falls on every African male over the age of eighteen years irrespective of whether he has an income or not, this Native tax was increased by 75 per cent for the financial year 1959-60, with further increases from 1960, when the burden of Bantu Education Bills was thrust on the African taxpayer. The fact that the Africans have protested against this system of education on the grounds that it is an education for Caliban has failed to impress the Government Department of Bantu Education.

The end of March of each year brings with it a concentrated campaign by the police against tax offenders; it is a criminal offence not to have paid the tax by that date, even if the African is unemployed and has no income.

This is the law.

The intention of this is to force the Africans out of the Reserves and the Bantustans in search of employment on white farms, in the gold mines and into domestic service, so as to keep up with the tax; under this system such minority paying jobs

302

are worked with cheap labour, which is even cheaper than labour in the urban areas. The land in the Reserves—which has long ceased to support the needs of the people who work it—is farmed by old women and children; the land is poor and exhausted, most of it eroding away, and because Africans do not own the land it is difficult to secure bank loans for improved farming methods; even if they could, the land hunger is so desperate that there is no room for crop rotation. Nine million Africans are settled on 14 per cent of the surface area of South Africa.

D: Bantu Authorities Tax

Over and above the Poll Tax tribal Africans who fall under the direct authority of tribal chiefs, the Bantu authorities, have to pay an additional Hut Tax, this too whether they have an income or not.

This is the law.

E: Additional Particulars (including concessions in respect to curfew, Native Law and customs, etc.)

In this section is written, in a legible handscript, this exemption:

'*William is exempted from the Urban Service Contract Regulations in terms of Section 3(4) of Act 67/52, having been exempted under regulations 14 bis Proclamation 150/341*

(signed) F. J. Labuischagne
asst. Pass Officer.

Except that it sounds impressive, larded with the appropriate official jargon, the provision of this exemption is meaningless—a point which was later conceded by the Pass Officer when I interviewed him for a magazine story. Because of the exemption written into my Reference Book I carry on my person a green-coloured Reference Book, green being the colour of exemption; the colour of the standard Reference Book is brown. I am allergic to brown, as a colour, you see. The principle of the Exemption Pass is to exempt me from carrying a Reference Book, as a result I carry a Reference Book into which is written a certificate exempting me from carrying a Reference Book.

According to the terms stated in the certificate I am 'exempted from the Urban Service Contract Regulations', which *should* mean that I am exempted from having to obtain permission to 'seek work in the proclaimed area of Johannesburg' and for permission 'to remain in the proclaimed area of Johannesburg until present contract is terminated', that in effect I am permitted to move from one area to another, to remain therein, to seek work and to take up employment without having to apply for the necessary permission. I should, further, be privileged to be unemployed until such time as I shall find suitable employment; but this is a violation of the very essence of Native labour in respect to control and movement.

The train puffed and coughed to a stop at Krugersdorp; I became conscious that my presence there was illegal and became restless and insecure. People were staring at me, they knew; there was accusation in their eyes, I was being reproached: the law is the law, you are deliberately breaking the law of the land. I nervously pushed the Reference Book on the seat and sat on it, my eyes fastened on a spot ahead of me, too nervous to look at the faces passing outside the compartment; my mind was screaming, the silence around me was maddening, I wanted to get out of the train and run back to Johannesburg, to prostrate myself before the authority of the law—repentant and contrite. But the train started to cough, to snail out of the station, and once in motion the fear subsided, the

Reference Book was warmed by the sitting on it. The confidence returned.

Before the passage of the 'Natives (Abolition of Passes and Co-ordination of Documents) Act' the certificates of exemption allowed to the select few freedom of movement and the right for the bearer to sell his labour at the best market, but this became an inconvenience to Dr Verwoerd as Minister of Native Affairs and architect of the Bill; however, a semblance of justice and fair play had to be pretended. To effect a sane and just compromise, the prestige and the respectability of the Exemption Pass was retained, but the principle was removed; the difference was emphasised by the colour of the Reference Book.

The African carrying a green Reference Book must apply for permission 'to seek work' and another 'to remain' in the proclaimed area, and in spite of the certificate which reads 'William is exempted from the Urban Service Contract Regulations' I am required, by law, to be registered under the Urban Service Contract, to have my Reference Book endorsed every month.

The principle of the exemption certificate is impractical, the economic structure of South Africa rests on the broad shoulders of cheap Native labour controlled and channelled by the Pass system; this labour must be kept in rotation all the time, and the demand for labour is supplied primarily by the migratory labour system—the redirection of surplus labour—and by convict labour. The official figures for the year 1958-59 revealed that 1,250,000 Africans were jailed for offences involving infringements of the Pass laws, liquor regulations, movement control and curfew restrictions; this is the manpower rotated around the farms at a fee of ninepence a day, per head, which is paid to the Government.

The 'Native Administration Act' No. 38 of 1927 is the authority which redistributes surplus labour, the African who is unable to secure approved employment within a period of three weeks is endorsed out of the area to a specified area with a labour shortage. If an African, thus ordered to leave an area, refuses to comply with the order, the Governor-General—or the equivalent authority under the Republic—has the unfettered discretion to order that, without trial in a court of law or further investigation of any kind, the African be summarily arrested, detained and removed from that area.

This is the law.

There are various variations on this theme. A rural African applying for permission to migrate to an urban area has to serve an eighteen-month service contract working in the mines, but after this term he is permitted to enter into domestic service only; in this manner domestic service is provided with the labour it requires which cannot be otherwise recruited in the urban areas where the Africans refuse—if they can help it— to work for an average wage of £5 a month. The average wage-scale offered by industry and commerce is £3 a week. The African male coming from his tribal home into domestic service or the mining industry is not allowed to bring his family out, but after a two-year service he is allowed to return to the Reserves to spend three months with his family. It has been observed that each time this African returns from the three-month reunion, he leaves behind a wife and a child he will not see for the next two years. His return to the urban area will depend on whether the employer is willing to re-employ this African; if not, then the process begins again.

Dr Verwoerd has a knack of reducing these things to their basic essential, he said: 'Natives should not be allowed to rise above certain levels of labour.'

The 'Natives Regulations Act' No. 15 of 1911, is used to regulate the labour into the depressed services. If an African recruited by a labour agent has undertaken to enter the service of any unspecified member of a group of employers by whom such labour agent is employed, but thereafter refuses to enter the service of the employer to whom he has been allotted, the African is guilty of a criminal offence punishable by a fine not exceeding £10 or, in default, to imprisonment for a period not exceeding two months.

These labour agents travel round the country with offers of high-paid jobs in the cities, and the unsuspecting African in the Reserves is dazzled by the prospects and signs a contract which the agent has been careful not to read and explain; the contracted African finds himself on a farm, to which he has been allotted, finds that it is illegal for him to refuse the job and is probably contracted for three years at a salary of £2 a month.

This is the law.

To maintain the labour requirements at the cheap level necessary for the sustenance of white prosperity, the State has erected protectives like the 'Natives Labour (Settlement of Disputes) Act' No. 48 of 1953, to safeguard itself against the bargaining power of organised African labour; trade unionism is illegal among Africans, and it is unlawful for an African worker to take part in a strike. If he does so he is liable, on conviction, to a fine not exceeding £500 or to imprisonment not exceeding three years or to both such fine and such imprisonment.

As an African journalist on *Drum* Publications I was not allowed membership into the Society of Journalists. I was therefore paid far below the minimum but with lots of prospects thrown in; the white editors never failed to explain to us that the paper was struggling, that it was not making money, so the African journalists subsidised it whilst the whites were paid the full rate.

The pass or the Reference Book is a life of its own, a kind of indestructable monster; its relationship to the African is one of an indecent intimacy, it controls his entire life, strangulates his ambition; it is his physical life. Only the Reference Book can

307

claim a registered letter or cash a Money Order; it is the Reference Book which gets married, the marriage ceremony might very well be conducted as something like this:

'Do you, Reference Book No. 947067, take Reference Book No. 649707 as your lawfully documented wife?'

Only the Reference Book can open a savings account and withdraw funds. The African with a Reference Book is anonymous, a faceless mask undistinguishable from the millions, and since Africans are invested with a propensity for lying, the policeman will not accept a verbal identification; in fact they show an unwillingness to negotiate directly with the African, who is like a robot with the Reference Book as the operational manual. It is the Reference Book which states that the bearer may be employed where, when and how long; it is the Reference Book which carries the permission which confers upon the bearer the right to take tenancy of a house, and it will list the people entitled to live in that house. If an African who was born in a town, where he has worked and lived continously for fourteen years, and has during the period worked for one employer, neither his wife—who lives in the Reserves—nor his unmarried daughter or his son aged eighteen years, although each is completely dependent upon him, is entitled, as of right, to live with him for more than seventy-two hours at time.

This is the law.

This is the essence of the Pass Law.

I cannot sell my labour to the highest bidder.

I cannot live in the residential area of my choice; I am committed by the colour of my skin to live in segregated ghettos or locations or slums.

Freedom of movement is restricted by the Reference Book.

The right to live in peace in my house is subject to the pleasure of any superintendent or Native Commissioner who is empowered to endorse me out of the municipal district if, in

308

his opinion, my presence is inimical to public peace and good order; public peace and good order is violated the moment I stand on a public platform to talk against increases in rent, thereby influencing others.

This is the law.

I am prohibited, by law, to challenge such summary endorsement; the 'Natives (Prevention of Interdicts) Act' of 1956, by which the Governor-General can, by proclamation, order an African to leave a certain area. Such an order must be honoured forthwith, and no court of law may grant an interdict preventing such summary endorsement or an appeal for a stay or suspension of the removal order. The terms of the Act are such that even if the order is served in error—intended for someone else—there is no way of correcting the error; the order must be fulfilled.

This is the law.

I may be detained for over sixty days without a charge brought up against me.

I cannot determine the kind of education my daughter shall have, and it is a criminal offence for me to give my daughter lessons at home; if it is proved that there was a blackboard, chalk, paper and pencil, then I am guilty of conducting a private school, thus contravening the Bantu Education Act.

This is the law.

I cannot worship in the church of my choice.

I cannot mix or consort, in a peaceful manner or for a peaceful common purpose with the friends of my choice.

This is the law.

I cannot object to all these restrictive laws, cannot cite the Declaration of the Rights of Man, that 'all men are created equal, they are endowed by their Creator with certain inalienable rights, that among these are life, liberty and the pursuit of happiness—that to secure these rights Governments are instituted among men, deriving their just powers from the consent of the governed, that whenever any form of Government becomes destructive of these ends, it is the right of the people to alter or to abolish it.'

The denials of these 'inalienable rights' are written into the constitution, are the laws of the land. These are the laws I am instructed to obey. Does a wrong become less immoral because it is written into the contitution? Am I to believe that only white men are created equal? Is this the morality of Western civilisation which I am told that I am not ready for? When I mature and become ready should I set up a parallel morality and declare that only black men are created equal? More equal than white men?

But this much I have learned, that whatever declaration I make I should be careful to surround it with the respectability of law and order; because it is only in the name of the law that man can outrage others, and the law is the law, it must be obeyed.

I must accept injustice and discrimination because they are written into the law; if that is all the reason I need to accept injustice and discrimination, then I can only reply in the words of 'Billy', the character in Robert E. Sherwood's play, *Abe Lincoln in Illinois*.

To hell with the law—the constitution. This is a matter of the rights of living men to freedom—and these came before the constitution! When the law denies these rights, then the law is wrong, and it must be changed, if not by moral protest, then by force! There's no course of action that isn't justified in the defence of freedom.

The train was slowing down for the entry into Mafeking, the border town separating South Africa from Bechuanaland. My attention was attracted by a noise outside the train, and through my window I saw African children, running barefoot alongside and scrambling for parcels which were being thrown out of the White coaches; the wrappings broke as the parcels bounced against the ground, and sandwiches, fruit and other food items scattering into the dust, and the children snatched and grabbed and quarrelled, all to the amusement of the benefactors. More parcels were being thrown out and all along the line white faces peered out of the windows to watch the amusement, and although I knew the hunger of the children I could not throw food at them. The pecking of vultures does not amuse me, but I reasoned with my heart and threw out all the change I had on me.

Then the train entered and puffed its way out of Mafeking, and South Africa and everything I had known, loved and hated remained behind me. I was out of South Africa. But it was no victory or solution, the compulsive agony was still with me, the problem was still with me; only its immediacy was removed, like an orgasm in bed, the tension was released but the filth slimed down my thigh dripping on to the sheet. My physical life in South Africa had ended.

Olive Schreiner

THE STORY OF AN AFRICAN FARM

The Story of an African Farm was first published in 1883, under the pseudonym Ralph Iron. Only later did it transpire that the author was actually a woman — Olive Schreiner. When the book first appeared it was received with mixed feelings by its Victorian readers, some of whom were shocked by the 'morality' of the author, and felt that it would have been better if the book had never been published. Schreiner's perseverance paid off, and today the novel, set on a farm in the Karoo, is considered important for South African literature, as the beginning of a national literary tradition. This new paperbook edition is introduced by Cherry Clayton.

281 pages, a paperbook

Olive Schreiner

THE WOMAN'S ROSE

The short stories and allegories in *The Woman's Rose* have been selected to provide a fuller and more varied picture of the achievement of Olive Schreiner, so often considered to be the one-book author of *The Story of an African Farm.* The pieces in this book offer an insight into nineteenth century feminism, which for the Victorians was a spiritual and educational revolution as opposed to the largely sexual one of today. Although the issues are different the principles are perhaps the same. Schreiner is of interest to the modern reader both as an example of historical conditioning and for her attempt to peer over the shoulders of her contemporaries into the future.

128 pages, a paperbook

Sarah Gertrude Millin

GOD'S STEPCHILDREN

First published in 1924, *God's Stepchildren* is no less relevant today. Miscegenation had long been a preoccupation of Sarah Gertrude Millin, and in this novel, the poignant story of segregation and people of mixed heritage, it is the dominant theme. The book begins in 1821 when Andrew Flood becomes a missionary in a remote section of the Cape Colony and, after failing to establish any spiritual contact with his Hottentot charges, marries one of them as a gesture of brotherhood. The marriage is a failure in all respects, and Sarah Gertrude Millin traces the lives of the next four generations, concentrating on one person in each, and emphasising their problems. These people question 'But is God himself not white?' and come to the final conclusion, 'Perhaps we brown people are his stepchildren.'

320 pages, a paperbook

Joseph Conrad

HEART OF DARKNESS AND TYPHOON

Conrad's *Heart of Darkness*, first published in 1902, has a particular fascination for readers at the southern tip of Africa today. It constitutes the most profound fictional rendering of Europe's attitudes to this continent at the beginning of the twentieth century, and now, in the closing decades provokes us to evaluate contemporary assumptions. The book investigates the institution of imperialism and the complex effects this has on the colonisers, and at the same time seeks to provide insights into an idealist conception of human nature which is, by implication, totally ahistorical and timeless. Behind such words as civilisation and enlightenment, *Heart of Darkness* reveals barbarism, exploitation and death. The book is Conrad's testimony to his stoical belief in 'the subtle but invincible conviction of solidarity that knits together the loneliness of innumerable hearts . . . the solidarity in mysterious origin, in toil, in joy, in hope, in uncertain fate — which binds men to each other and all mankind to the visible world.'

160 pages, a paperbook